Academic Equitation

General Decarpentry

ACADEMIC EQUITATION

A Preparation for International Dressage Tests
Translated from the French by
Nicole Bartle

Illustrations by
LT.-COL. G. M. MARGOT
(*former Riding Master in Chief of the Cavalry School*)
and by
CHEF D'ESCADRONS D'HALEWIN

J. A. ALLEN & CO. LTD.
1 Lower Grosvenor Place, S.W.1.

First published in Great Britain 1971
by J. A. Allen & Co. Ltd.

Translated from the Second Edition (Revised)
of ÉQUITATION ACADÉMIQUE by Général Decarpentry
published by Émile Hazan, 36 Avenue George V. Paris.

SBN 85131 036 2

PRINTED AND BOUND IN ENGLAND BY
HAZELL WATSON AND VINEY LTD
AYLESBURY, BUCKS

CONTENTS

DRESSAGE

APPENDIX

TRANSLATOR'S NOTE

For the sake of brevity, I have refrained from translating the following expressions each time they appear in the text. They succinctly describe certain reactions and effects which can only be replaced in English by somewhat lengthy explanations.

Each is in fact dealt with in the text under the appropriate section, but as they are frequently used in the first part of the book, whereas the explanations appear later on, it will be advisable for the reader to be familiar with their meaning before embarking on the book itself.

Ramener: flexing of the head at the poll; it is said to be complete when the nose is vertical. See Chapter IV, Part II.

Mise en Main: Yielding of the jaw, in the position of the Ramener. See Chapter III, Part II.

Rassembler: Collection, extending to all parts of the horse's body and affecting them all. See Chapter VIII, Part II.

Descente de Main: A yielding of the pressure of the fingers on the reins, on a balanced horse, who must not change his pace or modify his attitude. See Chapter VI, Part II.

L'Effet d'Ensemble: A special use of the spurs combined with a simultaneous traction on the reins. See Chapter VII, Part II.

Relaxation: The French use the word "decontraction", as the opposite of contraction. From the point of view that concerns us in equitation, I would have preferred this term to "relaxation", but it would not have been condoned by English linguists. Wherever the word relaxation occurs, it must be understood that it signifies an absence of sustained contraction, and not a total slackness of muscle.

AUTHOR'S PREFACE

From 1933 until June 1939, I acted as a Judge of Dressage Tests at all inter-national competitions in Europe, and at several national competitions abroad. Since 1947, I have had the honour of presiding over the Jury of the *Federation Equestre Internationale* for these same tests. On the other hand, fourteen years in the *Cadre* of the Cavalry School, eight of these as Ecuyer (Riding Master), have given me the opportunity of closely observing our military riders, who, up to this date, have been the only competitors selected for these tests.

By closely watching these champions in one competition after another, I have been able to make certain observations which I think it is useful to record, and here are the most important ones.

To start with, the French manner lacks uniformity. Within the same team, we often notice very different qualities, and almost opposite faults, which led one foreign critic—an unfriendly one, needless to say—to assert that a "French style" does not exist, and this is not true.

Secondly, in some of our presentations, in which the most difficult movements of the tests were performed better than just honourably, very serious faults in the most simple movements were noticed, as if the primary education of the horses had been neglected.

Between this primary education and the higher education which, however, they proved that they had received, there appeared to be no proper connection. Equestrian poetry was harmonious, but marred, here and there, by spelling mistakes. It frequently happened that one of our horses, having obtained a high mark for the changes of lead, or the passage, for example, would lose a considerable number of marks for a modest volte, too carelessly executed, or for a surprisingly faulty simple half-pass.

It is nearly always in this manner that complete success has eluded us.

These faults most certainly are due to causes of different kinds, and without presuming to unveil them all, some of them can be exactly pointed out.

The tests laid down in international competitions are far more difficult than the ones which are executed in our military schools, even the ones executed by the riding masters.

The education which our officers receive aims exclusively—and **very** wisely—at satisfying the requirements of military equitation, requirements much less severe than those of academic equitation.

The officer who decides to prepare a horse for international dressage tests is, therefore, going beyond the limits of his equestrian education. In his hurry to tackle new difficulties, he often neglects to make sure that his horse is "well-grounded" in the essentials of primary education and on this imperfect foundation he decides to develop an equestrian culture which has correctness and precision as its foremost qualities.

This initial mistake appears to have been frequently made by our teams, and it seems that the concept of "right and wrong" is not very clear to some of our competitors who, apart from this, show ability in the pursuit of dressage.

To attain high equitation it would be presumptuous on the part of the student trainer to rely solely on his own resources and his fortunate gifts. He needs a mentor.

He will have difficulty in finding suitable oral teaching. Academic Equitation has few adepts in France and, unfortunately, has become confused with circus riding, which is however completely different.

He must, therefore, resort to the printed word and it is often difficult to put into practice what one learns from books on equitation.

All great equestrian authors have been exceptionally gifted riders, for whom difficulties were practically non-existent. As they did not have to contend with these, they did not mention them, or hardly, and they mention even less any means of overcoming them.

Their readers, even those amongst them who are better than the average of experienced riders, at every step come up against these difficulties and find no answer to them, nor even a suggested solution.

Certain procedures used by great artists with the most marvellous results lead only to disappointment with riders of even considerable skill. "The spur", Baucher used to say, "is a razor in the hands of a monkey". However, it is not, by a long way, only to the spur that this applies, and it can truly be said that the greater the effective power of a certain procedure, the greater are the dangers of its application.

I was led to reflect that it might be helpful to our apprentice trainers to define, as accurately as possible, the concept of "right and wrong" that is accepted nowadays unanimously by international judges and is also entirely in accord with the traditions of the French school.

Furthermore, by indicating the successive stages of a progression adapted to the requirements of modern international tests, I thought it would be interesting to explain the various methods that help us to meet them, and I have always preferably advocated the use not of the most powerful, but of the safest method, i.e. that which is the least difficult to apply, and the least likely to produce irreparable damage.

I have almost invariably indicated the titles of the books and the names of the authors whose methods I explain, and have advised the reader to refer to these sources whenever possible. When I have not done so, this has been because I found it impossible to trace exactly the origin of some idea which could only have been a reminiscence.

There is therefore nothing of myself in this work. It is only a compiling, with suggestions, intended to guide the reader in his choice, from the arsenal of ways and means which I present to him.

My intention is to facilitate the task of those riders who wish to tackle artistic equitation.

My sole ambition is to have been successful in helping them, even in a very modest measure.

Amongst the many deserved criticisms of this work, the one of lack of simplicity, is, in my opinion, the most serious, and I cannot apologise too much for this.

The principles of equitation are simple, but the business of putting them into practice is not so simple. The methods used in equestrian art are numerous and varied. Some people have been able to sum them up succinctly and picturesquely in the formula: "Push and Pull" (Tirer dessus et taper dedans), but no great profit, obviously, can be derived from this sally.

Success in methodical schooling is made up of a thousand details, none of which is negligible. Without claiming to draw attention to all of them, it is certainly useful to indicate those which, by their neglect, seriously compromise the value of the expected results.

Furthermore, in equitation as in politics, we should beware of over-simplification; this nearly always complicates matters in the end.

This book is not, in any way, a corpus of doctrine. Neither does it propound a method, but it is a catalogue of procedures set out according to the order in which they should be used and amounts, after all, to nothing more than an equestrian recipe book.

General Decarpentry
1949

By the same Author

Piaffer et passage, 1932
L'Ecole espagnole de Vienne, 1947
Baucher et son école, 1948
Les Maitres écuyers du manege de Saumur, de 1814 à 1874, 1954
L'Essentiel de la Méthode de haute école de Raabe, 1957

FOREWORD by E. Schmit-Jensen

The Author's Preface being most elaborate another Foreword is hardly called for. However, as an old personal friend of the late General Decarpentry I feel it a dear duty to complement his Preface with some facets of his work and life. For many years we were in close equestrian contact serving together on the Dressage Committee of the Federation Equestre International and moreover as international Dressage Judges, and while he was preparing this book we were discussing many relevant points supported by interchanging of books from our respective "dressage libraries."

In his Preface General Decarpentry is explaining why, in his opinion, there was a real need for such an "equestrian recipe book" partly for the use of riders preparing for advanced Dressage Tests and partly "to facilitate the task of riders wishing to tackle artistic equitation", though lamenting that this latter form of equitation had only "few adepts in France" at the time (1949). This eclipse of interest in the equitation as an art once so famous and illustrious in France and reflected in a rich and outstanding literature on the subject was a source of much concern, not to say chagrin to him. As a sort of remedy he wanted to revive this literature and bring it within reach of the contemporary riding community and he did so by composing this book as an anthology of the readings of the most prominent riding masters of yore. With General Decarpentry's typical modesty he states in the Preface that "there is nothing by myself in this work". This may be right as far as the various procedures are concerned but certainly not when considering the way he is presenting and explaining them in his masterly and most lucid manner making it relatively easy for the student to turn theory into practice.

General Decarpentry was born in 1878 at Lambres near Douai and died in Paris in 1956 shortly before the Olympic Games in Stockholm.

As grandson and son of enthusiastic pupils of Baucher he developed, at an early age, a keen interest in equitation and decided on a cavalry career. The most important feature of this career from an equestrian point of view was his long connection with the Cavalry School at Saumur where he served in the Cadre Noir from 1904 to 1913, and later on as second-in-command from 1925 to 1931 just after having been in command of the Cavalry section at St. Cyr for two years. During the first World War he was badly wounded at Verdun which resulted in a stiff left elbow; however, as he used to say; leaving the arm bent in the right position for riding.

As will be understood from this book he was a fanatical student of the art of equitation, a great artist in the saddle and an excellent instructor. A very modest man, he had no desire to push himself forward nor to take part in competitions, but the above qualities combined with his absolute integrity and a most amiable and charming personality made him the ideal international Dressage Judge and President of the F.E.I. Dressage Committee, functions which he performed for a number of years until bad health forced him to give them up.

General Considerations

PART ONE

Chapter 1 · ACADEMIC EQUITATION

ITS AIMS

The first aim of academic equitation is to restore to the mounted horse the gracefulness of attitudes and movement which he possessed when he was free, but which becomes marred by the weight and interference of the rider.

To the solely utilitarian education which he has received in order to become serviceable, it adds, in the first place, in the exercises of the "low school", gymnastics intended to re-establish the regularity of his gaits and the straightness of his deportment.

It claims, thereafter, in the words of Newcastle, "to improve on Nature by the subtlety of Art".

It then subjects the horse to the progressive lessons of an aesthetic education destined to develop the rhythm and harmony of his movements, so that they are brought to a degree of "stylised" perfection which will gradually transform them into the "airs" of the high school, though their essential characteristics are scrupulously respected.

Equestrian art thus, is akin to choreographic art, and the high school to classical dancing.

The high school of the Circus is necessarily quite different.

Whilst the aim of the "academic rider" is solely the perfection of his art, the constant preoccupation of the circus rider, who is committed to fill his employer's cash box, is to draw at all costs the applause of a crowd to which art is only of the slightest concern.

It is of no concern to the circus rider if a few connoisseurs, enlightened by their equestrian education, are saddened by the perversion of their art as displayed in his presentations. They are a minute number and only pay for a few seats, whilst the uninitiated are a legion and it is they who swell the takings.

The circus rider must arouse the enthusiasm of the "philistines" by his stunts, acrobatics and airs of bravura. Extravagance of movements, sometimes even frenzy, are necessary to enchant the audience, rather than purity of style.

A.E.—2

However real his talent may be, the circus rider is obliged to twist his artistic conscience and, as General l'Hotte said: "sacrifices to false gods."

"For ten sous," Baucher used to say bitterly, "I must show off like a circus actor", and the greatest master of modern times, dressed up as an admiral, would perform on Neptune one of his most sensational acts, in which the "Head Wind" succeeded the "Becalmed Sea", and the "Ship in Distress" roused the crowd to delirious acclamations, whilst the last survivors of the School of Versailles bowed their heads in shame.

HISTORICAL ACCOUNT OF ACADEMIC EQUITATION

Springing from the Italian Renaissance, purified in France by the austere taste of the XVIIth Century, Academic equitation blossomed out during the XVIIIth Century in the Schools of Versailles and Vienna. The latter endured and survived all the vicissitudes of Austria, but the School of Versailles was destroyed by the Revolution. Re-established in 1815, only to disappear for ever in 1830, the famous French School has hardly left more than an oral tradition.

The last of its Riding Masters rapidly vanished from the equestrian scene, and only the strong personality of Count d'Aure could have rekindled the torch; but Count d'Aure had the spirit of an innovator and was more concerned with transforming than with transmitting.

What remains of the academic tradition was passed on by the subalterns of the Royal Stables and by the former grooms of Versailles, and that was how Saumur was able to benefit from it.

In 1814, when Saumur was founded, a "Manege Academique" was established there and entrusted to civilian riding masters who, after M. de Chabannes had left, all claimed to be heirs to the Versailles tradition.[1]

However, not one of them had ever been a member of the personnel of the Grande Ecurie or of the Petite Ecurie. The foremost among them, MM. Cordier and Rousselet, had merely received instruction in their youth at the Ecole Nationale d'Equitation, founded in 1796 for Cavalry troopers, and where all the instructors were former grooms (Piqueurs) of the Royal Stables.

It is therefore only by a somewhat tenuous thread of indirect transmission that the School of Saumur was linked in its beginnings to the School of Versailles. In those circumstances, it was inevitable that Baucher's brilliant achievements would divert devotees away from academic equitation towards

1. In 1817, Chabannes was a pupil of d'Auvergne, who himself had not been at the Versailles School but had received lessons from Lubersac, assistant riding master of the Grande Ecurie. Rousselet was his disciple. (Note of the 2nd Edition.)

the artistic conception of this master, with its qualities and its faults, and the Manege became "baucheriste", under the direction of Commandant de Novital.

The School, however, had an essential mission which had to take precedence over all considerations of tradition: this was to establish, to fix and to elaborate a Military Equitation, because Saumur is a Cavalry School rather than an Academy of Equestrian Art.

Count d'Aure devoted himself to this task and in this he was remarkably successful. Furthermore, he was neither an iconoclast nor a persecutor, and the riding masters under his command, besides giving the riding instruction prescribed by their chief, were allowed to continue with the dressage of their own horses far beyond the requirements of military equitation, just as Count d'Aure himself went on educating his own horse, "Neron", as far as the passage.[1]

Each one of them was free to use the methods of his earlier education; for instance, Guerin used those of Baucher, and Montigny those of Vienna, where he had been a student and a master, and they all upheld a classical correction and elegance of which the Riding Master in Chief was a shining example.

Thus, although it remained confined to the "Cadre" of the Manege, artistic equitation lived on at the Cavalry School.

Finally, General L'Hotte, faithful successor of d'Aure as regards the education of the students, himself practised on his own horses the highest difficulties of the art and succeeded in pouring into the mould of the Versailles tradition the most refined inventions of Baucher's genius.

He was later, in his book "Questions Equestres",[2] to give a corpus of doctrine to that modern French School that owes almost everything to him.

While the French School was going through all the vicissitudes of this evolution, the School of Vienna, equestrian metropolis of Central Europe, remained almost immovable in its doctrine.

It proclaimed its unswerving adherence to the principles of La Gueriniere whose book was still for it "the equestrian Bible", and it denounced Baucher as "the gravedigger of French equitation".

In fact, though the Germanic school preserved the method or rather the progression of this master who was not of its blood, it did not put his theories into practice without some modifications; these were less perceptible on the

1. According to L'Hotte, who had a limitless admiration for his master, this was almost his only attempt, and *Neron* never reached perfection in his passage. (Note of the 2nd Edition.)
2. Emile Hazan, Publishers.

banks of the Danube than on those of the Spree because of the racial difference between the people separated by the Danube and the Rhine.

Without resorting to as much as harshness, the masters of the Germanic school persisted too often in their direct opposition to forces of resistance, instead of having recourse to a skilful disassociation from them.

They demanded not just submission, but unconditional surrender of the horse, instead of seeking the latter's general co-operation towards perfection of the common task.

They attached greater value to strict exactitude of execution than to the joyous ease of their mount in his attitudes and movements.

For want of knowledge of the outside world and of instructive comparisons, for want of criticism and, above all, of competition, the Germanic school became a little torpid, basking in the admiration of the undeniably brilliant results that it obtained.

At the beginning of the 20th Century, both schools ignored one another, and it is to the honour of the F.E.I. that it has brought them together by giving them the opportunity to challenge each other from time to time in its competitions.

In the first contests, the differences of manner amounted to opposition.

The horses of the Romanic School, as the French School is known beyond the Rhine, showed more willingness than exactitude in their submissiveness, and facility rather than diligence in their work.

Their riders gave the impression of having avoided difficulties instead of having solved them and, in the course of their presentations showed a slightly negligent ease in their attitude and a rather nonchalant leniency in their demands on the horse.

On the other hand, in the performance of their task, the German horses evidenced an exemplary submission, a little constrained and sometimes dull, and a strict precision that was more mechanical than animated. Their results clearly proved the studious application of their trainers, but the riders in their presentations too obviously betrayed a persistently laborious effort.

The judges' differences of opinion were no less sharp, according to the School they belonged to, and the placing of the competitors gave rise to heated arguments.

But the competitors themselves rapidly took advantage of this opportunity for mutual observation.

Without forsaking what was good in their own method, they each tried to improve on it by adding something which they had admired in their neighbour's ways.

Year by year, the differences became less pronounced, the styles of both schools more similar, though fortunately for the sake of art, not entirely identical.[1]

In the same way, a similar concept of "right and wrong" was agreed upon by the judges under the high artistic authority of the President of the F.E.I., General von Holzing, and it is only in the scale of relative values that some minor differences of appreciation continue to exist amongst the judges.

This is how the Poetry of Equitation flourished after the Olympic Games of 1936, thanks to the fortunate artistic influence of the F.E.I.

It is to be hoped that the different national federations will vie with one another in organising these contests, which further the growth of the art of dressage so well, and that in a less troubled future the opposing teams will show ever greater perfection in their own particular style.

Spanish Riding School Rider,
from a drawing by L. Koch

A Saumur school rider,
drawing by Lt. Col. Margot

SPECIAL PLACE OF ACADEMIC EQUITATION IN
THE ART OF EQUITATION AS A WHOLE

The particular objectives of Academic Equitation, as they were set out earlier, are superimposed on the general objectives of Equestrian art: i.e., calmness, impulsion and straightness of the horse.

The first objective can only be achieved by a horse when there is perfect harmony in the play of his forces, exactly adjusted to its object. The horse is then said to be light.

1. This was written in 1949. We must regretfully state that, in 1964, no difference exists between "romanic" equitation and "germanic" equitation, in any case in international dressage tests. (Note of the 2nd Edition.)

Lightness is the essence of artistic equitation, and is its touchstone. Its nature and the form of its manifestation will be studied later.

*   *   *

The basic principle of equestrian art applies to academic equitation as well as to all other forms of that art: namely, submission of the horse to the will of the rider.

There is no essential difference between the obedience required of the horse in artistic equitation and the one he must show in utilitarian equitation. In both, his consent must be unconditional. But in the first, this must show in addition a character of joyous eagerness to please, that makes it, if one could express it thus, "smiling".

In the horse's education, this submission must be gained long before the point has come when time will be spent on his schooling for artistic equitation.

A description of the manner by which this submission is gained may appear to be outside the scope of this book.

However, the serviceable submission of the horse cannot be acquired as "a package" by means of a form of breaking that would give the rider, once and for all, the power to make his mount execute any new action he commands.

The horse can only execute orders the meaning of which he understands, and his mental constitution is of such a nature that man cannot undertake to teach the meaning of an order without at the same time winning consent to its execution.

In fact, to be understood and to be obeyed, amount to the same thing in Dressage, and the certainty of being understood never exists for the rider who is not obeyed.[1]

In academic Dressage, new demands are made on the horse, to each of which the same principle of submission applies, in conditions that vary only in detail but retain the following essentials:

(1) The execution of an act can only be obtained from a horse if he is placed in circumstances such as will influence his instinct to accomplish that act;

(2) Reconstitution of the same determining set of circumstances remains

---

1. Although the General writes with exceptional clarity, this paragraph is ambiguous. *Explanation* and *example* which are essential elements in the education of the rider cannot be applied to a horse. The *education* of the horse is based on *execution*. The art of the teacher resides in the choice and the progression of the exercises which prepare the desired movement; Beudant expresses this in the following general formula: "Obtain lightness; place the horse in a position appropriate for the movement; request; let the horse execute." (Note of the 2nd Edition.)

indispensable during the time it takes to form a habit which imparts to the execution of the act a character of *fatality*, similar to *reflex* in man.[1]

This character of fatality, which however can never give complete guarantees of certainty, is the only means the rider has of knowing that he is understood by his horse and also of knowing that he is assured of his submission.

The methods employed in Academic Equitation are in no way different from the ones used ever since the beginning of training, and they are in fact the only means man disposes of to train any kind of animal.

They consist in progressively developing applications of the principle of submission, by substituting for the means primitively employed to obtain it, other more convenient means that give scope for wider and more subtle applications.

The conventional language which has thus been gradually established between rider and mount becomes enriched with new signs. The understanding of the horse develops. The combined use of signs, the isolated meaning of which has been established separately, allows the rider to enlarge the scope of his teaching, which always proceeds from the known to the unknown.

This is the spirit of the method. It uses a conventional language to apply to the body of the horse the gymnastic progression of a series of movements intended to develop his agility rather than his strength, and his suppleness rather than his power.

This method remains unique in its principle, but with time variations concerned with choice of procedures and modes of application have appeared. One of these alone has deeply transformed the direction of Dressage, namely Baucher's contribution to equestrian art just over a hundred years ago. On the one hand, it systematically employs deliberately obtained flexions of the mouth as a factor of lightness, whilst the old masters regarded the same flexions merely as evidence of this lightness. On the other hand, it sets about suppling the horse by gymnastics as "localised" as possible, so that those parts of the body that are not the immediate object of each exercise remain inactive, whilst the old masters insisted on putting the whole body of the horse into activity.

*   *   *

In equestrian art, the *presentations* of the work of the riders are called "reprises". They can be collective or individual.

---

1. Similar, but surely not identical. The part played by the will is difficult enough to determine in the acts of human beings. In the acts of animals, man can only judge by analogy with himself, as he cannot have any certain knowledge of their psychological constitution.

In collective "reprises", everything must be subordinate to the whole. Precision of the figures described, exactitude of alignment and distances, uniformity of gait and attitude are more important than individual details of execution.

In individual "reprises", the composition of the display and its development still have their importance and the quality of each of its parts must be sustained, but the perfection of each detail plays a part in the value of the whole.

Therefore, the composer of "reprises" should take carefully into account the limitations in artistic aptitude of the performers so that the talent of none of the riders is over-taxed—particularly his own—in an individual presentation which should never, in any case, be imposed upon a performer of insufficient ability.

*   *   *

The competitions in Academic Equitation consist also of "reprises" but of a completely different character. Whilst the presentations aim at being spectacular, the competitions are purely probative. They are intended to be a means of assessing the relative quality of the work of each of the candidates. A necessarily common programme is imposed as a basis of comparison to determine the placing of the competitors. The tests include graduated difficulties, depending on the stage of dressage of the horses for which they are intended.

*   *   *

Academic Equitation is classified as *Low School* and *High School*.

In the Low School, the horse works on one or two tracks at all his *natural* gaits, which are brought to the highest degree of regularity at all paces, and also practises flying changes of lead at the canter in all changes of direction.

In the High School, the gaits take the elevated form of the *School* Walk, the *School* Trot, and the *School* Canter. (In English, these gaits are usually referred to as Collected Walk, etc: Translator's note.)

Some of these gaits are developed to a further extent and are then known as the *Airs* called "close to the ground".

No classical airs have been developed from the walk.[1]

The classical air developed from the trot is the *Passage*, which becomes the *Piaffer* when it is executed on the spot.

---

1. The so-called "Spanish" airs modify the proportions of the natural movement of forehand and hind-quarters. They cannot, therefore, be defined as academic airs, and neither can they be included in the airs of the classical High School. They are "fanciful" movements.

The airs developed from the canter are the *"Terre-a-Terre"*, (from the Ground to the Ground) and the *Mezair*, but they are not practised nowadays.[1] Alternation of the lead, after a limited number of strides on one leg and then on the other, no stride being put in at a different gait, constitutes the change of lead at every six, five, four, etc. strides and if the number of strides is reduced to one on each lead, it becomes the *Change at every Stride*, ("Du tact au tact")[2] or "a tempo").

The *Pirouette* can be performed at the Passage or at the Canter.

The High School also includes all the airs called "Above the Ground", which stylise the natural leaps of the horse, or his attitudes preparatory to them.

The airs above the Ground are not included nowadays in dressage tests, the preparation for which is the object of this book.

LIGHTNESS

Books of Reference:
GENERAL L'HOTTE: *Questions Equestres. Un Officier de Cavalerie.*

"The 'mark' of the High School, of scientific, artistic, high equitation, however one likes to call it, is not to be found therefore in extraordinary movements, but in those, whether simple or complicated, that are executed with perfect lightness." (General L'Hotte.)

Lightness, says General L'Hotte, consists in "the perfect obedience of the horse to the lightest indications of hands and heels".

1. In the "Terre-a-Terre", and particularly in the "Mezair", in order to lift up his forehand, the horse must unburden it considerably by translating a large part of his weight to the hind-quarters. On the contrary, in the changes of leg at the canter, the horse must remain in horizontal balance, and an overburdening of the haunches makes their execution awkward.

The old masters never practised the changes of lead "a tempo", which were invented by Baucher, and they only rarely practised repeated changes, even when these were separated by short intervals.

The introduction into Academic Equitation of the repeated changes, and the changes at every stride has brought about a change in the ancient form of the canter as it was practised by the old masters, and it is now executed in a position of equilibrium closer to the horizontal. This, no doubt, has been the cause of the disappearance of the Terre-a-Terre and of the Mezair. However, the first of these two airs occurs automatically when the pirouette at the canter is slow and very rhythmical, as perfection demands.

2. This expression, "du tact au tact", is used by the majority of good (French) authors. Its use could be frowned upon as implying some relationship with the popular sense of the expression "tac-to-tac", itself borrowed from the vocabulary of fencing. But in our technical, particular, if not unique, acceptation of the expression, it makes the sense quite clear: "touch to touch". This is why I have adopted it.

It *results* from the rider "arousing the horse to use only such energy as may usefully be employed to achieve the movement required, and still taking into account the fact that lightness requires the activation of all the muscles, as perfection forbids inertness of any part of the horse's body because of the instinctive co-relation between all muscular contractions".

This is *proved* not only by perfection of the movements, but also by the *mobility of the mouth*, and the *flexibility of the hips*, which are so intimately related in their mutual reactions that it is impossible to decide which has the predetermining influence on the other.[1]

Mobility of the mouth is felt by the *hands* of the rider. Flexibility of the hips is felt by his *seat*.

The nature of the feeling of lightness by the hands is explained later, in the section relating to the "mise en main".

The feeling given by the *seat* allows the rider to sense the efforts of the horse through the reactions of the gaits. These will be rough and jerky when the "play of the springs" is faulty, and will become smooth as it becomes correct and harmonious. Once the horse is perfectly light, the seat will give the feeling of riding on the "gentle waves of a quiet lake" (General L'Hotte).

The old masters, though they did not deny the value of the impressions received by the hands as evidence of lightness, attached far more importance to the impressions perceived by the seat. However, Baucher stressed the importance of mobility of the jaw to such an extent that his pupils forgot even the existence of the invaluable means of judging lightness given to the rider by the transformation of the horse's action.[2]

*   *   *

These two "feelers" are no more than a rider requires to keep him informed on the physical and moral state of his mount. Their indications complete and confirm one another. He must use them concurrently.

Feeling will be fully developed by always using both simultaneously.

1. And so we come to the crucial point. General Decarpentry is at pains to disclaim that he is propounding a *doctrine*. At the time he was writing "Equitation Academique", he was the President of the International Jury, and his obvious concern was to unite, instead of opposing, the germanic and romanic schools by convincing both of the merits of one another. However, if we consider Steinbrecht for the germanic, and Baucher for the romanic schools, to be the leaders of equitation during the XIXth century (d'Aure can be ruled out in an academic debate), we notice that although they are in agreement about the aims pursued, which is the *mobility of the mouth* and the *flexibility of the hips*, they do not agree on the subject of the means employed to achieve these objects. Steinbrecht tackles the problem as a whole; Baucher, and after him the General (who is not an absolute

"baucheriste", but one tending towards Baucher), obey the essential cartesian principle of dissociating the difficulties, as the General explains on page 21.

To this we can add that germanic equitation in its present state, which French riders are now trying to imitate, increasingly ignores the mobility of the mouth, even when it does not actually condemn it, while on the contrary Baucher made it the subject of his first lesson (from the ground, in the form of "flexions"). In his own personal manner, the General resorted to these procedures. However, we must again emphasise that the aim of "Equitation Academique" was to unite and not to oppose. (Note of 2nd Edition.)

2. With the exception of General L'Hotte, Baucher's pupils did not attach sufficient importance to the value of the impression received through the seat. A few merely mention it, others say nothing about it.

On the other hand, in countries where Baucher's influence was small or nonexistent—in Central Europe for example—the value of the mobility of the mouth as a proof of lightness is often neglected, while the one given by the feeling in the seat is carefully observed, often to the exclusion of everything else.

Chapter 2 · THE FUTURE RIDING MASTER

Books of Reference:
GENERAL L'HOTTE: *Questions Equestres*
RAABE: *Methode de Haute Ecole d'Equitation.*

To study ACADEMIC Equitation with any hope of success, the rider should be fully confirmed in the practice of outdoor equitation.

In this new study, he should be guided by a qualified instructor who has well schooled horses at his disposal and is able to explain the unity of principle common to all forms of riding and the differences in its application to the wide field of outdoor equitation on the one hand, and to the more precise and delicate demands of school work on the other.

In France, such instructors are few and far between, and there are even fewer horses schooled beyond the stage essential for current use. Our riding pupils are therefore obliged to supplement all direct, oral teaching by studying the writings of our masters, and are in the position of having to school themselves and their horses at the same time without having had the opportunity of first learning to handle a finished horse.

These are conditions that add considerably to the difficulties of a task sufficiently arduous of itself. They explain the perplexity of our riders when they are faced with the apparently contradictory opinions of the authors which they are obliged to consult, their hesitation as to choice of method, their anxiety concerning the effectiveness of certain procedures, the results of which they have been unable to ascertain and even their uncertainty regarding the requisite form and nature of the results which are, after all, the ultimate aim of their work.

This situation will persist so long as France remains without a Conservatory of Equestrian Art similar to the Spanish Riding School of Vienna.

Our military schools provide an education that embraces the most varied subjects but limits the teaching of equitation to its particular purposes. However, it is only in these schools that the majority of our riders acquire the few notions of academic art essential to their riding instruction which is, quite wisely, directed towards completely different ends.

The high stage of proficiency which they subsequently reach out of doors enables them partly to counteract the present difficulties appertaining to academic education by practising equitation as a sport and by preparing and schooling their horses mainly for that purpose.

Combined Training Competitions, sometimes called "Military" competitions, impose upon the participants a variety of tests that demands a harmonious development of every different form of equestrian skill.

Modern jumping courses often present difficulties of control that call for finesse and timing in the use of the aids rather than for strength.

To bring a horse up to the stage of dressage that will enable it to figure honourably in competitions develops, in a broad manner, all the aptitudes required for academic preparation.

Every act of dressage, even the most elementary kind, proceeds from the same principles as does the teaching of the most intricate difficulties of the High School, and demands on the rider's part identical moral and intellectual aptitudes.

No less power of observation, judgement, self-restraint and presence of mind, patience and tenacity are needed to win the confidence of a nervous colt than will subsequently be needed to teach it the piaffer. The rider who has been unable to gain the first is not likely to obtain the second, whatever may be his physical dexterity.

*   *   *

The cavalry officer, providing he has the right inclination and a feel for the horse is therefore fortunately placed to develop his aptitude for dressage.

He will find amongst the horses of his troop, on the whole, the sum of all the faults which he may later have to correct in the pursuit of academic perfection. He has permanently at his disposal a wide field of observation and action, which becomes almost unlimited if he is entrusted with the direction of the dressage in his unit.

Round about his thirtieth year, he will perhaps go through a course of "Lieutenant d'Instruction", at the end of which he should be well prepared, morally and intellectually, to undertake the academic dressage of a horse and to gain, with practice, the necessary skill in the use of the aids.[1]

The Riding Master of our military schools is in a happier position still.

He must receive from his chief a more thorough education than is provided in the programme of the students' classes and he will gain much by

1. This paragraph was written in 1937. Practically all of it is outdated in 1949, and the difficulties met with by army riders who want to receive an artistic education are considerably greater.

having the opportunity to watch the daily demonstrations of his more experienced colleagues.

The *Cadre Noir* is a world of equestrian ability and culture of the highest quality, where are to be found clear-sighted observers, shrewd critics and wise counsellors.

The "Reprises" of this Cadre, though they do not contain as severe difficulties as those laid down in international dressage competitions, are, nevertheless, valuable exercises. To take an honourable part in them, all the riders are obliged to pay the strictest attention to regularity of gait, precision in the execution of the different figures, whilst maintaining all the time the utmost correctness in their attitude and using the aids with the greatest discretion.

If he is worthy of his status, the riding master will display his horse every year at the "Reprise du Carrousel". ("The Carrousel of Saumur" is a yearly parade of the Cadre. The present Saumur Carrousel includes displays by the cadet officers whose final year's training includes a short equestrian course; this is followed by a display from the permanent staff, the N.C.O.'s giving a most spectacular display of work above-the-ground, culminating with a Grand Quadrille by Ecuyers of the Cadre Noir.—Translator's note.)

The high degree of dressage necessary to be able to take a faultless part in this is a first stage in school work. Amongst those horses participating in it, one will be found that possesses a special talent and which will be the chosen instrument for classical equitation.

*   *   *

Outside the Army, the pursuit of Academic Equitation and the preparation for dressage tests is far more difficult.

Those who wish to study the art will need a passionate devotion, a rare tenacity, and great ingenuity to surmount all the obstacles they will find in their way.

They will have to sacrifice time and money and worldly pleasures. In fact, they must have the courage to withdraw from the world, not to the extent perhaps of entering a "religious order of Equestrianism", but at least a "lay brotherhood of the Order of St. George". One cannot but admire those who decide to do so and who remain steadfast in their purpose.

And, as for the "spirit" that should animate the student, the formula used by General L'Hotte to describe the spirit of dressage in the sequence of its aims can be applied to it: "Calm, Forward, Straight" (Calme, En Avant, Droit).

The most perfect calmness is essential in any dressage operation.

However, despite the firmest determination, the rider will not always be able to avoid a shaking of his moral calm and he will never be able to recover instantly his physical calm once it has been ruffled by however slight and transient a loss of moral calm.

A flash of temper can be inwardly suppressed almost as soon as it is aroused, but its resulting effect on the rider's nervous tension will persist for some time and, what is more important, for longer than the rider himself realises. The horse, on the contrary, immediately feels this nervousness and immediately shares it, but needs a much longer time to forget than the rider. In this respect, the horse is gifted with an astonishingly delicate sensitivity, such that even the movements of his ears are a permanent indication of the "state of the horse's soul"—if this expression can be allowed, which provide the rider with the means of perceiving a change in his own state of nerves, so slight that he may remain unaware of it, and even if his loss of calm is unrelated to the horse's behaviour.

Therefore, as soon as the rider feels any disturbance of his serenity, it is absolutely imperative to allow *time* for his own physical calm, which determines that of the horse, to be completely restored. A pause, a halt, provided that submission is not in question, is necessary before the lesson can be continued.

After some strong vexation, even if it has nothing to do with the horse, the trainer must be sufficiently wise to put the lesson off until the next day, and be content with a quiet hack.[1]

In the trained horse, the desire for forward movement must be passionate and have the powerful rigour, the acute intensity of a permanent and imperious physical urge. To foster this and, if necessary, to develop this passion must be for the rider a haunting obsession, for he must be constantly aware of the helplessness of his situation as soon as impulsion is lost. At the slightest sign of fading, the rider must instantly fully restore it, leaving all other matters pending, by resuming without delay the lesson of the spur, adjusted to the seriousness of the case.

One consequence of the absolute necessity to foster with the greatest care the horse's instinct for forward movement—in the absence of which everything ceases to exist—is that the rider must avoid using the legs—in frequency, in duration and in intensity—more than is strictly necessary, except as agents of impulsion. Their use as agents of direction or disposition of the body is necessary at the beginning and during the course of dressage, but the progressive substitution of rein effects for leg effects to this end must be a permanent aim of the rider, so that, eventually, the business of channelling

---

1. The cigarette is of a great help in such circumstances. One old master, who was not a smoker, always had a packet in his pocket for students who were about to lose their patience.

the horse's impulsive efforts will be assigned to the hands only, whilst the maintenance of the development of impulsion will have become the sole object of leg action.

Finally, to permanent calmness and obsession with impulsion must be added the constant pre-occupation of the rider with the necessity of keeping the horse always constantly aligned on his course, so as to ensure a fully effective use of the output of the quarters.

Any lateral bend of the horse outside this straight line can only be justified as a momentary exercise intended to correct a faulty flexion in the opposite direction, as the final aim must always remain to keep the horse straight on straight lines, and bent only on curved ones ("Droit, s'il suit une ligne droite, et inflechi dans le cas seulement ou il suit une ligne courbe". General L'Hotte, Questions Equestres.)[1]

The student must acquire as broad an equestrian education as possible by studying the writings of masters of the art. He cannot remain indifferent to anything that has been written on the subject of equitation. He will always find some food for thought and critical appreciation.

In effect, all authors say the same things, but each one of them expresses it in a manner that is personal to him, and one of these "manners" will be found to be more particularly apt to help the reader grasp an equestrian truth of which he might have had until then but a superficial and rather vague concept.

For all that, one must still know how to read, first taking in the whole work "at one stretch", in order to discover, with the help of the table of contents and the Preface what its structure, composition and spirit are. Then the reader must tackle the chapters one by one, calling to mind recollections accumulated in the memory by previous studies, in order to compare, to note differences and similarities between the various methods and, finally, to form a provisional judgment on the book, a judgment which will have to be constantly modified subsequently according to the measure of experience gained.

In the progression detailed in this work, relevant books of reference will be indicated at the head of each chapter and in the course of the text. A list of such books will also be found in the biographical index, but it must be understood that this does not constitute an exhaustive catalogue of equestrian literature. It is only a list of essential reading. All that has been written concerning equitation, or almost all, is worth studying.

The student will however have to be most cautious when he puts into practice the theories which he has studied. The progression unfolded in the next chapters systematically discards certain procedures of dressage, and the

1. General L'Hotte: Questions equestres, p. 98.

reasons for their exclusion are explained and reside almost always in the difficulty of their employment and the serious drawbacks which a faulty use of them entails.

The riding student, at a later stage, must undoubtedly study these procedures, because their effectiveness and their quick results may well make up for the difficulties of their application, but prudence dictates firstly that one should proceed as far as possible with the dressage of several horses by use of the relatively easy methods advocated in this work. They may not be as rapidly effectual as the first,[1] but they require less skill and, furthermore, have the advantage of avoiding, almost surely, mistakes which are always difficult, if not impossible, to rectify.

However, the "mastery" to which the student must aspire calls for a certain "personal touch". This will depend to a great extent on the particular equestrian feeling of the rider. His temperament, nature, resourcefulness and deftness will be its foundations, but its form will progressively be established by experience gained through long practice.

Amongst all the procedures which he will have tried out, some will be more in accordance with his own aptitudes and will give him better results than others. He will naturally prefer to adopt these, but not to the exclusion, on occasions, of others which may be more suited to certain horses.

In the art of riding, there is no "omnibus" progression, neither for the rider nor for the horse.

1. Some of these practices, such as Baucher's use of the spur and his "effet d'ensemble" (combined use of spurs and hands) are so tricky to use that they cannot be learned solely by studying the written explanations of the author. The student must be given several demonstrations, with comments, by a competent person, and afterwards he should be guided step by step in his attempts to use these methods by a master who must be a skilled executant and a gifted teacher, able to give a warning of danger in good time.

Chapter 3 · CHOICE OF A HORSE

Books of Reference:
DE GASTE: *Le Modele et les Allures.*
G. RAU: *Aptitudes du cheval d'apres sa Conformation (in German).*

Notwithstanding the skill of the rider, the results which he will be able to obtain in the dressage of his horse will be narrowly conditioned by the latter's natural aptitudes.

Nobody can turn a bumpkin into a Serge Lifar.[1]

The conformation and the gaits, the temperament and the character of the individual that one decides to school necessitate therefore a thorough examination.

The perfect horse does not exist. Amongst the faults of the particular type under inspection, those that cannot be compensated for by other physical advantages, for instance those resulting from incurable ill-health, or old age, or sex, if they are at all pronounced, are a reason for rejection.

Others on the contrary are tolerable if they are sufficiently counter-balanced by the influence of a compensating factor.

The presence and degree of these compensating factors will guide the observer in his decision to take on or reject the horse which he is inspecting. In conformation, *the harmony of the whole* is of the utmost importance. A "beautiful shoulder", unless it is propelled by quarters in proportion, loses the benefits of its happy conformation. A powerful croup, with a forehand that is insufficient to turn to account the thrust of the hind limbs, will increase the difficulties of dressage without giving much hope of obtaining entirely satisfactory results. A sum total of "good averages" affords a better chance of ensuring the regular progress of the horse's education and at least the correctness, if not the perfection, of his work.

The first essential "harmony" resides in the correspondence between

---

1. Almost all rideable horses can provide good "study matter" for the rider and their schooling is often all the more instructive when their aptitude for dressage work is less favourable; horses intended for competitions should be chosen, nevertheless, from those which promise to make good instruments. The chances of their not living up to their promises are great enough.

forehand and hind quarters and the right proportion of reciprocal influence of both on the movements of the horse. However, the qualities and the defects of the one and the other must first be examined separately, and from the point of view of academic equitation.

In the hindquarters, the situation of the *hip-joint* is of foremost importance. The lower this is situated, the greater the ability of the hind limbs—on which depends the cadence of the gaits—to lift the mass. However, in repose, if the croup is well muscled up, or is buried in fat, the situation of this joint is not easy to detect and the position of the *point* of the hip does not give a clear indication of the position of the hip joint because the ilium which connects the two may slope more or less. However, if the horse is made to walk on slowly, the joint becomes visible and it is then possible to measure its distance from the superior outline of the croup. (Fig. i).

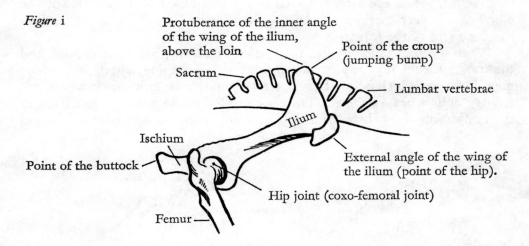

Figure i

Protuberance of the inner angle of the wing of the ilium, above the loin

Point of the croup (jumping bump)

Sacrum

Lumbar vertebrae

Ilium

Ischium

Point of the buttock

External angle of the wing of the ilium (point of the hip).

Hip joint (coxo-femoral joint)

Femur

The length of the ischium, i.e. the distance between the hip-joint and the point of the buttock, has a considerable influence on the form of the canter. When the ischium is too short, as is often the case with trotting horses, the canter lacks swing and assumes with difficulty the smooth oscillating movement that should be noticeable in the school canter.

Excessively obtuse or acute angles at stifle and hock are always a source of difficulties in the work of "fashioning" the hind quarters, but an over-acute angle is always more disadvantageous than an over-obtuse one, because it causes the horse to be in a permanent state of semi-collection which has no useful effect on the gaits and one which it is very difficult to improve upon in the measure required to produce a perceptible elevation.

In the forehand, the importance of the withers is paramount, because their disposition governs that of the entire front. If the withers are sufficiently long from front to back and sufficiently high, the tension of the topline, when the croup is lowered by the engagement of the hind limbs, will quite naturally produce a tension of the elevating muscles of the neck upon which the rider cannot himself exert any direct action.

In the examination of the shoulders, the most careful attention should be given to the disposition of the elbows. If these are too close to the chest, they make the horse clumsy and tend to impart to the movements an oblique, outward, direction, most detrimental to the development of all the gaits. Therefore, though excessive nearness of the points of the shoulder is, at least, not an evil, even if it may not be an advantage, elbows that are set too close are a serious fault. Their outward inclination, even if excessive, is not objectionable.

The direction of the arm, between the points of the shoulder and of the elbow has a very marked influence on the action of the forelimbs, and so has the *length* of the forearms.

When the arms tend towards the vertical and if the forearms are long, and the knee consequently low, the gaits are naturally sweeping, and their development in height which is sought in School equitation is difficult. However, the relative obliqueness of the arm must not bring the forelimbs too much under the body. This latter disposition results in the whole weight of the forehand

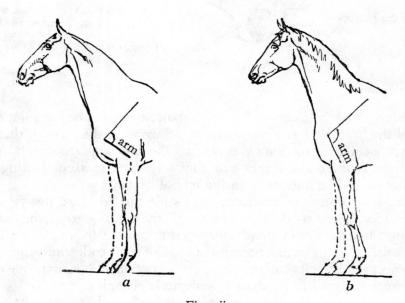

Figure ii

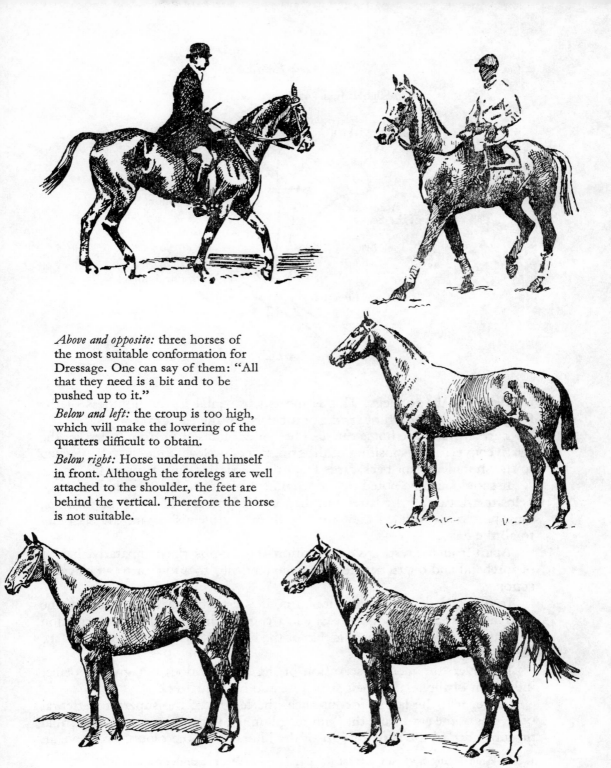

Above and opposite: three horses of the most suitable conformation for Dressage. One can say of them: "All that they need is a bit and to be pushed up to it."

Below and left: the croup is too high, which will make the lowering of the quarters difficult to obtain.

Below right: Horse underneath himself in front. Although the forelegs are well attached to the shoulder, the feet are behind the vertical. Therefore the horse is not suitable.

PLATE I

Drawings by Lt. Col. Margot from photographs

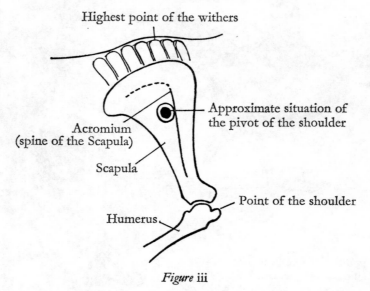

Highest point of the withers

Approximate situation of
the pivot of the shoulder

Acromium
(spine of the Scapula)

Scapula

Point of the shoulder

Humerus

Figure iii

overhanging the forelegs. This is most detrimental to the lightness of the front and to the length of stride, particularly in the canter.[1]

Furthermore, the horse can also be "under himself in front", despite the relatively vertical disposition of the arm, if the forelegs, though well attached to the shoulder, slant backwards from the vertical. (Plate 1, p. 23.)

It should also be noted that a prominent pissiform bone behind the knee helps the flexion of the latter and that, in the hind as well as in the forelegs, long pasterns, provided they are free from any blemishes, impart elasticity to all the gaits.

Apart from the respective disposition of the limbs, the comparative height of forehand and quarters determines the tendency to a low or to an elevated action.

In order to develop the School airs, it is essential that the efforts of the hind limbs are able to develop easily in a vertical direction. The conformation that favours this requirement is that of the horse that is built "upwards" (see Plate 1, p. 23).

However, the mere observation of the top line does not give a correct indication of the relative height of fore and hind quarters.

As regards the latter, for instance, the length of the superior vertebral processes of the croup and the "jumping bump", which is merely an abnormal protuberance of the anterior part of the ilium above the croup, may give an

1. The Arab saying is: "Never trust the horse whose feet are under thine own."

appearance of height which, from our point of view, is misleading because it is the situation of the *hip-joint* that influences the direction of the efforts of the hind limbs.

With respect to the forehand, the outline of the withers, formed by the upper edges of the first dorsal vertebrae, is much higher than the superior extremity of the shoulder blade, and it is towards the upper third of the latter that is situated the axis of oscillation of the shoulder.

It should also be noted that the line which runs from the apex of the withers to the point of the shoulder does not give either a true indication of the slope of the latter. It is the highest of the dorsal vertebrae that determines the height of the withers, but it is the ridge of the acromium of the shoulder blade that indicates the slant of this part. If the continuation of this line is not in line with the tip of the highest vertebra, the alignment of the apex of the withers and the point of the shoulder does not correspond with the real inclination of the shoulder—and that is frequently the case. A wither that is high at its rear extremity gives an appearance of slope to the shoulder, making it look more beautiful than it really is.

It is important therefore to examine not the topline, but a line that joins both these rather indistinct points: the hip-joint and the axis of the shoulder blade (Fig. iv). If the latter is lower than the first, the horse is built "downhill" and is not suitable for the elevated gaits. The reverse is true in the opposite instance.

Length of limbs is not an advantage in outdoor work, where a horse that

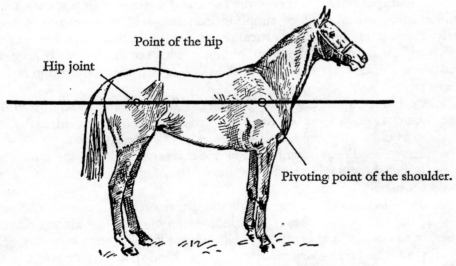

Figure iv

is "close to the ground" is to be preferred because he is more secure, but it is not a drawback in the manege horse who needs greater mobility and is consequently well suited by a centre of gravity placed slightly higher. The gaits of the whippet are lighter than those of the basset.

An examination of the tail gives some indication of the general suppleness. A high tail carriage, particularly if it persists in the slow movements and at the halt, is often a sign of abnormal stiffness of the spine. An insufficiently high one in energetic gaits denotes a lack of tone of the top muscles and slackness, if not weakness, of the spine.

The topline, through the intermediary of which the reciprocal influence of forehand and hind-quarters is exerted, must, in the prospective dressage horse, show promises of suppleness rather than of strength. It is not as important, in the horse destined for dressage, though it is essential in the horse intended for racing, that the spine should be able to transmit without loss of energy the efforts of the motor to the whole of the mass, but rather it should facilitate, by its suppleness, the many different inflexions which enable us to vary the direction of the output of energy of the hind legs. A rather long back, providing it is well attached to a good loin, need not be a worry, on the contrary. The important thing is that it should flex easily, in a vertical plane, upward and downward, but without any marked tendency to do so one way more than the other. A tendency towards hollowness of the back is certainly not desirable, but—for the purpose considered here—is less objectionable than the opposite one. Even a slight tendency to a "roach-back" should make us reject a horse; he will always be a frustrating beast for manege work. A very short back and a massive loin always entail a stiffness that no amount of suppling exercises will ever overcome completely, either laterally or in a vertical plane. And the lateral suppleness of the spine, which is limited in the horse because of his conformation, is however essential for the easy performance of the various attitudes required in artistic manege work.

The neck must also be studied attentively. Its direction, in relation to the trunk, where it comes out of the shoulders, must be examined first. This should be as close as possible to 45 degrees above the horizontal.

A greater elevation, providing it is not excessive and that the loin is not too weak, can be compensated by a flexibility of the poll which facilitates the correct placing of the head.

On the other hand, a congenital and permanent hanging of the neck below 45 degrees predisposes to heaviness in front, which is always difficult to correct and can, in any case, only be corrected if it is compensated by great flexibility of the higher articulations of the hind-quarters, permitting the hind legs to engage easily under the mass, and the croup to be well lowered.

It is particularly just at the point where the neck grows out of the shoulders that its direction is important. When the point of attachment is too low, the trainer's efforts to lift the neck will be restricted to the upper part. The horse then becomes "pigeon throated", and he will always find it difficult to maintain the carriage necessary for the unburdening of the forehand.

At its other end, the disposition of the neck is no less important, as it affects the ease or the difficulty of correct head carriage. If the space between the jaw-bones is constricted, if the jowls are too massive, if the poll is too short, a horse with otherwise good conformation, loses all the advantages of his good points. He will always be a mediocre instrument for manege work, as no compensation exists for these faults. It is possible to obtain a vertical position of the nose by a flexion of the neck in the region of the third or fourth vertebra instead of the poll, and thus give the horse *an appearance* of having a correct head position, but the reaction of this bend of the neck on the natural curvatures of the spine does not produce the same powerful effect as does correct flexion at the poll which by compression of the vertebrae, constitutes collection of the back, i.e. the real essence of collection.

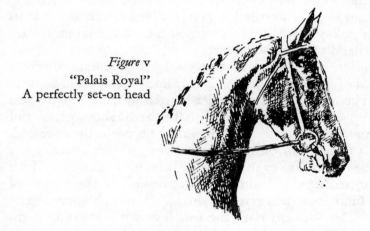

Figure v
"Palais Royal"
A perfectly set-on head

Furthermore, the mastoido-humeral muscles, which command the movements of the fore-legs, and are attached *below* the poll, are not given full play by this false head carriage and cannot assume the disposition which, when there is correct flexion of the poll, produces an elevated gait.

This flexion of the poll determines all the flexions of the spine and without the former, the rider cannot obtain the latter. We cannot be too demanding on this score. A horse with a badly set on head will always be a frustrating one, and his attitudes will always lack grace in the school airs.

A head that is small and light will obviously facilitate a correct position of the front end, but the proportions and beauty of the head matter far less than the way it is articulated with the neck, and the way it is coupled to it.

The set of the limbs must be carefully examined. In profile, in the hind-quarters, a line dropped from the point of the buttock to the point of the hock should be as vertical as possible and continue through the posterior projection of the fetlock. A forward or backward deviation from the vertical of the lower part of this line is always unfavourable to collection. When the horse naturally stands with the hind legs stretched behind the vertical, he finds it difficult to bring them forward sufficiently to a position under the body which produces the advantages of this general attitude. If the hind legs are naturally placed in front of the vertical, under the horse, they will advance beyond a position favourable for collection and all the articulations of the hind-quarters are then submitted to an excessive flexion which paralyses them.

Excessively angled, or excessively straight joints of stifle and hock, for the same reason, are unfavourable to collection, and so are insufficiently muscled buttocks or split-up thighs.

In the forehand, the importance of the position of the limbs in relation to the mass of the shoulders has already been emphasised above. If the arms are too short, the legs will not be able to develop sufficient elevation. If they are too long, the forehand will be too heavy.

This latter disposition is greatly aggravated when the general direction of the forelegs, instead of being vertical, inclines from front to back, starting from the shoulders. The horse which is "under himself in front", regardless of the position of the upper part of the limb in relation to the shoulder, cannot be collected along his *topline*, and therefore cannot be correctly collected. When the hind legs advance and push the spine forward, the latter is not arrested in front by the opposition of the forelegs. It is this opposition which should, by its resistance, cause a closing by compression of the curves of the spine when the hind legs deliver their thrust. In the absence of any resistance, the body slides forward over the fore-legs without being compressed, and the forelegs tip forward from the feet up.

The horse, which is "under himself in front", "collects his feet" and no advantage is gained as regards his general attitude on the modification of the gait which should result from the transformation of his whole attitude.

Viewed from in front or from behind, the limbs of both hind and fore pairs of legs must be rigorously parallel, and the distance between the legs of either the fore or the hind pair can only increase at the expense of mobility, particularly in the case of the fore pair. A horse with a wide breast, and shoulder points which are too far apart, lacks lateral mobility and has difficulty in changing the lead at the canter.

A divergence from the parallel, from top to bottom, in the hind limbs, is particularly objectionable. As the limbs move forward, they also spread apart and away from the body, instead of advancing under it as they come to the ground. This is a conformation most detrimental to collection, and so is the one in which the points of the hocks are too close (cow-hocks), which produces the same results despite the possible parallelism of the legs in their upper part.

On the other hand, a contrary disposition of the hocks, facilitates collection and increases its useful effects, but in this case it frequently happens that in a piaffer the hind legs cross to the extent of the shoes cutting the inside of the feet, and sometimes painfully wounding the coronet, so that the horse takes a dislike to this air.

The natural gaits of the horse are never completely transformed by dressage. They can be made more regular and developed to a certain extent, which is difficult to foresee and which we should not presume too optimistically.

Cramped paces, a short and trailing trot, a rolling canter without a good swing will never acquire the amplitude and rhythm demanded in manege work.

Regularity and symmetry in the natural gaits are essential in a horse intended for academic equitation. It often happens that an asymmetry barely noticeable at the trot becomes very conspicuous in the passage and completely mars a piaffer. A slight difference in the play of the limbs between the canter on one lead and the canter on the other may go almost unnoticed until a stage is reached when changes of lead at close intervals require a rapid alternation, and this can be an unsurmountable obstacle in the execution of changes at every stride.

In both fore and hind pairs of legs, viewed from the front, or in profile, the action of both limbs, at the trot and at the walk, must be perfectly symmetrical.

Correspondence between the movements of the forelegs and the hind legs is also important. A slightly excessive lifting of the forelegs is no great fault, on the contrary, providing the hind legs do not display an excessive tendency in the opposite direction. Conversely, if the hind legs are lifted higher than the fore legs it usually reveals a conformation unsuitable for manege work, and almost always precludes the execution of high school airs in their classical form.[1]

---

1. In "Piaffer and Passage," the General points out this natural defect of his horse *Professeur*, but he does not point out that he was able to neutralise it, not permanently, which is almost impossible, but at least in the very collected school airs. (Note of the 2nd Edition.)

At the walk, ample oscillations of the neck and the tail indicate good overall suppleness, to an extent shown by the amplitude of their swinging.

At the trot, the natural elevation of the neck gives an approximate indication of the limit we can hope for in the school trot and in the airs developed from this gait.

If we want to examine the gaits of the horse, it is useful to see him ridden, if possible by his usual rider who can show him from the front or the back better than he can be shown in hand, and also demonstrate how the horse behaves when he is mounted.

However, it is particularly when the horse is *at liberty* that his gaits should be observed. At the moment when he is let loose in the manege, still under the influence of his "stable freshness", the horse naturally assumes the air of joyful pride which dressage must eventually make habitual to him; he composes himself of his own accord, and displays as much as we can expect of his "future brilliance" as regards attitude, gaits and school airs.

After he has calmed down, we can get valuable indications of his aptitudes at the canter, and it would be a bad sign if he returned too soon and too willingly to the trot which is only used normally by the horse at liberty as a transition between the canter and the walk.

By moving about in the manege, the observer will get the horse to turn and change direction.

If the horse turns towards the side opposite to his leading leg, remains on the same lead and continues to canter on the outside leg, we may take it as a sign of some natural awkwardness at this gait. If he becomes disunited, and remains disunited, this awkwardness should be considered with even more concern. Finally, if he changes from one lead to the other by putting in a stride at the trot between each change, it would be wiser to give up the idea of dressage, as the work at the canter would always remain disappointing.

Natural changes of lead at liberty must be easy, light and instantaneous if they are to give any guarantee about their future execution on demand.

As regards the nature of the horse, viciousness and inveterate temper are unacceptable defects. Even after years of methodical work, of firmness allied to kindness, after long periods of apparently perfect submissiveness, the rider will never be certain of having obtained the total obedience, confident, cheerful and obliging, which is required in a presentation. Even if the domination of the rider is assured, the possible necessity of resorting to coercion risks provoking at least a laying back of the ears, or a lashing of the tail which a conscientious judge will feel obliged to record in his note on "submission".

For academical work, the "cold" horse is often a frustrating animal. His lack of natural impulsion will oblige the rider continually to sustain the action, or even to over stimulate it. Very often his efforts will be obvious. This will influence the judge's note on "impulsion". Furthermore, a continuous and strong use of the legs always spoils the correctness of the rider's position to some extent, and loses him marks on "correction".

The excessively sensitive horse is also often very difficult to present, particularly when the audience increases his nervousness, as he frequently becomes confused and inattentive. However, to have permanently at ones disposal a slight excess of tension is preferable to being under the constant threat of an easing off in energy.

If a choice has to be made, and if we discard the mulish horse and the incurably apathetic one on the one hand, and the frenziedly agitated, the congenitally crazy, the demoniac, on the other hand, a hot horse is preferable to a cold one.

The timid horse, particularly if his poor eyesight is the cause of his permanent anxiety, is also a frustrating animal. Sooner or later, the sight of some too brightly coloured flowers will cause him to spoil a change of lead, or the sound of the judge's bell will make him panic.

In conclusion, as regards moral qualities, we want a "decent sort", a horse which is generous but not fanatical, who has good eyesight, is well mannered and civilised.

Breed and breeding only matter when they have an influence on conformation, action and temperament.

Many thoroughbreds are built "downwards" and their limbs are directed in a manner that favours a low, sweeping action, which is the reverse of the one required for school work.

However, a thoroughbred with almost the right kind of conformation is nearly always a good instrument, an energetic and sensitive one. Furthermore, thoroughbreds have a very remarkable way of compensating for the faults of their natural movements by some other qualities. They usually do their work seriously and attentively. They are, in the present state of breeding in France, the best instruments for artistic equitation.

Anglo-Arabs are nearly always endowed with the right action for manege work. Unfortunately, some of them have very badly set on heads[1] and their

---

1. The upper part of the cheek bone is very broad from front to back and at the top; as a result the parotid glands are painfully compressed between these bones and the lower part of the first cervical vertebrae when the poll is flexed.

Collection of the head (ramener) is very painful for them. This regrettable conformation, and also the insufficient spacing between the cheek bones is inherited from their Eastern ancestors, whose notorious "star-gazing" attitude was often attributed to the severe bits used by the Arabs, although this is far from being the principal cause.

inability to flex at the poll causes them to be models from which we can never obtain rigorously correct results.

Amongst the half-breeds, those with strong trotting heredity are seldom suitable for manege work, despite the natural elevation of their gestures. Their hind-legs are usually directed to allow them to move *outside* the trace of the forelegs, without hitting them as they advance in front of them. Their aptitude for collection is therefore almost non-existent. They often show a flashy and rhythmical trot which can be mistaken for a passage, but the spreading out of the hind-legs when strong engagement is required, makes the piaffer almost impossible.

Furthermore, for generations their ancestors have been so severely punished for breaking into a canter, that through selection this gait has become unnatural to them. A correct transition to the canter always remains difficult for them. In the change of lead, they often put in a trotting stride between the first canter and the new one. This serious fault is difficult to cure, and makes the changes of lead at every stride almost impossible.

From all these remarks, the rider can draw but a small number of approximately certain conclusions. For the rest, he must remain content with presumptions which can only be verified by trying out the horse, first in his usual work, then in some more testing evolutions than those required in outdoor riding.

If the results of sufficiently long and repeated trials are satisfactory, the horse can begin Dressage.

PART TWO

Generalities

Chapter 1 · THE AIDS

The aids are the legs, the hands, the weight of the rider, the whip, the caress, the voice, and the use of extraneous circumstances.

The legs have the duty of creating impulsion; the hands, that of regulating and directing the impulsion.

The modifications which the rider can effect in his position will move the point of application of his weight on the horse, and thereby influence the equilibrium of the mass, rider/horse.

The whip is an additional aid to impulsion. It can also be used to activate certain groups of muscles when it is applied to particular parts of the body, thereby influencing the whole play of the locomotive system.

The caress and the voice help the rider to influence the morale of the horse, either to excite him or to soothe him, to scold or to reward.

Outside circumstances influence either the moral disposition or the physical disposition of the horse. By making a judicious use of them, the rider is able to modify the one or the other in the manner he wishes.

The use of these aids is essentially the same in dressage as it is in outside or ordinary riding. It is however more subtle and discreet.

THE LEGS

To create and to maintain impulsion is the *essential* duty of the legs. Accessorily, they form, with the reins, a corridor of direction, within which the impulsion must be delivered.

Impulsive action of the legs

It is of the greatest importance that the legs should create as exactly as possible the degree of impulsion desired by the rider, and which is necessary if his orders are to be obeyed.

If there is *insufficient* impulsive leg activity, the execution of the rider's commands will be listless and sluggish. The directing actions of the hands are only effective because of the partial opposition they set against impulsion and they become indistinct when this opposition does not receive sufficient thrust from behind to be clearly felt. If the rider makes the mistake of pulling on the reins, to make the indications more emphatic, the insufficient activity of the horse would be diminished even more, and he would come behind the bit. From only hesitantly obedient, he would become unreliable and, ultimately, disobedient.

An excess of impulsive leg action causes disorders that are hardly less serious. To keep the excessively "impulsed" horse at the desired speed, the rider is obliged to increase the opposition of the hands. Compressed between legs and hands, the generous horse "collects" himself more than in the measure required to execute the movements commanded by the rider. He loses his poise, squanders his energy, and gets into the habit of going permanently in a more or less complete state of collection, to get him out of which is very difficult. If the horse is lazy, he will choose to obey the one of the contradictory commands of legs and hands that requires the lesser effort. The little drive he ever possessed will be diminished. He will become "cold to the legs", and "go to sleep on them".

From the start of academic dressage, the rider must strive to feel exactly the degree of sensitivity of his pupil to the leg. As he should by definition be a good willing ride, he must not only respect the leg, but generously obey its indications, which should not be brutal but given frankly and clearly.

That is a good starting point for further dressage, and there is no point in demanding a finer responsiveness to the legs until the horse is ready to be taught the Rassembler.

To produce impulsion the legs always act by brief *contacts* with the horse's body. Any prolongation of this contact, any pressure with or without increase in strength, is detrimental to the creation or the development of impulsion.

It is the briefness of these successive contacts, this series of shocks produced by their repetition that is the essence of the impulsive action of the legs, and pressure is used only to maintain the degree of impulsion that has previously been obtained by the "attacks".

According to the measure of force employed to produce them, these "attacks" of the legs will graduate from the blow to the mere vibration, with the "taps" in between.

Striking with the heel, particularly when the heel is armed with a spur, is the most severe form of impulsive indication of the legs; normally, the calf is used. The taps should never be prolonged, but as elastic as those of a spring hammer on an electric bell. The intensity of their force will vary depending on the effect we wish to produce and on how close the lower part of the leg is to the horse's body, and according to the energy used to deliver them. Assuming the use of the same force, the effect is greatest when the leg is in the normal position, its weight on the stirrup. It diminishes as the leg is brought closer to the body of the horse before it contacts it.

The impact of the leg could be greater still if it were brought away from the normal position before striking, but the small increase of power thus obtained would not compensate the rider for the consequent loss of fixity nor for the disturbance to the correctness of his position.

The minimum effect is obtained by repeated, short pressures of the foot on the stirrup, with which it must not lose contact, while the leg remains in the same position. A finer gradation is still possible, depending on whether this pressure is done by opening the joint of the ankle or by merely lowering the toes. Even when these actions are so discreet that they become invisible, which is as they should be in academic equitation, they are perfectly perceived by a finely schooled horse that has become really "light to the legs". Between the two extremes, the legs act in their impulsive action by a vibration of the calves which is produced by brief contractions of the muscles, without noticeable displacement of the lower legs. This is the normal form of impulsive activity.

According to the needs of the moment, the rider will alternate the taps with pressures on the stirrup, or the threat of the spurs when necessary, this being done by turning the toe out without displacing the heel; the latter only strikes in the last resort, as the "supreme expression" of the leg.

All these shades are not usually perceptible to the ordinary riding horse. However, they do become so without difficulty in the course of dressage if a light indication of the leg is followed quickly by a markedly stronger one if the first was not immediately obeyed, until the first indication is sufficient to produce immediately the results that could only be obtained originally by the second.

Pressure of the legs becomes impulsive only by using this procedure when the horse knows that the pressure warns of an "attack". If the rider does not use this succession, pressure of the legs signifies a call to the horse's attention, and an order not to change his output of energy.

It is in that form only that simultaneous pressure of the legs is considered in the following progression.

The place where the legs act has some influence on their effects, but it is a small one compared to the influence of the "manner" in which they are used which has just been described.

A.E.—4

The completely opposed opinions of Raabe and of Fillis on the effects of the legs used in the region of the girth is a convincing proof of this.

Raabe believed that the legs used far behind the girth produced forward movement; in front of the girth, backward movement, whilst in the intermediate position, just behind the girth, the action of the legs is without any modifying effect on the impulsion.

However, Fillis, whose girths used to get torn to shreds, held that it is exactly the rear edge of the girth that is the most suitable place for the legs to produce impulsion.

This total difference of opinion is undoubtedly due to the fact that at the same spot on the body of the horse, Raabe used pressure of the legs, whilst Fillis, at that spot or any other, always used a tapping leg.

The *manner* of using the legs is therefore much more important as regards the result, than *the place* where they are used.

Nevertheless, as Raabe maintained, pressure of the legs, at the normal place, does tend to prevent variations in the intensity of the impulsion—specially to prevent decreases—and to preserve it at the rate achieved by the *previous* impulsive actions. At the halt, a sustained pressure of the legs at this place maintains immobility.

If the pressure is applied a little further back, it confirms the horse in his direction by forbidding any lateral evasion of the hind quarters.

Finally, closed firmly backwards, against the flanks, the legs compel the horse to remain in a state of collection, by making the hind legs engage well under the body when they alight.[1]

Use of the isolated leg

Used singly, one leg produces effects which vary according to the manner and the place of application.

In the same way as when both legs are used simultaneously, taps of one leg only, wherever they are done, tend to increase impulsion. Its pressure has little effect on the degree of energy delivered by the horse, but has some on the form and direction of this output.

For instance, the right leg, used in a series of taps, does tend to increase impulsion, mainly because it intensifies the energy of the right hind leg's movements.

1. The last way of using the legs should only be practised in the course of schooling. The schooled horse, until he receives a contradictory command, must willingly keep a collection which is produced by the impulsive action of the legs regulated by the hands—which alone determine the form of the output of energy created by the legs. The horse must work "of his own accord", so that the rider keeps a correct position and the presentation then loses none of its quality.

When it is applied in the normal position, with a pressure perpendicular to the horse's body, it causes the latter to curve, as it yields to this action by moving away to the left the part that is being pressed against, thereby "hollowing" the right side to escape the contact. The resulting flexion has the effect of bringing right hind and right fore closer to one another, of collecting the right pair.

Further back, pressure of the right leg tends to push the quarters over from right to left, and the whole mass forward and to the left. That is if the hand does not oppose, and furthermore assists that displacement.

The more acutely sensitive and responsive the horse has become to the leg (through dressage) the less will be the necessity to draw the leg back to obtain a displacement of the hind quarters. Eventually, the direction of the pressure will be enough to achieve the desired effect. Used perpendicularly to the horse's body, pressure of the right leg will cause it to flex and become concave on the right side; directed backwards, towards the left, it will displace the hips towards the left, particularly if the hands contribute to produce the same effect.

At the beginning of schooling the horse to respond to this command of lateral displacement of the hind quarters one should not hesitate to bring the leg sufficiently backwards, to a place where the horse clearly perceives its intention. This place will vary with each horse, but it is seldom that it will be found beyond the middle of the body. If the leg is brought further back the chance of being better understood is unlikely, but there is a much greater chance of provoking lashings of the tail, or cow-kicks.

The amount of pressure necessary to achieve the effects of a single leg will become less as the horse's lightness to the legs increases. Once this lightness is perfect pressure of the foot on the stirrup will be found to be sufficient.

Combined use of both legs

As the rein effects are insufficient to make an incompletely schooled horse assume the positions commanded by the rider, the legs will have to be used not only to create impulsion but also to complement the commands of the hands.

An infinite number of combinations can be used for this purpose, according to the difference in intensity, in manner and place of application of each leg.

Work on two tracks, for instance, always requires, at the beginning, combinations of this kind. From left to right, the left leg drawn more or less further back, acts by pressure to push the horse's mass forwards and towards the right, but the horse, upset by this lateral progression which is unnatural, tends to slow down; then the *tapping* right leg prevents him from doing so.

Besides that, there often will be a tendency to incurve the left side under the pressure of the left leg. This faulty curvature will then have to be corrected by *pressure* of the right leg on the girth. In the half pass to the right, for instance, the left leg, drawn back to a greater or lesser extent acts with a continuous pressure, of varying intensity however, and will alter its point of application according to the horse's reaction, while the right leg—on the girth, or immediately behind it—acts by "taps" or "pressures" depending on the circumstances. The actions of the hands will necessarily also have to vary in order to sustain those of the legs, but furthermore they will progressively substitute themselves for the legs in all matters that are not concerned with impulsion.

The necessity of constantly straightening the horse in single track work, which should be the rider's concern at all times, requires, no less than does the half-pass, the use of similar combinations.

THE HANDS

Contact

For the indications of the hands to be perceptible to the horse, the reins must necessarily be *adjusted*, that is stretched *by the rider* in the exact measure required to bring the hands in contact with the horse's mouth.

The firmness of the contact depends on the degree of tension that corresponds to this measure, and is peculiar to each rider depending on the degree of his touch.

Tension

Tension is the support taken *by the horse* on the reins adjusted by the rider. It varies according to the conformation and the ardour of the subject. A horse that goes on his forehand leans on the hands. If he brings his weight excessively on his haunches he will not give enough tension.

Too hot, he pulls, in an attempt to go faster than the rider wants him to. Too cold, he refuses to come up to the bit.

In all equestrian uses, the tension applied by the schooled horse must be definite and continuous. It increases in intensity with the development of the drive or push of the hind legs and the resulting speed. Outside, it is desirable for the tension to be firm at extended paces and to remain clearly felt at moderate paces without ever going to an excess or a deficiency, beyond the limits imposed for the comfort of the rider.

In academic equitation, the tension must be as light as possible, closely resembling the mere contact which must never be lost.[1]

1. See Part II, Chapter VI: The Descente de Main. Note: 2nd Edition.

The Half-Halt

A firm, upward action of the hands, on taut reins, with the fingers firmly closed, followed quickly by a progressive opening of the fingers and yielding of the hands.

This action is somewhat similar to the action used to lift up a heavy flagstone lying at the foot of some stairs in order to put it down on a step above, without damaging in any way the surface of the step or making a noise.[1]

Vibration

Quivering action of the finger tips, lightly closed on the reins, rather like the one the violinist uses on the strings of his instrument to produce a "vibrato".

The *Mise en Main* or relaxation of the mouth in the Ramener reduces tension for a moment to the degree of minimum contact. This is the subject of another chapter.

The Descente de Main

Prolongs and maintains this reduction of tension to minimum contact. However, even when the hands have yielded, it is not prudent to abandon all contact by dropping the reins on the neck. The weight of the reins gives a contact despite their looseness so long as they are still held in the hands by their end. Complete surrender of the reins on the neck must be reserved for periods of rest.

* * *

The hands regulate the *output in speed*, *the form*, and the *direction* of the amount of impulsive energy produced by the horse.

Because of the positions he takes up under the influence of the actions of the hands, the horse is able to obey their indications.

Control of Speed

For a set amount of energy produced by the horse, the speed is regulated by the position, in the vertical plane, of the head and neck.

When the horse is using himself properly, without resistance or distraction, at the given speed, he quite naturally places his neck at a set height.

---

1. This text was also in "Piaffer and Passage". It is necessary to make it clear that the comparison between the half-halt and the act of lifting up a heavy flagstone does not apply to the *vigour* required by such a feat of strength. For then the half-halt would not be a business for young ladies. It does depict strikingly the slowness of the movement, the curving line followed by the hand, the tightening and very gradual opening of the fingers. Note: 2nd edition.

When he uses the amount of energy that corresponds exactly with the speed required by his rider the latter will let him take this natural attitude, which varies with every horse but which should always be one in which the mouth of the horse is approximately in the same horizontal plane as his hips, allowance being made for the vertical oscillations of forehand and hind-quarters. The horse is then balanced in his speed.

When the impulsion wanes, because of fatigue or laziness, the horse can, for some length of time, keep up the same speed by disposing his mass in a manner that helps him to obtain a rather better output from the same amount of energy than he would obtain in a normal attitude; he puts his weight on his forehand by lengthening and lowering his neck. His balance then becomes precarious because of the excessive burden borne by the shoulders and a fall can occur as soon as the forelegs make a mistake. That is a risk which it is sometimes necessary to run in "sporting equitation", when the effectiveness of the aids is exhausted, but it is absolutely excluded in academic equitation, which will not bear with laziness and should never be practised to a stage where fatigue sets in.[1]

It is often the case, on the contrary, that because of his ardour the horse uses more energy than is necessary to obtain the speed wanted by the rider. Diet, rational exercise and proper schooling may well help in restricting this ardour within a proper measure, but with some horses this is sometimes almost impossible and the rider is left with no other resource than that of modifying the horse's attitude to diminish the output of this excessive energy, by drawing to the rear some part of the weight of the mass.

He may attempt to achieve this by pulling on the reins to shorten the front of the horse, to draw the nose closer to the chest, but the horse soon learns that he can pull in the opposite direction and that his strength out-measures considerably his rider's. He becomes at best uncomfortable, and sometimes uncontrollable. In any case the contractions to fight the hands extend to the whole muscular system making the gaits irregular. The horse may be usable for ordinary outdoor riding, but it would remain impossible to obtain correct results in academic equitation so long as his resistances are not destroyed at their roots, i.e. the fight against the hands.

The most effective method of regulating the speed of the excessively "hot horse" with the least effort consists in lifting his neck.

1. The lowering of the neck obtained by pushing the horse on to the point of fatigue can be employed in the breaking-in and elementary dressage stage with a view to using the horse for ordinary riding, to correct a persistent habit of going in the opposite attitude. There is no room for this practice in academic equitation, where it is required that a horse should still be alert and fit at the end of every lesson, so that fatigue does not blunt his sensitivity to the aids.

To "push" his head down, the horse has only a limited force at his disposal. He cannot possibly use it continuously, and can only struggle to free himself from the elevated position of the neck which the rider tries to impose by "plunging" on the hand at more or less frequent intervals. The persistent "leaning" on the hands is not produced by an effort of those muscles that push the neck down but on the contrary by the absence of effort of the opposing ones. It is by getting the hands to support the forehand which he will not carry himself, that the horse is able to put this pressure on them. If the rider refuses to give this support and unflaggingly repositions the head each time it is abandoned, he will gradually get the elevating muscles to work until they can support it by their own effort. As for the horse that "plunges" on the hands and tries to "wrench" the reins away, he automatically receives a punishment that soon effects a cure, provided the rider is able to meet these plunges at their depth on immovably fixed hands, instead of resisting them at the start.

The skilful rider can, therefore, obtain a lifting of the head without painful effort and moreover without causing the persistent contractions that result from a backward pull on the reins.[1]

FORM OF THE GAITS

To reduce speed, the method of lifting the neck is therefore more effective and convenient than the one that consists of shortening it by backward tractions on the reins. It does not impair, as the latter does, the regularity of the gaits, it does however have some influence on their form.

The reduction in the output in speed of the horse's impulsive energy is obtained by getting part of this surplus energy to spend itself upwards. As the head carriage rises, the gaits become higher too, thus covering less ground. Beyond a rather narrow limit, this may be a disadvantage outside. In academic equitation, the school movements call for greater elevation than the natural movements, and the "airs" demand the loftiest elevations. Consequently, the lifting of the neck is a frequent practice in high school work, but it is nonetheless essential that even when a horse has reached that degree of dressage he can still be kept by his rider at natural gaits without any more elevation than they require.

This stage is reached gradually as the horse progresses in his submission which shows itself not only by his prompt obedience, but also by his more exact and more complete comprehension of his rider's wishes.

1. However, when it is a case of contending with the strong resistances of a horse going full out over country, this lifting of the hands is difficult, and the use of a gag instead of an ordinary snaffle gives more comfort to the rider.

The closeness of the relationship that progressively becomes established between rider and mount enables the horse to penetrate more deeply into the intentions of his master, who will then be able to act directly, almost by "persuasion" on the cause of the disorder, i.e. the excess of energy, instead of being limited to transforming the effects of this excess.

Once the horse's moral submission is complete, it will be necessary to prescribe an attitude that by itself determines a certain speed. An imperceptible beginning of an indication becomes a threat to the horse, or rather a warning preparatory to coercion, and the warning is sufficient to obtain obedience.

Such a result can only be obtained by much skill and perseverance. Every time an order to slow down is given, the intensity of the new indication must be less than that which was sufficient on the previous occasion to obtain submission. If, however, it is insufficient, it must be increased by almost imperceptible degrees, and cease at the first sign of obedience. It is only by practising this calculated parsimony for a long time—as the slightest impatience would compromise results—that absolute domination over the horse's mind can be obtained and that persuasion can replace constraint.

Direction

When the horse, through ignorance or unwillingness *resists* the directing actions of the hands, the rein effects are only predictable to a very limited extent, according to the following remarks.

(1) If hips and shoulders are not in the same direction, the hips always determine the direction of the horse's mass.

(2) The articulation of the spinal vertebrae does not allow the spine to flex laterally more than one way at a time. A marked "S" position is quite impossible, except in very restricted measure at a free walk.

(3) The flexion ascribed to the spine by its fore-end is communicated to the whole of the spine, from front to back to its very tip.

(4) The lateral flexibility of the spine is very limited.

The moment the horse is bent to his limit he finds that he is obliged to straighten himself out again. If he cannot straighten his neck which the hand forces to remain bent, he throws his quarters out in the opposite direction, to escape the bend.

Usually the horse attempts to straighten himself out from the hips before he reaches this extremely bent position, in fact almost always as soon as even a slight flexion is demanded.

It is only on the well schooled horse, i.e. the submissive and educated horse, that the actions of the hands can be exactly defined.

If both reins are equally adjusted and placed symmetrically on either side of the neck, and the rider relaxes the pressure of his fingers on the left rein and increases it on the right rein, without moving his hands, the "feel" of the mouth on the bit is disturbed. The horse tends to withdraw the right side of his lower jaw, and to advance the left side to escape the discomfort. The manner in which the upper jaw is articulated with the head makes it impossible for him to do so unless the head follows the movement of the jaw. The head therefore inclines to the right, and the neck has to bend to the right in its upper part. This bend extends from front to back along the whole length of the spine, and causes the hips to move over towards the left. At the same time, the weight of the forward extremities is brought to bear on the right shoulder, causing the forehand to move in that direction.

All those tendencies will be more or less marked according to the difference in pressure felt by both sides of the mouth. The horse is "placed to the right" and the amount of bend will depend on the difference in pressure. He is prepared for any change in direction to the right. If the left hand advances a little or allows the rein to slip through the fingers, the horse will enter a wide turn, the curve of which corresponds to that of his neck, and he does this by displacing equally but in opposite directions, his forehand and his quarters. When the direction of the right rein is modified by moving the hand to the right, the head turns in the same direction. The curve of the spine increases as does the loading of the right shoulder. The turn will be more or less sharp depending on the extent of displacement of the hands. The further the rein approaches the perpendicular to the horse's median plane, the more the displacement of the hips towards the left will exceed that of the shoulders towards the right, and the turn be made on the forehand.

When the direction of the right rein is altered by a displacement of the hand towards the left, the curvature of the spine to the right is accentuated at the fore end, diminished from front to back and tends to be localised in the neck. The tendency of the hips to escape to the left is reduced, while the weight of the forehand is transferred to the left shoulder, causing the shoulders to move in that direction. The horse turns to the left, more or less on the haunches.

Between these two opposite effects, infinite variations make it possible to control the direction and amplitude of the respective movements of fore- and hind-quarters and to determine quite accurately the disposition of the body in relation to this direction. Those variations are influenced not only by the extent of lateral displacement of the hand, but also by the height imposed upon the neck, because its lateral suppleness decreases with its elevation, though it improves as the Ramener becomes more complete. The effect of the difference in the tension of the reins remains the same as when the hand is not displaced laterally.

Finally, other rein effects can be added to the purely mechanical ones as the conventional language between horse and rider improves and becomes enriched with new signs. Thus, in perfect lightness, the touch of a rein on the neck initiates a turn in the opposite direction without causing any concave bend of the neck on the side of the touch but with a slight bend in the direction of the turn. (F. de Kerbrech p. 83.)

In the half-pass also, the simultaneous displacement of fore and hind-quarters in the same direction can be obtained by an effect of pressure of one rein only on the opposite side of the neck and although this effect is not identical to the first, it differs from it in a degree so fine as to be accessible only to a skilled rider and perceptible only to a well schooled horse.[1]

During dressage and with incompletely schooled horses the hand effects are insufficient to determine the positions the rider wishes to impose upon the horse. They can only do so with the co-operation of the legs used in a different manner from that which induces impulsion. The necessity of this co-operation diminishes as dressage progresses. As it approaches perfection the role of the legs is increasingly confined to the production of impulsion, and can progressively be restricted solely to this role as the horse becomes more eagerly submissive to the actions of the hands, which must eventually be able to determine by themselves all the positions required of the horse by academic equitation.

Handling of the reins

To give to the reins in relation to the mouth the directions that determine their effects, the rider is compelled to move his hands in all directions. The extent of their movements is fairly considerable in ordinary riding and at the beginning of dressage. It diminishes as dressage progresses to the point of giving an illusion of immobility of the hands to a spectator, whilst in reality on the contrary they are almost continually, though unnoticeably, moving.

Theoretically, the hands should never move backwards, as all tractions on the mouth are a fault. If the horse releases the tension on the reins by bringing his mouth closer to the hands, the rider should—in theory—adjust

1. This is the neck rein or bearing rein. The artist does not confuse it with the "Indirect Rein" of French Manuals of Instruction, or the "Indirect Rein of Opposition", though General Decarpentry occasionally uses the latter term. The indirect rein acts on the outside corner of the mouth and flexes the neck to that side; the indirect rein of opposition acts simultaneously on the corner of the mouth and by lateral pressure on the neck. The neck rein acts by pressure alone on the neck, which it does not bend. Used in combination with the inside direct rein of oppposition it allows the slight bend to the inside that is desirable in school riding. Note: 2nd edition.

his reins by shortening them. This is in fact what he does if the horse gives him time to do so. Some horses, however, alter the flexion at the poll so frequently and rapidly that it is physically impossible for the rider to keep on adjusting the reins. He must, however, try to retain a continuous feel by following the mouth in all its changes of position, either backward or forward. In the elementary schooling stage, the pursuit of this feeling may bring the rider to advance and withdraw the arms from the shoulders because of the extent of the movements of the horse's head. Later on, as the stability of the head becomes better established, the rider's movements can gradually be limited to a play of the wrists, the suppleness of which is sufficient to follow the displacements of the horse's mouth. Finally, with the schooled horse these displacements are minute, and the play of the fingers, more or less flexed on the hands, permits the utmost precision in following the very small variations of contact.

The same remarks apply to the actions of the hands that tend to lift the neck. At the beginning of dressage it may be necessary to lift the arm up from the shoulder and to extend it horizontally until the hands are close to the ears, so that the reins are given as near a vertical direction as possible. The results obtained in that manner may later be achieved by a progressively restricted elevation of the arm, and a less vertical direction of the reins. The elbows can stay closer to their normal position, level with the hips, only advancing very little to prevent the hands being drawn back at all when they have to rise.

The ordinary riding horse should have reached that stage of schooling and the further education he must then receive to transform him into a school horse must reduce considerably the necessity of extensive movements of the hands to oppose an excess of speed. Gradually, the movements of the elbow joint diminish until they cease and the forearms can stay in their normal position level with the waist, while an upward flexion of the wrists becomes all that is necessary to regulate speed. Finally, as the horse progresses the play of the wrists can also be reduced and at the end of dressage it will be sufficient to lift the flexed first finger, upon which the thumb holds the reins, to determine the displacements in height of neck and head, limited themselves now but still retaining an influence not so much on the horse's balance as on his mind.

Weight of the body

The rider displaces the centre of gravity of the mass Horse-Rider by altering his own position.

When he *maintains* his upper body forward, he also moves the centre of gravity forward. When he grips upwards with the thighs he lifts it. In both cases he increases the horse's instability; from back to front in the first in-stance, in all directions in the second.

However, the influence of the new position on the balance is totally different from the influence of *the movement* made by the rider to change his position. In fact, these influences are *directly* opposed. For instance, the move-ment that brings the shoulders back causes, by reaction, the seat to push forward, but the pushing effect only lasts while the shoulders are *moving backwards*. If the shoulders stay back after they have completed the backward movement, they also fix the centre of gravity backwards, which is *unfavourable* to forward movement, whilst on the contrary the action of pushing with the seat was *favourable* to it.

Again, the horse does not passively accept these changes of balance. His compliance, and not by any means a wholehearted one, can only be obtained by a progressive education. At the beginning of dressage, he reacts instinc-tively and more or less vigorously in the *opposite direction*. Even when he is schooled, he only submits to a certain extent, and beyond that he starts by retarding the displacement forced on his centre of gravity, then he openly resists it and finally reacts against it when his instinct gets the upper hand over his submission.

Those considerations help one to understand why it is so difficult for the rider to make a judicious use of changes in his own position in order to influence the balance of his horse. Every change produces two opposite effects usually of unequal intensity: the one sudden and fugitive, the other longer lasting according to how long the new position is adhered to. There-fore it is often very difficult for the rider to obtain with certainty and precision exactly the result he desires. In fact the results which he imagines that he has obtained *because* of his body's displacements are often achieved *despite* them. Far from helping the horse they hinder him, but nevertheless the horse bravely tries to overcome the obstacle, so that he can be left in peace.

It is therefore prudent in academic equitation to restrict displacements of the body to the strict minimum required to overcome the effects of inertia and to keep the rider's centre of gravity—which is not in the same vertical plane as the horse's—in the direction of the movement, neither more nor less than in the measure required by the speed. Even then the displacement of the rider's body must accompany that of the horse's and neither precede it nor come after it.

In lateral movements, the best manner in which the rider can conform to these conditions is by putting his weight on the stirrup that is on the side of the displacement. This causes his seat to shift slightly in the same direction and his body to lean imperceptibly that way also.[1]

1. This weighing on the stirrup must not be confused with the *pressure* of the foot on the

Even without altering appreciably the position of his body, the rider can displace the point of application of his weight on the horse's back. When he relaxes his leg grip until his legs are merely in contact with the horse's flanks and taking as little support on the stirrups as is necessary to avoid losing them, the rider brings the whole of his weight to bear on his seat bones and consequently on that part of the back that is situated under approximately the rear third of the saddle. Conversely, if he puts most of his weight on the stirrups and lifts his seat imperceptibly out of the saddle, the weight of his body is borne by the part of the back that is situated below the stirrup bars, towards the front third of the saddle.

All horses can feel these displacements of the point of application of the rider's weight, and with some the activity of the "top line" is greatly conditioned by them. The lighter seat frees the loins and facilitates the flexions of the spine. It considerably assists horses that have difficulty in reining back, and at the beginning of the piaffer facilitates the moments of suspension between the beats.

To sum up, the perfect accord between the rider's position and the horse's movements must give the spectator the illusion of stability, the line formed by ear, hip and heel of the rider being vertical at the halt, and in motion inclining forward in the direction of the movement according to the speed and to the inclination of the horse's body.

THE CARESS

The caress is of cardinal importance as an instrument of dressage. All horses are naturally sensitive to it in some degree and their sensitivity can be greatly increased if, in the beginning of dressage, it is followed by a more tangible satisfaction, such as tit-bits, dismounting or taking the horse back to his stable. This first "association of sensations" greatly enhances the potency of the caress as a means of dressage. It should not be neglected.

However, the caress must be discriminatingly used in dressage and the rider must not expect it to produce better results than it can. The horse is not conscious of his actions in the same strictly precise manner as man is. He is only rather vaguely aware of them, and in a succession of actions is capable of distinguishing one from another only after much groping and hesitating

Therefore, to teach the horse anything the rider never has more than one means at his disposal, i.e. to place his horse in a situation which produces

stirrup which is the minimum form of impulsive action of the leg on the perfectly schooled horse. The latter is achieved purely by lowering the toes, or opening the ankle joint without altering the amount of weight brought to bear on the stirrup. These effects can be used simultaneously, but should still remain distinct.

instinctively and precisely the reaction the rider wishes to obtain. Neverthe-less, it is almost impossible, however great the skill of the trainer, to create a set of conditions which will provoke *one* reaction only. Nearly always the horse will try several different ones, and the trainer must be on the look out for the right one to appear, which he immediately rewards, namely with a caress. The horse, however, is slower in discerning precisely which of the reactions he has tried brings with it a reward in the form of a pleasurable sensation. His hesitations will gradually diminish as the rider repeats his requests, and only then will he be able to associate a particular act with a caress.

It must be noted, however, that this association "works" (if one may use the word) in reverse also. For instance, a horse that has taken a very long time to grasp the association: rein-back—caress, because he found that movement difficult, will subsequently show a tendency to move backwards whenever he is patted, whatever may be the new action the rider wants him to associate with a caress.

This frequently causes surprises and misunderstandings in dressage.

For example, when a horse starts to learn the piaffer, his first attempts must be rewarded immediately. Supposing that the horse was by nature "cold to the leg", and that this "coldness" had necessitated frequent lessons of the spur, the last one quite recently in the course of which sudden tran-sitions had been amply rewarded—as they should be—with caresses; then the bestowing of these at the first appearance of a piaffer may well produce an abrupt transition and this would be detrimental to the regularity of the piaffer and later on to the transitions from the piaffer to the passage.

In this hypothesis no great harm really would be done, as the disorder occurs in a forward direction. The situation would be far more serious if the horse instead of being cold and apathetic had been naturally agitated and nervous and at the beginning of dressage had shown difficulty in learning to stand still and had been generously rewarded every time he had succeeded in doing so. In this case, the horse would immediately come to a halt if he were caressed at his first successful attempt at a piaffer. That is one of the greatest difficulties one can encounter in the study of this air.

The foregoing examples show how prudent one should be in using the caress in the process of dressage. The rider is often inclined to think that it is just a means of letting the horse know about his master's satisfaction. How-ever, as far as the horse is concerned, a caress is only a pleasant sequel to some definite action with which it becomes linked in his mind to a greater or lesser extent.

Therefore, before using the caress when starting on some new work, one must be certain that the horse will not connect it with an action that would be unfavourable to this work. If such a connection exists, it will have to be attenuated by repeated exercises that will establish a mental link with the opposite action, and the new work will only be started when the caress has lost any influence that would be detrimental to success.

In any case, whether in ordinary riding or dressage, one should avoid the all too common mistake of attributing to the horse human ways of feeling and thinking, and avail oneself instead of the little that is known with certainty about his mental constitution.

The Whip

In the preparation of the horse by work in hand, the whip, as Raabe so justly said is "veritably a magic wand".

When he is mounted, the rider must most often be content to use his whip solely to produce impulsion by applying it to the shoulders. One must therefore see that this impulsive effect of the whip is fully developed, so that the slightest touch, the mere tap of the whip on one shoulder or the other immediately produces an awakening or quickening of impulsion. This development must go on at the same time as the education to the spur and to the clicking of the tongue. Once it is perfected, it should be possible to use the whip solely by a more or less rapid contraction of the little finger, without any displacement of the hand that would affect the tension on the reins or be conspicuous to spectators.

In exceptional circumstances, the whip can be used just behind the leg, in the form of an embracing and stinging blow, the arm outstretched, but this is a severe measure, the use of which should be restricted to the punishment of very serious faults. If these attacks are renewed, particularly at frequent intervals, the horse becomes alarmed at the slightest movement of the rider's hands and in academic equitation disorders due to this manner of using the whip exceed any advantages.

Once the horse has learnt by work on the ground to increase the activity of his hind-quarters when tapped by the whip either on the point of the croup or the point of the hips, the rider can resort to the same effects from the saddle, but only in the course of schooling. He should never use this method in presentations; it would be incorrect and a proof of insufficient training of the horse that is being presented.[1]

THE VOICE

The human voice has a great influence on the horse. It always attracts his

1. Furthermore, riders are not allowed any more to carry a whip in dressage tests. Note of 2nd edition.

attention and therefore prevents the *surprise* that his timid nature so often transforms into justified or unjustified measures of self-defence.[1]

The horse's sense of hearing is extremely acute. He clearly discerns intonations of the voice and maybe also some of its modulations. It is however a very common mistake to attribute to the intonations of the human voice an influence on the horse corresponding to man's intended meaning. If, for any length of time, the utterance of insinuating, affectionate words is followed by a stinging lash with the whip, it would not be long before, in the horse's understanding, these affectionate words would signify an imminent attack. If the feeding of oats immediately followed the most threatening shouts, soon these would mean to the horse the coming of one of his greatest satisfactions.

Undoubtedly, his reactions to the voice would be determined accordingly and be quite the opposite of those which one usually expects.[2] One must therefore first study the effects of the voice on the horse that is being schooled, then either confirm them or correct them by the usual method of associating sensations, which is the only one that enables man to influence the moral disposition and the mind of the horse.

In any case, we should always take advantage of the acuteness of the horse's sense of hearing, and avoid raising the voice unnecessarily as even the quietest tones are perfectly well heard by him.[3]

Tongue clicking as an impulsive agent is extremely convenient to use as much in dressage as in ordinary equitation, because it is directly perceptible to the horse and need not be accompanied by touches on the body which are liable to produce other, at best unnecessary, reactions besides an impulsive effect. With gradual practise, this tongue clicking can become so discreet as to be unaudible even to the rider's closest neighbours and yet remain clearly heard by the horse who must be trained to obey it immediately.

1. On the stable walls of the German cavalry, the following inscription used to be found: "Tritts du an ein Pferd Heran, rufe es stets mit Namen an."—"When you approach a horse, always call his name."

2. It is significant that the natives of North Africa use the clicking noise of the tongue to soothe the horse, just as we use the "whoa", therefore in exactly the opposite sense which we give to our tongue clicking. They use it continuously, when strapping and even when riding, and it is almost impossible to get them out of this habit. As a result, horses in their care soon come to disregard the impulsive character of our tongue clicking. This is all the more regrettable because North Africans usually make excellent grooms, providing they have not got too much Negro or Kabyle blood in their veins.

3. It is in the stable that the horse first learns to understand the human voice and its intonations. His first impression will always remain the most firmly-rooted. A brutal groom should be mercilessly sacked, but a "loud" groom, however gentle, should be avoided: he ruins the effect of the voice as a means of dressage.

The meaning of this tongue clicking must, of course, be made clear and compulsive, particularly by using it in conjunction with the education to the spur.

EXTRANEOUS INFLUENCES

The effects of the rider's aids are only a part of the extraneous influences that can be brought to bear on the horse, whose senses are continuously impressed by numerous other causes.

Amongst the effects of these causes are those which assist and those which oppose the effects of the aids.

As dressage progresses, the effects of the aids progressively predominate over other influences. The unfavourable ones are gradually neutralized, and it then becomes unnecessary to support the authority of the aids by making use of favourable influences.

It is quite a different matter, however, at the beginning of dressage. It is then imperative not only to avoid as much as possible all unfavourable influences, but also to secure the assistance of all those that can co-operate with the trainer in achieving his aims.

As far as moral disposition is concerned, calmness and attentiveness are favoured by silence, and by solitude, once the horse has become accustomed to it. They are disturbed by noise, by the company of other horses, by the sight of unusual objects, etc. All riders know this, but sometimes it happens that the trainer, intent on his work, omits to pay as much attention to it as is necessary, and that is a fault which he will always have to pay for.

As regards impulsion, one should always take into greatest account the natural attractions and revulsions felt by the horse. The stable, the door of the manege, the proximity of other horses are magnets towards which the horse is always drawn and which are favourable to forward movement, whilst this is diminished when he is taken in a direction away from them. If the door of the riding school is to his right, the horse will turn, move, and start into a canter more easily in this direction than in the other. Advantage should always be taken of this at the beginning of schooling.

The physical development of the horse no less than the moral one is influenced by extraneous conditions. On sloping terrain, he will instinctively put more weight on his shoulders on the upward grades, thereby developing the thrust of the hind legs and improving the diagonal action of his walk. On downward grades, he will "brake" with the forelegs, lessen the thrust of the hind legs, which are further engaged under the mass, thereby transferring some weight to the hind-quarters, while simultaneously his lateral actions are developed; when going across a slope, two-track movements and striking off at the canter are facilitated on the upward side. Both are more difficult on the downward side. In deep and heavy going, the horse is obliged to develop the effort of lifting his limbs, etc.

The art of combining extraneous influences with those of the aids is a great measure of the trainer's skill.

Chapter 2 · THE MOUTHPIECE

Book of Reference:
WACHTER: *Apercus Equestres*

The conformation and the structure of the parts on which the bit bears have necessarily some influence on the nature and intensity of the sensations felt by the horse through his mouth.

Horses certainly show considerable differences in the structure and conformation of the mouth.

This may be more or less deeply split, the corners of the lips being more or less close to the first molars or to the tushes (or incissors).[1]

The lips may be thin and smooth, or thick and wrinkled. Sometimes they have a tendency to roll over towards the inside of the mouth, thus covering to some extent the bars or the edges of the tongue. The corners of the mouth themselves may be either thin and smooth, or thick and wrinkled on their inner or outer aspect.

In the upper jaw, the height of the arch of the palate varies, either because of the structure of the maxillary itself, or because of the thickness of its fleshy covering and transversal ridges. The width of the arch also varies and therefore the room available above the tongue, when the mouth is closed, depends on the shape of the palate. The amount of space available is also limited by the tongue itself, which can be thick or thin. The lower part of this lies in the channel between the branches of the lower jaw; the upper part spreads over the bars, as far as the lips.

The narrower the space between the jaws, the less room will there be for the tongue to lie in its channel, and that part which is spread over the bars will be so much the thicker. The space available for the bit is accordingly reduced.

The bars can be either thick and fleshy or thin and poorly covered on their ridges.

Generally speaking, the lips are relatively insensitive, unless they are

1. Some mares have rudimentary tushes. In any case, the part of the bars in mares where the tushes grow in horses is particularly sensitive.

pinched by the bit; the tongue is more sensitive and the bars are the most sensitive part of this region; however, that is not invariably the case.

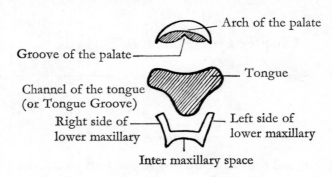

Figure i. Section of the mouth showing the bars
(section perpendicular from top of the head).

THE SNAFFLE OR BRIDOON BIT

A great number of horses accept the snaffle without fuss.

Those, however, that have a thick tongue, or a narrow tongue channel, or a combination of both, resent the pressure of the bit on the tongue, and try to escape it by getting the latter over the former. If the height of the palate permits, this is what in fact they are content to do and an inexperienced rider may not notice it.

But when the arch of the palate is too low the horse cannot do this, and he thrusts the tongue out to one side or the other, at first only occasionally but later on continuously.

In the first case, when the palate is sufficiently arched, one can successfully use a snaffle with a port, invented by Fillis which gives particularly good results when it is employed without a curb bit.[1]

However, when the palate arch is so low as not to accommodate the port of the Fillis snaffle without being touched by it, the port only increases the discomfort, and causes the horse not only to thrust the tongue out, but also to keep the mouth open.

1. In 1907–1908 a Russian officer, who had previously been a pupil of Fillis at the St. Petersburg Cavalry School, and was on a course at Saumur, had to school a mare who constantly stuck out her tongue, sometimes to the left, sometimes to the right. Returning from leave in Russia, this officer brought back a Fillis snaffle and used it on the mare. When used alone, this snaffle produced very good results. When the mare was ready to be ridden in a double, a curb with a port of the same size was used, and the effects, though still appreciable, were less satisfactory. It is probable that the total volume of iron in the mouth, of the two bits with their two ports, was more than it could hold.

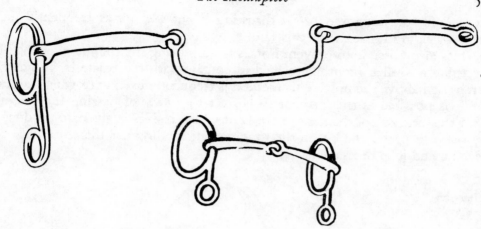

Figure ii. Baucher snaffle and Fillis snaffle with tongue groove

One can then try a very thin snaffle, particularly in its middle part, with very slender joints; the tongue, however, could be cut by this if the horse strongly stretched the reins. This procedure could therefore only be resorted to if the horse is naturally light on the hand or is very well schooled.

In the early training of a horse with such a mouth, the best thing is to substitute for the ordinary Bridoon a Mullen mouthpiece,[1] arched like the German driving bit. The regulation bit of the English cavalry which is used without a bridoon is of this pattern and often gives good results. The reins of course must be attached to the centre rings to prevent any tipping of the bit in the mouth.

Figure iii

English Cavalry bit: angle-cheek

Pelham (2)

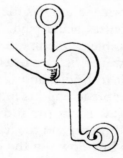

Because of its unbroken arch, this kind of bit allows the tongue to spread out and flatten itself accordingly. Many horses that fear the snaffle go well in this and it should be noted that carriage horses that evade the bit, either

1. Baucher also designed a thin mouthpiece without a joint which he used towards the end of his life. Note of the 2d edition.

by passing the tongue over, or thrusting it out are not as frequently met with as riding horses with this fault.[1]

It is also possible to prevent horses from putting the tongue over the bit by using a Mullen mouthpiece held in contact with the palate by means of straps tied above the nose. This method is frequently used in trotting stables.

It is possible in this manner to correct the *effects* of passing the tongue over the bit, but not the *cause* of the fault which resides in the pain produced by the pressure of the bit on the tongue. The method has therefore little to recommend it in dressage.

Figure iv

One could also tie the tongue down by passing a noose around it, the free ends of which are tied under the chin. This is a makeshift device that can be used if one has willy-nilly to use an unschooled horse. Thus compressed, the tongue swells up and the pain caused by the noose increases the pain caused by the bit.

Finally, in dealers' yards, one never sees a horse that puts his tongue over the bit. The method used is as simple as it is brutal. The tongue is seized firmly in one hand and jerked upwards, while at the same time the jaw is drawn forcibly down with the other hand. The fraenum of the tongue is thereby partly torn. As long as the wound remains unhealed, any movement of the tongue causes acute pain. The horse therefore keeps his tongue as immobile as possible, sometimes even to the extent of refusing to eat.

Healing, however, is rapid. The habit reoccurs. In addition, the horse becomes difficult to bridle, and lifts the head as high as possible as soon as he sees a hand approaching his mouth.

If the lower jaw is narrow and if, in addition, the bridoon is too wide (a frequent case in France) and the leather cheek-pieces are too long so that the bridoon lies too low down in the jaw below the narrowest part, the mouthpiece of the bit forms a more or less acute angle at the joint, which then

---

1. The old masters used a straight, unjointed mouthpiece called a "billot" for horses with an excessively mobile tongue who constantly toy with the bit—a vice called "snaky tongue". When, however, the tongue is heavy, numb and insufficiently mobile they used on the contrary a mouthing bit with keyes suspended to the joint of the bit, which hang on the tongue. Both these bits were used only for breaking in and therefore without a curb.

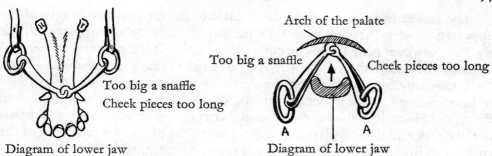

Diagram of lower jaw — Diagram of lower jaw

Figure v

presses against the roof of the palate.[1] Under the influence of the pain, the horse opens his mouth as wide as possible to avoid the contact of the offending point with his palate. He "yawns". (Fig. v).

When the reins are stretched, the rings "A" come closer together, the bit slides up onto the narrowest part of the jaw (Fig. v). The angle of the mouthpiece at its joint becomes more acute and increasingly presses on the roof of the palate.

It is possible to prevent the opening of the mouth by tightening the nose band, but this aggravates the cause of the trouble instead of eliminating it. From the point of view of dressage the procedure is useless. The cause itself must be eliminated by using a suitable bit, properly adjusted, either in one piece and arched, similar to the German driving bit, or else with a double jointed mouthpiece that gradually tapers towards the centre, with joints that protrude as little as possible.[2] In the case of a horse with a sensitive tongue, it is advisable to use a snaffle with cheeks, such as the Baucher pattern, which keeps the arms of the mouthpiece in their proper position and prevents pressure on the tongue.[3]

THE CURB BIT

The curb bit is a lever which like all levers transmits and multiplies the force applied to the extremity of the longer of its arms.

It is therefore an instrument that helps the rider to produce an effect of a certain intensity with a lesser effort.[4]

1. This bit is not provided with rings for the lip-strap. The bend of the cheeks, under the mouthpiece, is designed to prevent the horse from seizing them with his lips or his teeth.
2. This wedge-like disposition of the bridoon is inevitable when a curb with a port is used in conjunction with it. In such a case it is essential to use a double-jointed bridoon.
3. Like the (French) Army regulation bridoon.
4. That is why some of the old Masters called "harsh" some bits which we call "mild", and conversely. Their point of view was that of the rider while ours is that of the horse. (A "Treatise" (in Latin) on the mouthpiece by Simon Stevin, dedicated to the Bishop of Liege (end of the 17th Century), makes this point clear.)

The power of a curb bit is in direct ratio to the difference in length of the upper and lower parts of its cheeks measured from the mouthpiece; this is the case however only when the curb chain, which is the point of pressure of the lever, is attached to the upper ends or bridle eyes of the cheeks.

With many bits, particularly the Army ones, the curb hooks are attached to holes pierced in the upper part of the cheeks, between the bridle eyes and the mouthpiece. It is then the difference between the length of the lower part of the cheek and the length of the upper part to the point of attachment of the curb chain hooks, both being measured from the mouthpiece, that determines the power of the bit.

Figure vi

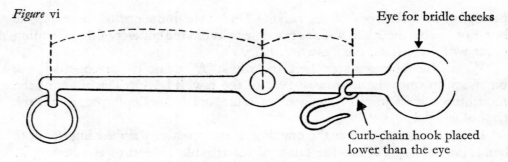

Eye for bridle cheeks

Curb-chain hook placed
lower than the eye

A bit which may appear innocuous because of the slight difference in length of the upper and lower parts of the cheeks may, in fact, be severe, according to how close the curb chain hook is to the mouthpiece.

The bit must rest on the bars, and not on the tongue, for pain is caused if the latter is compressed between the bars and the mouthpiece and resistances are then unavoidable. The compression must be avoided by the shape of the mouthpiece. In the case of a horse possessed of a thin tongue and a deep inter-mandibulary space (within the mouth), all bits are suitable. The tongue has plenty of room to rest in the channel. (Fig. vii.)

Figure vii

Bars of the
mouth

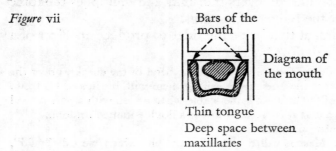

Diagram of
the mouth

Thin tongue
Deep space between
maxillaries

If, however, these conditions are absent, we must increase the space in which the tongue can lie to avoid it being pinched.

An arched mouthpiece is often sufficient to allow enough room beneath the arch for that part of the tongue that cannot be lodged within the channel. (Fig. viii.)

Figure viii

Extra room for the tongue is afforded by the space between the dotted line and the apex of the curve of the bit

When this is not sufficient, a "port" or tongue groove is incorporated in the mouthpiece, the shape and size being carefully adapted to each mouth.

The port must be sufficiently high and wide to give room for all that part of the tongue that cannot be lodged in the channel.

However, the height of the port must be limited by the height of the palate. If it touches it it can injure it or at least provoke a gaping of the mouth which a noseband can prevent but without, however, eliminating the cause.

The width of the port is limited by the space available between the bars. If it is too wide, its lower angles rest diagonally on the outer edges of the bars and injure them. (Fig. ix.)

Figure ix

Too broad a tongue groove

This can be remedied by a manner of construction well known to the old masters. It was known as a "Col d'Oye" (Goose Neck)—the lower part of the port being narrower than the space between the bars of the mouth but wider at the top. One can thus make more room for the tongue without increasing the height of the port.

Figure x

A "Goose-Necked" ("Col d'oye") tongue groove

The curb chain is an essential part of the bit which, without it, ceases to act as a lever as there would be no point of pressure. The curb would then act only as a very badly fitted unjointed snaffle.[1]

The position of the curb chain cannot be arbitrarily chosen. It is dictated by the shape of the lower jaw and of the chin and it must rest in the groove between the two, in light contact with the chin. Thus placed, so long as the curb hooks are not attached too high, it exerts pressure when the bit pivots on its fulcrum, without coming out of the groove and sliding up the lower jaw. There is a limit therefore to the height at which the curb hooks should be attached to the cheeks—and this limit is exceeded if these hooks are affixed to the bridle eyes when the upper part of the cheeks are too long. It is precisely to permit the use without disadvantages of longer cheeks that the hooks can be fixed in holes pierced below the bridle eyes. If the hooks are too high the curb chain rubs the lower jaw when the bit tilts. This is the cause of more curb-chain galls than is the excessive tightening of the chain.

CHOICE OF THE BIT AND FITTING OF THE BRIDLE

Snaffle or Bridoon

Unless the corners of the mouth or the tongue are unduly sensitive, there is no reason to use a thick bridoon. On the contrary, it is preferable to use a thin one that takes up as little room as possible.

A double-jointed bridoon is never objectionable, and in fact should always be used with a curb bit that has a port, to avoid the danger of the port getting under the bridoon, and lifting it, and thereby injuring the palate which can occur if the bridoon is of the single jointed type.

Cheeks with keepers are not essential on the bridoon, but are an advantage in that they hold the bridoon up in the mouth and thus prevent pressure on the tongue; they are never objectionable.

The bridoon should be of such a length that when the mouthpiece is laid out flat the ends should protrude from the mouth sufficiently (1 or 2 mm.) to prevent the rings pinching the corners of the lips.

The leather cheekpieces must be just long enough to hold the bridoon against the corners of the lips, if possible without wrinkling them.

This is not difficult when the mouth is deeply split up. However, when it is not, one must choose between the lesser of the two evils. If the bridoon hangs too low, it lies over or under the curb bit and this interferes with the

---

1. A curb bit without a curb chain is like a bicycle without its cog-wheel, chain and pinion, with the pedals mounted on the axle of the wheel, as they were on the penny-farthing.

The curb bit can be used without a chain in the preparation of flexions, especially with horses which bore on the bit because of excessive tightening of the curb chain. It is a device that can only be used temporarily. It should never be a normal procedure.

action of both bits. If it is suspended high enough to avoid this disadvantage, the corners of the mouth will be drawn up. The latter fault is not as serious as the former. It can be minimised by placing the curb as low as possible, but only within the limits imposed by the conformation of the mouth, and these limits are very restricted.[1]

The mouthpiece of the curb bit must be chosen according to the observations made earlier on the individual shape of the mouth. An arched mouthpiece is suitable in a great number of cases, and cannot cause any discomfort to horses that could even bear a straight mouthpiece.

Its width must be exactly the width of the mouth at the place where it rests, therefore a little less than the bridoon's. A millimetre of clearance, on either side, between the cheeks of the bit and the lips is sufficient. If the bit is wider, it slides through the mouth when a single rein effect is used, and can injure the bars of the mouth, particularly if the bit has a port. The width of the mouthpiece is not necessarily the same as the width between the higher extremities of the upper part of the cheeks. It frequently happens that the upper jaw is wider externally than the lower. The upper cheeks of the bit must then be sufficiently wide apart to pivot freely forward without rubbing the sides of the upper jaw.

The fitting of the bridle depends wholly on the right place for the bit. As this can only vary by a few millimetres upwards or downwards, it may be necessary, with insufficiently split-up mouths, to wrinkle the corners of the lips when fitting the bridoon, so as to avoid the two mouthpieces being superimposed.

This fitting must be done with the greatest care and it is seldom that perfection is achieved the first time. Very often alterations have to be made after the first fitting. No consideration for the preservation of the leather or disinclination to pierce more holes should prevail on the absolute necessity of obtaining a perfect fit.[2]

However, the horse one intends to train for academic dressage should be capable of being described as a perfect outdoor ride. In most cases it will have to be ridden in a double bridle.

("L'accoutumance est la meilleure garantie de convenance")—Custom is the best guarantee of suitability—and once again experience matters more than theory.

---

1. Horses with a small mouth, or rather an insufficiently split-up mouth are therefore difficult to bit.
2. The leather cheek-pieces are usually pierced by the saddler at intervals of 2 cm. They should be obtained pierced at intervals of 1 cm., or additional holes must be made in used cheek-pieces. Stirrup leathers should have holes pierced at intervals of $1\frac{1}{2}$ cm. instead of the 3 cm. of ready made ones.

If a horse goes well in his usual bridle, without showing any signs of discomfort, that is the bridle to use in his School dressage, even though it does not conform entirely to the conditions described earlier.

Furthermore, nothing prevents one from improving on it later on in minor details that might be of advantage.

For the kind of work that is referred to here, and with a horse that has been properly prepared by the use of an ordinary snaffle, a severe curb-bit would not only be unnecessary, but would be definitely objectionable.

Cheeks about 5 cms. long above the mouthpiece, and of a maximum length of 8 to 10 cms. below it, give the bit a quite adequate power, if the curb hooks are attached to the bridle eyes (round eyes, such as those incorporated in most modern English bits).

The curb chain, of course, must be twisted to lie flat, and must be fitted so that it comes into action in the chin groove, without sliding up, when the cheeks incline 25 or 30 degrees in relation to the mouth. The cheek pieces of the bridle must allow the bit to tilt to an inclination of up to 45 degrees but no more, so that the mouthpiece cannot slide up on the bars.

It is advisable with all horses to use a lip strap, which must be sufficiently tight, without however drawing on the curb chain, to prevent the horse seizing with his lips, and even more so with his teeth, the lower cheeks of the bit.[1] The cheeks of the bit must therefore be provided with special eyes for the attachment of this strap, which is not at all as effective when it is fixed to the bridle eyes.

---

1. It is very rarely out of annoyance that a horse starts to seize the cheeks firstly with his lips, and later on with his teeth, but usually more in play when he is tied up, held in hand or otherwise bored. The vice, however, is quickly acquired and soon becomes a resistance.

Chapter 3 · THE MISE EN MAIN

The "Mise en Main" is the relaxation of the mouth in the position of the ramener, defined in a later chapter.

The relaxation of the mouth essentially consists in a movement of the tongue similar to that which it does in the act of swallowing, when upper and lower jaw separate only to the extent required to permit the movement of the tongue.

This movement, a slow and supple one, causes the parotid glands to come out of their lodging, induces a slight salivation, lifts the bit or bits which the tongue draws towards the rear of the mouth and then drops as it resumes its place in its channel. As they drop, the bits chink, producing a typical clinking noise.

Any exaggerated lifting, or excessively prolonged lifting, any convulsive movement, or twisting of the tongue is a sign of contraction or insufficient relaxation; likewise, any exaggerated, jerky, spasmodic or persistent opening of the mouth. The head must remain set, not even giving a hint of movement, not even a "yes" nod, while the lower jaw softly relaxes in the small measure necessary to allow the tongue to move.[1]

It is without demur or bad grace that the horse must "give in his mouth", but he must do it with neither irritation nor ostentation, so that this evidence of perfect agreement with his rider remains, according to General L'Hotte's expression, "a discreet murmur" and does not become a "tiresome chattering".

Value and Significance of the Relaxation of the Mouth
All the old masters have drawn attention, in one way or another, to the significance and the value of the action by which a horse "gives in his mouth".

Once the horse has found the attitude suited to the work demanded of

1. In the beginning quite frequently the molars can be heard to grind sometimes noisily. This is a sign of incomplete relaxation. Start again, with indefatigable patience, at the halt first. (Note of the 2nd edition.)

him and can hold it without unnecessary effort, with complete control of his balance and perfect ease of movement; once, to quote the old French masters: "Le cheval se plait dans son air", (the horse is happy in his work), the muscles, which were cramped by the horse's attempts to adapt himself to his rider's demands, relax and their relaxation is progressively communicated and extended to the entire muscular system.

The stage of rather uncertainly directed efforts during which the horse, just as man, had clenched his teeth, is succeeded by a state of harmony in the use of energy, of relaxation, which causes the jaws to unclench and the horse to salivate; he "savours" his bit, he becomes "Gallant in his mouth", to quote the old masters again.

Thus, for them, what we call the yielding of the mouth was equivalent to a kind of logical proof of an "equestrian process".

Baucher entirely agreed with this view, but nevertheless based his method not on this proposition but rather on its "converse", which could be formulated as follows.:

"By *first* obtaining a relaxation of the mouth by means of special exercises called flexions of the jaw and getting the horse, by shrewd progression, to move in all directions without deterioration of the relaxation, the rider will have the certainty of keeping his horse constantly and perfectly balanced."

It was certainly so as regards the horses trained by Baucher himself. Possibly too as regards the horses trained by his pupils under the Master's eye.

However, those amongst them who have had to work alone, solely "by the book", have had a different experience. The excessive use of these flexions makes the jaw become more supple than the rest of the body. It yields too quickly and too easily, before the rest of the muscular system relaxes, and sometimes even when it does not relax appreciably.[1]

Because of this excess, which can be aggravated further by the trainer's

---

1. Those of Baucher's students who had received an extensive equestrian education before taking lessons from him did not fail to point out this danger.

De Lancosme-Breves, ex-pupil of the Manege des Pages—a subsidiary of Versailles— exposes it plainly in his "Guide de l'Ami du Cheval". As he was already treated more or less as a Schismatic by the "frenzied sectarians' of Baucher who disliked independence of mind, Lancosme-Breve had free scope to express his opinion of the value of the yielding of the jaw which, he said: "because of the excessive use of flexions, loses all significance".

Others, with more regard for the master's susceptibility expressed the same opinion though less forcibly.

A paragraph was devoted to the "danger of flexions" by De Sainte-Reine, who was moulded by seven years of education at the Hanover School during the famous Ayer brothers time, and later was Riding Master at the Sardinian Court, before he received lessons from Baucher.

lack of skill in the practice of flexions, the value of the yielding of the jaw as a proof of submission and perfect balance is much diminished and can be very small indeed when it is induced even more artificially by a pinching with the spurs, as was Raabe's practise, after de la Broue and Frederic Grison.

One can then validly object that the yielding of the mouth is accompanied by characteristic faults, namely those described above concerning the jaw.

But often these can only be observed by a very experienced trainer, after long practice. For the less experienced, even when advised by the former of his error, it is often too late to rectify this completely. In most cases it is therefore prudent to try to obtain the "Mise en Main" indirectly, by means of comprehensive gymnastics which will lead the horse to use his forces as harmoniously as possible in all the movements required of him.[1]

The mobilisation of the mouth, which is the essential part of the Mise en Main, then occurs almost always spontaneously. In order to preserve its character as evidence of the perfect adjustment of energy to movement, i.e. of perfect lightness, it will be enough to avoid interfering with its occurrence.

The numbness of some horses' mouths, despite the correct distribution of forces that shows in the ease of their movements and the softness of the reactions felt by the rider's seat—nearly always originates in their distrust of the hands, if lack of tact has discouraged their first relaxations. Most of the time, all that is needed to regain the confidence of those horses is a generous "yielding of the hand" at the slightest sign of mobility in the mouth, which one must learn to await with patience and to watch for with unflagging attentiveness. Nevertheless, these signs must at least show themselves for us to be able to encourage them, and it may be necessary to induce their appearance by using special methods which predetermine the mobility of the mouth.[2]

1. De Montigny, formerly a Riding Master at the School of Vienna, states: "Excessive practice of suppling is very injurious".

The military, who because of their profession had the opportunity every day to observe pupils of on the whole mediocre ability came to the same conclusion, and Lieut. Col. Gerhardt, undoubtedly the most practical of all, after having prescribed all Baucher's flexions in 1857, eventually in 1872, in his "Traite des Resistances", replaced them almost completely by a comprehensive gymnastic of the whole of the horse's body.

As for General L'Hotte, who drafted "L'Ecole du Cavalier" of the Army Regulations of 1876, he did not even mention the word flexion in it. In his double capacity of Riding Master in Chief and of General commanding the School he conformed to ministerial orders by purely and simply forbidding the use of Baucher's methods to the Cavalry School, and he does not express anywhere the regrets that this loyal submission might, supposedly, have made him feel.

2. This is the liaison which General Decarpentry, with such admirable wisdom, recommends to the German and French schools. (Note of the 2nd edition.)

On the other hand, Baucher's "converse" which is explained above, renders signal services in dressage. Although the mobilisation of the mouth, practised prior to a comprehensive gymnastic, presents undoubted drawbacks, its moderate and opportune use, *once dressage is sufficiently advanced*, offers advantages which could never be obtained by any other means. For although a perfect distribution of forces does bring about a yielding of the mouth, experience shows that conversely once this distribution is sufficiently close to perfection, the yielding of the mouth will bring it even closer to this, because of its particular effect on the whole of the body and will finally achieve it, at least temporarily, so long as the yielding is skilfully obtained by the persuasive influence of a cleverly "insinuating" hand.

This persuasive effect of the hand may, in fact, be due partly to its skill proper, but is greatly assisted if the mouth's receptiveness is perfected by the special exercises mentioned above.

The conditions in which these are used will be explained further on, in the chapter devoted to suppling exercises, called "flexions". (See Volume 2, Part 2, Chap. V.)

USE OF THE MISE EN MAIN

When the head and neck, together with the rest of the body, has been suppled by exercises, and its suppleness has been perfected by flexions, the Mise en Main then assumes a capital importance in the handling of the horse.

It brings about between man and mount an intimate relationship which the language previously established between them can never achieve without it.

In the first place, it gives the rider the most certain and the most subtle indications regarding his horse's mental state. Distraction, negligence, nervousness, reluctance to obey, in the slightest degree, immediately react on its production. When the horse, "neither mute nor garrulous", works in perfect lightness, he "falls" spontaneously into the Mise en Main, at more or less frequent intervals with a frequency particular to each animal, which it is essential that the rider should be perfectly cognisant of.[1] As soon as this normal frequency changes, the rider receives an infallible indication of threatening disorder.

Inattention, laziness, sulkiness, delay the appearance of the Mise en Main, which is on the contrary precipitated by irritation or anxiety. The form itself is modified by these, to a degree often unnoticed by the onlooker but which cannot fail to impress itself on the feel of a skilled rider.

From the physical point of view, which is in any case inseparable from

1. Hence the difficulty even a very skilled rider may experience in riding however well-schooled a horse for the first time.

the mental one, the slightest modifications the horse brings to the right disposition of his forces affects the frequency of the Mise en Main, usually by diminishing it and always by modifying it.

The spontaneous execution of the Mise en Main thus is an element of liaison with the horse, and a permanent source of information for the rider.

When the frequency changes the rider is himself compelled to provoke the Mise en Main in order to complete, by the observation of its form, the indications received by his seat on the nature and the extent of the incipient disorder.

Finally, and it is in this that Baucher has enriched equestrian art with a truly capital discovery: when the horse does not offer a spontaneous Mise en Main sufficiently frequently, or refuses a requested Mise en Main, he is manifesting a deterioration of his physical or mental balance. Once the Mise en Main is eventually obtained, it restores this balance because of its particular effect on the whole body of the horse, and does so far more rapidly and with greater precision than does any other effect of the aids.

When exceptionally, the unruliness is too serious for the Mise en Main alone to suffice to check it, it ensures a preparation for the action of the other aids, helps the rapidity and potency of their effects, which it completes and finally bears witness to as soon as it has itself resumed its normal frequency.

Chapter 4 · THE RAMENER

Books of Reference:
BAUCHER, RAABE, GENERAL FAVEROT DE KERBRECH, DE MONTIGNY: *Manuel des Piqueurs*.
LE NOBLE DU TEIL: *Cours d'Equitation*.
GERHARDT: *Traite des Resistances*.

The Ramener is the closing of the angle of the head with the neck, the poll remaining the highest point of the latter.

The Ramener is said to be *complete* when the nose reaches the vertical; if the nose comes behind the vertical, the horse is no longer "ramené", he is overbent.[1]

The Ramener can be achieved by drawing the head towards the body or by pushing the body towards the head, or by combining both movements.

Whichever way it is obtained, the Ramener presents the following advantages:

(1) It shortens the lever constituted by the neck, through which the weight of the head bears on the forelegs, and consequently unloads the latter.[2]

(2) By bringing the upper insertion of the mastoidohumeral muscle, which is attached at the poll, closer to the vertical line through its lower insertion at the arm, it increases the elevating action of this muscle on the fore limbs and thereby develops the amplitude of their movements.

But the intrinsic advantages of the Ramener are accompanied by serious drawbacks when it is obtained by drawing the head and neck towards the trunk, because the Ramener then necessarily communicates this backward movement to the trunk itself. To start with, the feet remain in the same

1. This attitude is only possible by a lowering of the poll, so that the highest point of the neck is situated further back.

2. This leverage effect of the neck is generally recognised; however it is not absolutely real because there is no fixed point (fulcrum) at the shoulders. No bony articulation exists between the spine and the forelegs such as there is between the spine and the hind legs because the horse has no collar bone. The spine rests between the shoulders in a cradle of muscle and cartilage which is relatively flexible. A lightening of the forehand produced either by the Ramener or by lifting the neck is therefore only to a certain extent true and is considerably less than is generally believed.

position, the limbs incline backwards from the feet up; the horse tends to squat on his haunches. Then, to avoid the instability of this awkward position, the horse moves his hind legs backwards; he becomes stretched out with a hollow back, ("il se campe")[1] whereas the whole progression of dressage aims at driving the horse forward into the opposite attitude of collection.

When the Ramener is obtained by means of progressively tighter side reins worn in the stable, the horse almost inevitably assumes one or the other of these two faulty attitudes. If the horse is walked in hand, or lunged with side reins, those dangers can be partly avoided if the trainer is very skilled and vigilant.

When, by a more discerning, delicate and nicely graduated process, one executes flexions of the poll, at the halt, as Baucher used to practise them in his first manner, their dangers can be nearly completely avoided, as long as the trainer by a careful preparation with the whip, has managed to secure the *irresistible* means not only of sending the horse forward, but also of preventing any drawing back of the body behind the vertical line of the limbs, which is much more difficult.

However, even in those conditions, the practice of flexions of the poll, amounts nonetheless to teaching the horse the art of coming behind the bit, of escaping its contact by drawing away from it as little as may be, whilst in all the previous course of dressage the aim has been to "push him on to his bit", by making him "go into his reins", and "draw his cart". At the very best, there will be a reversal of direction in the conduct of dressage, and the slightest fault against impulsion committed by the trainer will completely contradict the whole of the horse's previous education. It is therefore prudent to give up methods that aim at drawing the head back towards the body, and to avoid trying to obtain the Ramener on a stationary horse.

It is the opposite procedure that we will adopt.

In all the lessons that precede the direct seeking of the Ramener the whole body of the horse has acquired a certain degree of suppleness, and the elasticity of the spine has already reached its terminal joint—the jaw.

Furthermore, every time the horse, having become balanced in his work, has given a hint of yielding of the jaw, he has been immediately rewarded by his trainer by an opening of the fingers, a caress, or being allowed to rest.

---

1. This attitude ("Le Camper") was formerly taught to carriage horses. Its purpose was to avoid sudden departures of the horses in harness and to ensure that they stood still while the footboard was lifted and the door was closed.

If the side reins worn in the stable failed to produce this posture, little taps of a stick behind the pasterns of the forelegs caused these to step forward, rather in the same way as dealers nowadays tread with their toe on the horse's heels to get him to show himself.

He already knows that far from being a forbidden action, "giving in his mouth" will earn a reward.

A few flexions of the jaw, without any attempts at modifying the head carriage, will help to confirm the horse in his certainty that this relaxation is not just permissible, but always earns a reward, and thus the yielding of the mouth at the rider's request will become a "*habit*".

Only in the case where a local stiffness should persist in the mouth—this is very rare—could flexions of the jaw be made the object of particular insistence, in order to restore uniform suppleness in the whole of the body, including the mouth.

However, one should make quite certain that this local stiffness is not just an "appearance" but a reflexion of either an overall stiffness or lack of suppleness in some part of the body, the haunches for instance, as is more often the case.

These flexions will be executed *in motion*, as the momentum of the mass makes it then more difficult for the horse to squat on his haunches than it is at the halt.

Before going on to the direct pursuit of the Ramener the trainer will obtain a few lateral flexions of the poll, with the aim above all of equalising flexibility of both sides.

Here again, previous work on circles and the shoulder-in will have developed the lateral flexibility of the entire body, from which the poll cannot have been excluded. As was done for the jaw, it is then a matter of testing the results obtained, of perfecting them, and confirming them by creating a habit.

In the same way as flexions of the jaw, flexions of the poll will be demanded *in motion* and without attempting to draw the head closer to the chest.

Finally, and very gradually, the trainer will try to obtain the Ramener by practising variations of speed and transitions, but always without destroying forward movement.

When decreasing speed and halting, the rider will endeavour to prolong, at first imperceptibly, and later more positively, the forward progression of the horse's body, and having secured relaxation of the mouth, he tries to stop the head *first*, so that the limbs arrest their movement more slowly than do the head and neck.

When lengthening the stride and moving off, his hands will yield, after his legs have acted, less readily than formerly, the fingers opening to allow the impulsion to go through only after the horse has given in his mouth.

The softly mobile mouth will open for a fraction of a moment as it meets the bit under the influence of the thrust of the hind legs, so that the rider's hands receive the "impression that the poll, the neck and the whole of the upper part of the body tend to go over the mouth". (Le Noble du Teil.)

As is classically expressed, the horse will have "passed across his bit" ("franchi son mors") to come into the Ramener.

In the case of horses with a short, thick, massive poll, lacking in suppleness, there may be no alternative but to seek the Ramener by simultaneously drawing the head back towards the body and driving the body towards the head. It is necessary then to allow the second and third vertebrae to participate in the flexion that should normally be limited to the joints of the occiput and the atlas, and of the atlas and the axis. In this case some lowering of the poll must be tolerated, and we must be content with only a small degree of Ramener. Such horses are not really suitable for academic equitation, and their schooling should not aim at more than turning them into good ordinary outdoor rides where they often become excellent.[1]

The suppling exercises aimed at preparing the Mise en Main and the Ramener will be explained in the chapter on flexions.

1. The use of a running rein generally gives good results in the schooling of those horses, the centre of the rein being placed somewhat behind the Axis vertebra.

(a) The running rein is called a "Rein Colbert". Without altering the ordinary bridle, a thin cord is passed through one ring of the bridoon, over the neck behind the Axis, and through the other ring of the bridoon; both ends of the two cords are joined at a length that suits the rider, who works on this makeshift rein, while just holding the leather one with the tips of his little finger. (Note: 2nd edition.)

Chapter 5 · LIFTING OF THE NECK

Books of Reference:
FAVEROT DE KERBRECH
RUL: *Le Baucherisme Reduit a sa plus simple expression*
STEINBRECHT

It is frequently asserted that the lifting of the neck without Ramener necessarily unloads the forehand and loads the hind quarters. The spine being held to act as the arm of a pair of scales, with its fulcrum situated at "M" in the region of the withers.

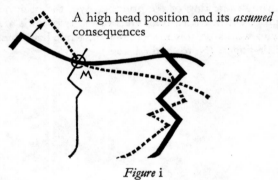

A high head position and its *assumed* consequences

Figure i

Granted, if the spine were rigid and this famous fixed point "M" really existed.

But it does not exist, because the horse has not got a collar bone. Admittedly, his spine is firmly attached to the hind limbs through the intermediary of the pelvis, but it has no bony joint with the forelegs. In other vertebrates, in man for instance, the spine is joined to the upper limbs (forelimbs) by the collarbone, through the intermediary of the breast-bone. Therefore, there exists a joint of bones, in man, between the spine and the "forelimbs" as well as between the spine and the hindlegs".

In the horse, this joint with the forelegs does not exist. This fulcrum M, which would allow the spine to act as the arm of a pair of scales is purely imaginary.

The spine of the horse, through the intermediary of the thorax to which it is joined, lies between the two shoulders in a kind of cradle constituted of muscles and cartilage. This cradle is neither rigid nor of a fixed shape, it has the elasticity common to all muscular tissue. It can stretch downwards and thereby allow the thorax, and therefore the spine to descend by taking advantage of the elasticity of its cradle.

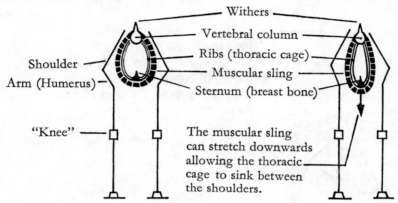

Diagram of front view of a horse

Figure ii

If one lifts the neck bodily its lower part sinks in the cradle, the withers sink between the shoulders, and the spine, behind the withers, sinks under the saddle.

The weight supposedly transferred to the hind-quarters, through this famous fulcrum which however does not exist, in fact simply remains on the forehand—whilst the back caves in. The lower part of the neck is thrown out: the horse becomes "pigeon-throated".

This is not entirely true, because the elastic property of the cradle is not very great and it does not occur to the horse to take full advantage of it until he is inconvenienced by the attitude enforced upon him; but it suffices to diminish to a greater extent than is often realised the effect of unloading the forehand by lifting the neck, with the head held horizontally, as advocated by General F. de Kerbrech.

The whole situation is different, if this elevation is accompanied by a suitable Ramener. The poll moves forward to align itself vertically with the nose, the first vertebrae, axis and atlas, move from back to front, flexing over one another and over the head; the succeeding ones are drawn up because they are joined to the others which pull them and from bottom to top they draw with them the rest of the neck which therefore can no longer sink between the shoulders.

Furthermore, all the other muscles of the neck which were slackened when the neck was lifted without Ramener now are tensed and their tension is communicated to the muscles of the back, the tension of which in turn prevents the sinking of the rib-cage.

It is clear that forcibly pulling up the neck only, with the head in a horizontal position, produces misleading results in the first place, and difficulties in the end.

————— Outline of the natural position of the vertebral column

• • • • • • Effect of elevating the head with collection (ramener)

- - - - - - - Effect of elevating the head without collection

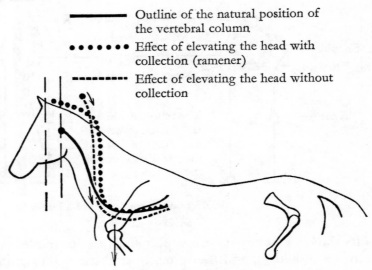

Figure iii

Furthermore, the loin as well as all the joints of the hind-quarters must be adequately prepared by proper gymnastics for the true burden imposed upon them by a lifting of the neck in the position of the Ramener. Otherwise, they lose their activity and their suppleness.

The elevation of the neck must therefore be achieved very progressively, during the course of schooling; as all the joints of the hind-quarters become better capable of flexing they facilitate the lowering of the quarters.

It is not the elevation of the neck, but the lowering of the haunches that is the aim to pursue. Lifting the neck is only a part of the whole work that contributes to that end.

Part of the advantages of the Ramener is that it shortens the lever arm at the end of which the head is suspended, and it consequently diminishes the combined weight of the head and neck on the forehand. However, the mere elevation of the neck, without any Ramener also shortens the lever arm and also unloads the forehand, but only in a restricted measure as has just been explained.

Unloading the forehand by shortening the lever, and the advantages that result from this in getting the horse to find his balance, can be obtained either:

By the Ramener alone (Baucher, first manner);

By the lifting of the neck alone (Baucher, second manner, Beginning of dressage);

By combining both methods (Baucher, second manner: Continuation of dressage).

The Ramener on its own, without a corresponding lifting of the neck, entails a serious risk of overbending the horse and getting him to go behind the bit, with all the harmful consequences.

Lifting the neck without a Ramener causes the muscles above the neck to slacken, and their slackening is communicated to the rest of the spine which tends to collapse. In this manner, it diminishes the elasticity of the whole of the spinal column, limits the play of the hind legs and considerably reduces their ability to engage under the mass.

It is therefore only logical to try to combine both those unloading effects so that either can be used to the best advantage and their respective drawbacks avoided, by lifting the neck to a height which makes overbending impossible, and by keeping the Ramener within limits beyond which the horse would try to escape it by allowing the base of the neck to collapse.

It is, however, possible either to pursue both methods separately, to the extent of waiting to proceed with the one until the other had produced results, or to use them simultaneously and in harmony.

Baucher, in his second manner, clearly opted for the first solution, and ordered a complete lifting of the neck before making any attempt at Ramener.

One may well imagine the drawbacks of this procedure when it is applied as a matter of course and indiscriminately to all horses.

When one pulls up the neck bodily—"the head almost horizontal" writes Faverot de Kerbreck—not only does the head rise, but it also tips backwards, and its angle with the neck opens, because the lateral processes of the Axis are brought closer to the top of the cheek bones and crush the parotid glands. In order to avoid this painful constraint, the horse lifts the nose and moves the poll backwards. The occiput then presses against the Axis and the Atlas, which are situated in an almost horizontal plane when the neck is in a normal position, and pushes them backwards.

As these two vertebrae are joined at an angle with the following ones, which are almost vertical, the pressure of the occiput on the axis and the atlas is transmitted through this angle and the other vertebrae (the third and the subsequent ones) are compressed in their own particular direction, that is downwards. The last of the cervical vertebrae transmits this downward pressure to the first dorsal one which is itself lowered by this pressure and this lowering gradually proceeds step by step along the whole spine as far as the haunches. The withers sink between the shoulders, the back drops behind them and finally involves the loins in its "hollowing".

That, likewise, explains how lifting the neck bodily is the best means of correcting the arching of the back in horses that are "arch-backed", "mule-backed", or "roach-backed".

But all horses are not roach-backed, and when they have a normal topline, the bodily lifting of the neck hollows the loin, reduces its suppleness, relatively overloads the hind-quarters and consequently compresses the hind limbs.

If this lifting is attempted at the beginning of dressage, before appropriate gymnastics have developed the suppleness of the joints of the hind-quarters, the hind legs as a whole under this constraint become unable to bend.

The haunches may in fact be lowered, not, however, because the hocks flex, but because they spread out and that is the most detrimental attitude to the success of dressage and to the obtainment of Rassembler in particular.[1]

However, the pressure of the occiput on the cervical vertebrae and all its consequent disorders diminish in the same degree as the opening of the angle formed by the head and neck and the resulting backward tipping of the head diminish. The smaller the angle at the poll, the less the spine is pressed downward in the process of lifting the neck. (Fig. iv.)

In other words, the better the horse can be flexed at the poll, without pain, the fewer the disadvantages entailed by lifting the neck. For in the Ramener the head moves in the opposite direction to the one produced by the lifting of the neck: the poll advances in relation to the nose. Far from forcing the Axis backwards, on the contrary it pulls it forwards and lifts the whole of the spinal column instead of forcing it down.

It must again be noted that it is not the elevation of the neck of itself that is so important in dressage, but its elevation in relation to the haunches.

Practised skilfully, in moderation and progressively, lifting the neck reacts upon the haunches and contributes to their useful lowering, *once the hind legs have been suppled*. But conversely, the lowering of the haunches obtained independently of any direct elevation of the neck by means of appropriate exercises produces by reaction a relative elevation of the neck that is far more important than its absolute elevation.

1. The following experiment is easy to make and conclusive. Get someone to mount a horse with a normal back on which the saddle usually keeps its position. Have the girth very slack and instruct the rider to drive the horse forward at a rather brisk speed, and to hold its head up high. At the end of a few hundred yards, the pommel of the saddle will be resting on the withers, and the whole saddle on the shoulders; it will have followed the slope of the dropped back, and the withers having sunk will have been unable to prevent this. Furthermore, it is easy, by observing the horse's tracks, to notice how those of the hind legs are all outside those of the forelegs, because the hind legs are spread out.

Figure iv   Diagram of vertebral column in natural position

Effect of elevation   Effect of elevation
without Ramener   with Ramener

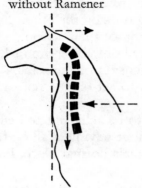   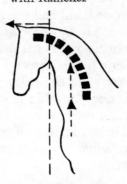

WITHOUT RAMENER

—the poll is drawn backwards
—the chain of cervical vertebrae
is compressed downwards
—It flexes forwards at the lower part,
thus causing a ewe-neck
(Pigeon Throat).

WITH RAMENER

The poll is advanced
or (in front of the perpendicular)
The vertebrae are curved and
stretched correctly from
the bottom upwards.
The neck is correctly carried
from the base upwards.

When the Ramener is obtained by progressively causing the body to advance towards the head, as is advocated here, by driving the whole of the horse's body towards his neck from the beginning of dressage and during the whole of its course, the hind legs develop precisely at every moment their ability to flex in their joints so that they engage under the mass. The haunches constantly tend to lower themselves, progressively causing by reaction a *relative* elevation of the neck.

It is only when the Ramener has been sought by drawing the head back towards the body (Baucher's first manner) that overbending or the threat of overbending may make it necessary to lift the neck up in a marked manner. When the Ramener is obtained by the reverse procedure, followed here, the degree of lifting that may be necessary is always small and is obtained without difficulty.[1]

1. These observations were made a very long time ago. Fifty years before Baucher moved from his first manner to his second, the regulations dated 1825 of the Prussian Cavalry ordered the almost total elevation of the neck before any attempt be made at obtaining the Ramener. Experiments covering thousands of horses and several decades had caused the Prussians to abandon this method completely. Furthermore, they sinned in the opposite

Finally, it must be realised that lifting the neck produces the intended results only if it remains in that position *without the support of the rider's hands*.

The lifting only becomes effective and helpful when the elevating muscles of the neck on the one hand and the flexing ones on the other, fix the neck in its proper position solely by the combination of their action.

So long as the horse keeps his neck lifted only by more or less propping himself on the rider's hands through the tension of the reins, so long as he drops his head every time the rider ceases to act on the reins by lifting the hands, the horse is not "lifted in front".

This elevation can only be considered to be achieved and effectual when the horse can hold it by his own effort without relying at all on the assistance of his rider whose hands must remain in their normal place, level, more or less, with his waist.

direction, and Plinzner, the Emperor's Riding Master, systematically lowered his horse's necks and overbent them completely; and that at a time when Baucher in his "Derniers Enseignements" prescribed the systematic elevation of the neck.

Elevation of the head does not *necessarily*
produce a lowering of the quarters.

Chapter 6 · DESCENTE DE MAIN

The "Descente de Main" is a relaxing of the pressure of the fingers on the reins which are allowed to slide and gradually lengthen, whilst the horse, having first been balanced and placed so that he achieves perfect poise, rigorously keeps this poise, without modifying his attitude in any way.

This is how La Gueriniere, and Baucher later, have defined this action.

More recently, the same expression has been used to describe a completely different procedure, in fact an almost completely opposite one, in which the horse, on feeling the same relaxation of the rider's fingers, seeks his bit and lengthens his neck as the reins become looser.[1]

This equivocation is most regrettable and could easily have been avoided if the term "Descente de Main" had been allowed to keep the meaning given to it by La Gueriniere, and preserved by Baucher, and if the procedure advocated by Montigny and Dutilh had been called "Descente d'Encolure" as it was called later on anyhow.

Montigny, having explained his conception of the "Descente de Main" which is in reality the "Descente d'Encolure" adds: This comes from Count d'Aure. However, Count D'Aure mentions neither the "Descente de Main" nor the "Descente d'Encolure" in any of his books (unless I am mistaken). It is probably in his oral teaching that he discussed the matter.

Each of these procedures has some advantages but from very different points of view.

The "Descente de Main" (La Gueriniere and Baucher) enables the rider to give his horse greater freedom and greater ease in an unchanged attitude, once this attitude has become familiar to him and is willingly held. It allows the horse to use all the resources of his instinct to make good any local weaknesses of his muscular system by resorting to certain "compensatory" efforts which remain invisible but nevertheless free his movements of any trace of stiffness.

1. This second meaning of the "Descente de Main" was very prevalent, particularly in France, during and after Commandant Dutilh's period of direction at Saumur (1873–77). It seems that it was first formulated by Count de Montigny who was Riding Master at the Cavalry School at the time (1852–55) when Dutilh was an assistant riding master there.

Without ceasing to remain entirely under the domination of his rider, he remains a prisoner, but a prisoner "on parole", to use General Detroyat's expression.

The "Descente de Main" adds to the grace of the attitudes and movements of the horse, and in that respect, should not be neglected in academic equitation.

As for the "Descente d'Encolure", it allows the horse instantly to lengthen his neck to a degree corresponding to an increase of speed or to a relaxation in his general attitude as authorised by the rider.[1]

Unfortunately, to teach both these lessons to the horse it is not possible to use any but identical means, to obtain completely opposite results.

In order to teach the horse the "Descente de Main", the rider yields and if the horse advances his head, the rider replaces it, as many times as may be necessary to obtain his understanding of what is required of him, and rewards him as soon as he obliges. For the "Descente d'Encolure", the rider yields, just as for the "Descente de Main", but when the horse advances his head, the rider yields again, allowing it to stretch out, and immediately rewards the horse.

Therefore it is not possible to teach the horse the completely opposed "Descente de Main" and "Descente d'Encolure", or even to obtain a partial understanding, without adding to the rider's indications some other disposition that will help the horse to distinguish unhesitatingly between the two kinds of submission that he is supposed to show.

The legs provide a means of reaching a compromise that enables the rider

---

1. General F. de Kerbrech (a pupil of Baucher in his second manner) writes: "Lightness and 'Ramener' must remain constant in the medium gallop, and the pace must be progressively extended . . . the horse keeping the same position of the head."

On the other hand, of the extended trot, the General writes: "Out of doors at an extended trot . . . it should be considered sufficient for the neck to be kept up, and the head to have a position *approximating the perpendicular*."

Though one is prepared to accept this demand for the trot, in a measure where the "approximation" to the "perpendicular" is left to the horse's choice, and the horse remains submissive to the hands even when using himself to the utmost, it is impossible to suscribe to the view that the Ramener should be held regardless of the speed of the gallop. Innumerable racing photographs show that the position of the head with the majority of horses is definitely not a vertical one, the inclination being closer to 45 degrees, and even beyond this in the final effort.

It is true that Le Noble du Teil, another pupil of Baucher in his second manner, for his part writes: "What we have just seen . . . shows that at extended paces one must allow the angle of the head and the neck to open." This shows how the same teaching can be contradictorily understood by two different pupils, both undeniably of good faith. It is to the opinion of Le Noble du Teil that we will subscribe.

to benefit from some of the advantages of each of these two practices, and prevents the horse from confusing them.

From the beginning of schooling an understanding, which there is no need to modify, has been established between the rider and the horse: when the legs have by their action commanded a set rate of speed and the horse has taken this speed, the legs cease acting and remain passive as long as the speed remains constant.

Thus, the legs remaining passive and the horse at a set degree of speed and elevation, nothing prevents the rider from teaching the "Descente de Main" to the horse.

In this way, at ordinary paces the rider will have a horse that walks freely, on a long rein as one says. The position of the head which has no reason to be "ramené" will be one that conforms to the natural attitude corresponding to the speed of the movement.

At collected gaits or in the school airs, when the legs must also cease to act as soon as the necessary impulsion has been obtained, the rider, as he loosens the reins to teach the "Descente de Main" will demonstrate his trust in the horse—a trust that soon becomes mutual, and thereby will enjoy all the benefits in ease of movement that result from this practice.

In both cases, it is quite unnecessary to lengthen the reins beyond the extent needed to allow them to act by their weight alone, and they should not hang in interminable festoons.

In fact, this way of teaching the "Descente de Main" is not that of Baucher in his first manner, i.e. independently of a yielding of the legs (descente de jambes). It is the one described and advocated in his "Derniers Enseignements" (Last Instructions), the simultaneous yielding of hands and legs, with the reins loosened no more than to the necessary extent.

As for the "Descente d'Encolure", the old convention remains valid: While acting with his legs to create forward movement or a lengthening of the stride the rider opens his fingers, not only to allow the impulsion to develop but also to allow the neck to assume an attitude suited to the speed required.

This attitude, however, does not demand that the neck should be lowered to the level of the knees, as Dutilh required, but merely that it should be lengthened with the nose stretched almost horizontally. So the horse will have no cause to become confused.

When the legs act and the fingers open, he already knows that he must increase his speed accordingly, and assume a neck position adapted to this speed: what is essential is the lengthening of the neck.

When the legs are not active, when they are already, and remain passive, opening the fingers will grant the horse merely "freedom on parole", and this he will have been taught to use solely to maintain his pace and his attitude: this is the "Descente de Main".

As for the lengthening of the neck allowed during intervals of rest, it will be easily obtained by completely loosening the reins, after coming back to the walk at the end of a brisk and sustained gallop.

There are few horses, with trust in their rider, that will hesitate to respond to this invitation to relax.

To confirm these conventions clearly, the rider will carefully avoid requesting a "Descente de Main" when his legs are active, and a "Descente d'Encolure" when his legs are passive.

The "Descente d'Encolure" for relaxation will never be *requested* from the horse. It may be granted to the horse when he himself requests it, and to the extent judged suitable by the rider.

Chapter 7 · L'EFFET D'ENSEMBLE

Books of Reference:
LA GUERINIERE
BAUCHER
FAVEROT DE KERBRECH

". . . By drawing on the curb rein and closing the legs rapidly and progressively to the point of a positive, continuous and emphatic pressure of the spurs, one produces what is known as the "Effet d'Ensemble sur l'Eperon" (the effect produced by a combined and simultaneous use of hands and spurs: translator's note).

"One is then able to overcome all resistances, and to guide the horse as one wants, and at the speed one desires." (Faverot de Kerbrech.)

The "Effet d'Ensemble" can be very useful therefore, especially in the schooling of difficult horses, particularly with the aim of riding them in the open, so that they can be dominated, for instance in the event of their being frightened by something. For this purpose it can even be indispensable.

However, its use can, in certain circumstances, be inconvenient and, from the point of view of dressage as a whole, it presents drawbacks that are not negligible.

EXECUTION OF THE EFFET D'ENSEMBLE

At slow paces, its execution does not present any difficulties. The horse's action is not strong enough to prevent the rider from graduating as necessary the activity of his legs and hands, and especially the *continuity* of his leg action.

But difficulties crop up as soon as the pace quickens. At the sitting trot, if the horse's action is at all strong, it is difficult for the rider, however supple he is, to keep a strictly uniform pressure with his heels. At the rising trot, the rising and lowering of the seat cause the amount of pressure of the foot on the stirrup to vary considerably and it is difficult to avoid communicating these variations to the pressure of the heels on the horse's flanks.

At the canter, as soon as the pace becomes faster, the alternating and powerful contractions and extensions of the muscles of the abdomen, as well as the movements in contrary directions of the ribs during inhalation and

A.E.—7

expiration make the flanks of the horse move in rhythm with the pace, so that they are at times drawn away from the rider's heels, at times pressed against them. It is then extremely difficult to follow exactly those movements of the flanks, and the pressure of the heels, instead of remaining constant, is almost inevitably changed into a series of more or less brief contacts.

Modern dressage competitions however, although they do not habitually include fast paces, all require some lengthening of the gaits which must be as pronounced as the dimensions of the arena permit, and these lengthenings are precisely the occasions of possible disorderliness due to untimely bursts of gaiety.

USES OF THE EFFET D'ENSEMBLE

The uses of the "Effet d'Ensemble" are undeniable, for it provides a means of enforcing obedience, and this is sometimes necessary even with the best schooled horse.

It must be noted, however, that such a necessity ought to be of rare occurrence in academic equitation.

For, in the first place, the selected horse should be, by nature, generous and of good temperament. In the second place, his academic dressage should not have been started before he has been confirmed as a good ordinary ride, and although one should not expect him to "lick a steam roller", he should already be familiar with all objects that frighten young horses.

Lack of co-operation should, therefore, not arise in the course of higher dressage, because the essence of the art excludes any element of surprise and all efforts beyond the actual capability of the particular horse.

Nor will there be many occasions for fright, as the causes will be lacking; at the most, in public dressage tests, one could be apprehensive of the startling effects of bursts of music, of the rustling of papers in the wind etc., but the preparation for these tests is intended precisely to accustom the horse to these happenings and they should leave him "blasé" by the time he is ready to take part in such competitions.

Furthermore, the lesson of the spur, which should have been given at the beginning of secondary dressage[1] and repeated many times during the course

1. See page 34—This lesson is not the same as the one explained by General Faverot de Kerbrech.

(a) Faverot, who was a pure Baucherist of the second manner, prescribes that one should prevent *any forward movement* by using the bridoon rein, whilst one applies a pressure: (1) of the calves; (2) of the heels; (3) of the blunt spurs; (4) of the rowelled spurs, the object being to obtain "lightness at the halt". "Once this result is obtained, *and this is most important*, one must get the animal into the habit of moving forward resolutely on an action of the spurs". This is a confusing contradiction, that is also found in the present doctrine of "taut" reins.

of the latter, will secure for the rider complete power to maintain or develop forward movement, to forbid any deviation of the haunches and consequently to prevent the horse from changing his direction. One can fear at the most that obedience, although unquestionable, might be rather sudden in its execution, if the means used to obtain it are not sufficiently progressive.

The "Effet d'Ensemble", in the particular case considered here, is not therefore essentially useful, and presents some disadvantages that can outweigh its advantages and are often difficult to avoid.

From the beginning to the end of dressage, the horse has been, and must be confirmed in the immediate development of impulsion upon any action of the legs, and the "Effet d'Ensemble" amounts after all to forbidding this development of impulsion upon an "emphatic" action of the legs, as the legs are undeniably active in the "Effet d'Ensemble" all the while that they are closing "rapidly" and "progressively".

One may of course argue that this contradiction with the rest of the teaching is at least compensated for by an unusual and completely novel use of the hands, for the rider, who up to this point had to endeavour never *to pull* on the mouth, now finds that he has to do so and is told to "draw the hands closer to his body". This novel use of the reins, however, is not devoid of risks of confusing the horse on the meaning of the indications of the hands.

Even if one views it in the most favourable light, and assumes that teaching of the "Effet d'Ensemble" is perfectly successful, which is not an easy task, this procedure is nonetheless completely different, if not altogether opposed, to the progression of dressage as it is contemplated here. Owing to its special purpose of domination, one may, however, countenance it like the taming achieved by Rarey's method or Barnum's lunge.

However, perfect results in the teaching of the "Effet d'Ensemble" are difficult to achieve, and it is equally difficult to assess the results obtained from it. To start with, it is at the halt, on the standing horse, that this training is practised. One can accept that the horse, even the "cold" one, at the start must feel a traction of the hands "equal" to the leg pressure to make him remain stationary and, unless his natural or his acquired desire for forward movement is absolutely "frantic", very soon he will learn to require a less than equivalent action of the hands to absolve him from obeying the contradictory command of the legs. He will quickly come to the stage of stopping

Beudant, a less rabid Baucherist says, "Dissociate: (obtain) lightness—yield with the hand, close the legs, upon obtaining one forward stride, yield with the legs, halt with the hands only".

It is evident that Beudant's method should be preferred, and more so Decarpentry's when he is "Baucherising". (Note: 2nd edition.)

on an increasingly soft hand action, despite the greater energy of the leg action.

However, the forces expended by the rider through his hands on the one hand and his legs on the other are not of the same nature and are therefore incommensurable, and the rider has no other proof of their equality but the immobility of his horse.

What happens at the halt will soon happen at all paces; gradually, for the same action of the legs, a less and less powerful action of the hands will be required to prevent an increase in speed, the horse will become more and more "cold" to the legs, to the point of "coming behind the legs", and he cannot be put into a more dangerous frame of mind.

Fewer risks are entailed with a "hot" horse, but conversely we may have to pull more strongly on the reins to get him to "disobey" the legs and thereby he becomes heavy on the hands.

In School gaits, the risk is no less. In the Rassembler, which, as General de Faverot de Kerbrech says, should: "animate, awaken, *over-stimulate* activity", the spurs must "act by successive pressures, repeated, even alternated but never continuous", whilst in the "Effet d'Ensemble", which "calms, extinguishes or regulates, their pressure must act in a continuous and graduated progression".

The horse, however, is frequently only too willing to become bewildered by these actions, however, perfectly the rider may differentiate them. If the horse is hot, he will be inclined to confuse "graduated" pressures with "successive" pressures, and if nonetheless the rider manages to preserve by force the same gait and the same speed, he will find it difficult to moderate the horse's "overstimulation". It may, for instance, be possible to force him to remain on the same spot, but be almost impossible to prevent him from "prancing" or doing a piaffer if he can (see further on, the note about the horse that went into piaffer at the hunt).

If he is cold he will fall into the opposite confusion: he will go to sleep, "fade" on the spur, and very soon increasingly energetic leg action will be needed to "animate" him.

That is perhaps the reason why it used to be said of Baucher's horses that they "worked with clockwork regularity and mournful despondency" (Aubert), even though they were not spared attacks of the rowelled spurs.

The "Effet d'Ensemble" with the spur certainly enforces obedience, but a forced obedience is not suited to academic equitation because it can never be gracious. What is required is a generous, trusting, eager, smiling submission.

As regards the kind of dressage considered here, it is felt that the advantages of the "Effet d'Ensemble" do not counterbalance its disadvantages sufficiently to warrant recommending this procedure in all cases.

If, however, the trainer deemed it necessary to use it as a last resort in desperate cases, he could not do better than to follow General de Faverot de Kerbrech's slow and careful progression in the teaching of the "Effet d'Ensemble", and to use it as little as possible as soon as he has obtained the desired result.

Chapter 8 · THE RASSEMBLER

Books of Reference:
BAUCHER
GENERAL DE FAVEROT DE KERBRECH
RAABE
GERHARDT
STEINBRECHT

The Rassembler (collection) is the disposition of the horse's body which affects all of its parts and places each one in the best position to ensure the most efficient use of the energy produced by the efforts of the hind legs.

Those efforts can have an immediate and special purpose, or can be a preparation for several eventual purposes.

The race horse before the start, the show jumper before going over an obstacle, the dressage horse before performing a courbette, all collect themselves, but the disposition of their body, i.e. the form of their collection, is different in each case, and so is the direction in which their energy is spent ultimately.

But collection can also prepare for an output of energy that can be used for several purposes.

The "rogue" who wants to resist and prepares himself to do so, adopts a general disposition that makes it possible for him to shy, to rear or to turn about, depending on the vicissitudes of his struggle with the rider. He assumes an intermediate attitude a median disposition that he can instantly modify. He also is collected, but his collection can serve several ends.

The kind of collection suited to academic equitation belongs to this last category, though it must not be confused of course with a preparation for resistance.

In the first place, it must ensure to the horse the maximum mobility in all directions and the ability to make rapid changes of speed. Furthermore, it must enable him, in answer to his rider's command, instantly to impart to his gaits the maximum elevation compatible with the length of stride that the rider wishes to maintain.

On the one hand, mobility requires a short base of support and this is possible only if the hind legs touch the ground further forward than they would at a free pace, i.e. that they engage.

On the other hand, it requires that the mass be held constantly in a mean position so that the centre of gravity of the body will remain as close as possible to the vertical line passing through the centre of each of the successive bases.

ENGAGEMENT OF THE HIND LEGS

Elevation of the gaits, or of the school airs that derive from them, is a result, not of the engagement of the hind legs, but rather of the opportuneness and the vigour of their extension.

Because it diminishes the breadth of the base of support, engagement of the hind legs is favourable to mobility, but only to a certain extent.

Beyond this, it diminishes the horse's capacity for forward movement which always remains an essential element in his mobility.

The startled horse stops dead, and engages "fully"—frequently so much so that he over-reaches; the excessive forward slant of his hind legs constitutes a braking attitude. If the rider provokes this attitude as he tries to obtain collection, he also provokes a marked diminution of impulsion. This braking, which at first is purely mechanical, is soon used by the horse to oppose the impulsive actions of his rider.

There is then a limit to the *useful* engagement of the hind legs. Beyond that limit, it turns into a resistance—often taught by the rider himself to the horse.

Excessive engagement of the hind legs produces still further disorders. It locks the coxo-femoral joint; to free himself from this constraint, the horse disengages his coxa by lifting it, consequently lifting his spine at the same time; he arches his back, which always tends to provoke, by reaction, a lowering of the neck and an advance of the trunk over and in front of the forelegs.

The horse is then *under himself in front and behind* and he overbends.[1]

The diminished impulsion, the arched back that lifts the saddle under the seat, and the heaviness of the head can warn the rider of the excessive engagement of the hind legs. But these warnings are only faintly perceptible at the beginning of the disorder and by the time they become obvious, it is too late to start correcting it.

The rider must therefore remain on the look-out for these signs, and should

---

1. This is Baucher's collection, in his first manner—dangerous as regards impulsion, when the horse is not ridden by Baucher himself. It is this form of collection that the Germans sarcastically compared to the position of a chamois perched on the summit of a rock.

avoid trying to obtain collection at the halt, as this often provokes that faulty position.

The proper remedy, to be applied without delay as soon as this position is produced, is to re-establish impulsion fully, by driving forward energetically with the legs, without any opposition of the hands.

EXTENSION OF THE HIND-LEGS

It is the extension of the hind legs, and not their engagement, that produces the elevation of the school gaits and of the airs that are derived from them.

The more the hind-limb, as a whole, approaches the vertical at the moment it extends, the more it thrusts the body upwards.

(The hind-limb, in general, can be said to be practically vertical, when the foot is on a plumb line with the point of the hip, allowing for some minor variations of position due to the particular conformations of certain joints, especially of the hock).

The further the hind-leg is behind the vertical at the moment of its extension, the more the resulting thrust is delivered from back to front: the greater the *speed* (Fig. i).

Figure i

When the hind-leg extends from a position in front of the vertical, the thrust is delivered upwards and backwards: the horse leans back or steps back, with or without a period of suspension of the body, depending on the force of the components of his effort.

The degree of elevation of the body during the moment of suspension

RASSEMBLER (Complete Collection)

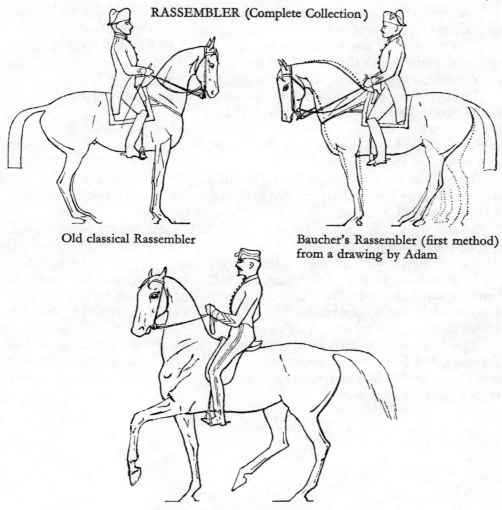

Old classical Rassembler   Baucher's Rassembler (first method)
                                        from a drawing by Adam

Baucher's Rassembler (2d method)

In collection, the Old Masters wanted pronounced lowering of the
quarters and a correspondingly lightened forehand. The forelimbs' movements were much higher than those of the hindlimbs. In Baucher's first
conception of Rassembler, quarters and shoulders were equally loaded
and the movements of front and hind limbs were equally high. In his
second manner, Baucher's conception of Rassembler ressembles the Old
Masters', but the forehand is lightened principally by elevating the head.
The flexion of the hind limbs and lowering of the quarters is not as great
as in the old school. In his notes on the second manner, Baucher does not
mention any difference in the height of the movements of the fore and
hind limbs.

will depend likewise on the vigour of the effort of the hind legs, and consequently on the amount of previous compression of their joints.

It is precisely at the moment when the hip, in its forward course, passes over the vertical line through the foot that the compression of the springs, i.e. the bending of the joints of the hind-legs, is greatest.

Finally, the elevation of the body during suspension will also depend on its proper disposition in relation to the limbs.

If the whole of the mass of trunk and forehand is excessively in advance of the hind limbs, these can only lift the croup, regardless of the direction and energy of their thrust.

The closer the hips are to the centre of gravity at the moment the hind legs extend, the more effectively the body, as *a whole*, including the extremity of the front end, is lifted.

Therefore, it is not only the underpart of the horse that must be shortened, but also his *topline* which must be compressed by the closing of all the natural curvatures of the spine; the collection of both must proceed in harmony.

From the beginning of dressage, the rider has endeavoured to push the horse towards his own hands, to make him "go into the reins", to bring progressively the whole of the body closer to the head, and the haunches closer to the centre of gravity of the mass.

The pursuit of collection is not limited therefore to a special period of dressage, but from the very first lesson it must be the object of each day's work, so that the rider can master eventually all his horse's forces and control their output as he wishes.

Dressage

PART ONE

Progression of Dressage

Chapter 1 · CONDUCT AND PROGRESSION OF
ACADEMIC DRESSAGE

Books of Reference:
LA GUERINIERE
BAUCHER
GENERAL FAVEROT DE KERBRECH
RAABE
GERHARDT
STEINBRECHT

Dressage, with academic equitation in view, is a higher education that must be based on a properly assimilated primary education. It is therefore necessary to define with exactitude the elements of this basis and to determine clearly the nature and the limits of the minimum education that the horse must have acquired before the second stage of dressage is entered upon.

To profit from this complementary education and to be in the best state to receive it the horse must be already a good outdoor ride.

He must be frank and generous, obedient and comfortable, completely used to being ridden alone or in the company of other horses, even of many horses, accustomed to all objects and noises of town or country; he must always be willing to give of his best without hesitation and to obey without dispute. His gaits must be free and smooth, he must gaily take all jumps within his capacity, be capable of going perfectly calmly on quiet hacks, or of hunting with enthusiasm but without pulling frantically.[1]

1. To all the above qualities, no better one can be added than his familiarisation with marching quietly at the head of a troop with music playing and flags flying, and the crowd milling around.

He must confidently come up to, and remain in contact with the bit, without using it as a fifth leg, and move forward willingly at the invitation of the legs.

The isolated action of one leg, though not often required at this stage, must principally determine forward movement, with a very small deviation of the haunches to the opposite side, and the horse must not show any tendency to lean against it.

If the horse one wants to school for the purposes of academic equitation does not already possess all those qualities, they will have to be imparted to him first.

It is possible to take a "green" horse and, by confining him between four walls, to put him through a whole progression that would lead him to execute school airs within a relatively short time. He will appear to be schooled, but his moral education, as one may say, will be lacking in all that is essential not only for ordinary service under the saddle, but also for turning to account what has been taught in the manege.

No sooner taken out of there, all the unfamiliar things that will surround him will be so many causes for surprise, uneasiness, fear or excitement. The latter, in particular, will inevitably bring his youthfulness to the surface and the tension of his nervous system will display itself, together with other disorders, by the execution of the finest airs of his repertoire against which none of his rider's objurgations will be of any avail. If the rider succeeds in preventing this, he will find that when he tries to obtain the same airs on a further occasion, the horse very naturally will fear the punishment which they earned him on the previous occasion. Irregularities or at least anxieties will ensue in his school work.

However, most of the time, the rider will be unable to prevent entirely those untimely and ridiculous displays. The horse will become intolerable in the open. Furthermore, his agitation will quickly turn to resistance. In his school work he will get into the habit of collecting himself against his rider's wishes, whenever he feels like it, and of executing any air that he finds more to his liking than the one he is asked to perform. He is well on his way to "nappiness".[1]

1. One of the horses considered for inclusion in the French Olympic team in 1936 had been schooled in those conditions. In an attempt to make him usable out of doors, the owner entrusted him to a huntsman who used to ride him out hunting. At all the checks, and even at the meet, the horse would go into an interminable piaffer, and his unfortunate rider could do nothing to prevent this frenzy. The horse has never been cured of this vice, which had become for him a kind of St Vitus's dance.

It is in these sort of circumstances that the precariousness of the "effet d'ensemble" is revealed. In theory, it should immobilise the horse at the halt, and, during motion, it should constrain the horse to limit his output of energy to the measure prescribed by the rider.

In fact, a skilful rider may well be able, without much difficulty, to make his horse remain in one place, but will experience much greater difficulty in enforcing complete immobility, especially when his horse knows the "piaffer", as he will then, nearly always, prance on the spot when he is over-excited. During motion, the "effet d'ensemble" may enable the rider to prevent his horse from gaining too much ground and force him to stay in the appointed place fairly easily, but the gait will remain frenzied, and the horse will squander his energy beyond all measure. In any case, it is physically impossible to use the "effet d'ensemble" indefinitely. It has to be given up eventually and, after it has ceased producing its compression, the succeeding explosion is even more violent.

Chapter 2 · ROLE OF THE GAITS

THE WALK

The walk is the gait most favourable to the explanations of the rider to his pupil.

At the walk, the rider, through his seat, remains in close, constant and almost invariable unison with his horse. There are no violent reactions that can prevent him from giving the utmost precision to his indications. The development of the effects of the latter being relatively slow, the rider has plenty of time to observe them and can modify his actions accordingly if necessary.

The horse is calm and his attention is easily fixed. His nervous system is not considerably stimulated, and his muscular system is not greatly tensed. He is in a permanent state of peaceful receptivity, he is little exposed to surprises, and is able to try out quietly the various reactions to the sensations he feels, and can grope without haste to find the one his rider desires.

This is also the gait at which resistances, owing to the relaxation of the overall tension, are more easily confronted as they are less intense, but likewise the effect of surmounting them is reduced in similar measure. The walk, therefore, allows one to begin the work of suppling the horse, which is continued later in the less favourable conditions of the faster gaits and the advantages procured in the walk can then be exploited.

The walk then is the most suitable gait for teaching the language the rider must create from the beginning of dressage to communicate with his horse, but this stage of the education should have been passed long since by the horse that is ready for academic equitation.

The walk is not the gait most favourable to gymnastic development. To impart to a bar of iron the elasticity needed to turn it into a spring, requires first that it be "steeled"; it must be hardened by tempering. Similarly, the horse: in his gymnastic exercise, a greater output of energy and greater activity must be demanded than are required in the walk, and also greater firmness in the muscular tension.

It is only at the trot and at the canter that the activity and the general tension are sufficient to ensure that the physical development of the horse will lead to the aims of academic schooling, and that contractions which oppose the use of "only those forces necessary for movement" become clearly apparent.

In the pursuit of those twin aims, the trot presents important advantages over the canter. It is therefore essentially the gait for academic dressage.[1]

At the trot, the movements of the limbs are symmetrical, and the oscillations of the neck in all directions, are less extensive. The horse's general attitude remains more or less constant, especially with regard to the disposition of his spine.

It is at this gait that the rider can be most constantly and surely made aware of the form and the degree of poise achieved by his pupil and that he can most consistently intervene when necessary, because the faults which require his intervention show few variations of form and are usually very persistent.

The same does not apply to the canter in which the movements of the limbs are not symmetrical, and the oscillations peculiar to this gait cause a continuous succession of changes in balance and attitude.[2]

However, precisely because of its "asymmetry", and providing it is wisely used, the canter makes it possible to counteract directly the opposite "asymmetries" of the horse. Thus, in the example of a horse whose left diagonal lacks, at all the gaits, activity and scope in its movement, these will be perceptibly developed by frequently practising the canter on the left lead, especially the counter canter. However, the oscillations of the neck and the undulations of the spine are too marked at the canter to permit the work of stabilising, of confirming posture, which constitutes the basis of academic equitation.

The School walk, which is shorter than the ordinary walk, though it preserves the regularity of its rhythm, has some of the characteristics of both the walk and the trot, but in a restricted measure. The general attitude is steadier than in the ordinary walk, and the overall tension is less than in the trot. It can therefore be used in preference to the ordinary walk to increase suppleness, and also to maintain, in conditions already less favourable than at the trot, the attitude obtained at this latter gait.

1. Read La Gueriniere's chapter: "Of the utility of the walk, and of the necessity of the trot."

2. One can nevertheless press on to quite an advanced stage with the work of the canter, independently of the work at the trot, for in some regards it is unrelated to the latter, and not harmful to it. Taine, the winner in the Olympic Games of 1932, performed changes at every stride long before having done one step of the piaffer, and when he could do only a very sketchy passage.

But the School walk, if it is obtained directly from the natural walk by opposing with the hands the impulsive effects of the legs nearly always assumes a faulty form, detrimental to its purpose. The hind limbs remain extended in the development of their action instead of stepping higher, engage too far under the mass, well ahead of their proper position for useful collection. Instead of flexing in all their joints, they extend with their hocks unbent, and the flexion of the upper joints is not noticeably increased. The spine is not at all shortened by the pressure that should result from this flexion, and it is precisely this "packing" of the spine from back to front, and not the forward engagement of the hind legs, which constitutes the essence of collection.

In this defective form of the School walk, the horse collects himself only underneath, and his top does not participate in the least in the increased tensing which imparts its value to this attitude.

Furthermore, the *cadence* of the gait is vitiated by the hurrying of the strides of each diagonal pair of legs. Instead of the regular four time beat of the correct walk, two series of two closely succeeding steps are audible, each series separated by a shorter or longer interval of time. (1, 2—3, 4). The gait tends towards and frequently turns into a walking *trot*.

On the contrary, a regular form of the School walk can be obtained easily when one endeavours to develop it from the trot. The breaking up of the diagonals occurs then just as it does in the transition from trot to ordinary walk, and the horse, whilst falling into the four time cadence that characterises the walk, easily preserves at the same time the flexion of the haunches, of the back and of the neck achieved at the trot, which are the essence of collection and which determine the effective flexion, without excessive engagement, of the limbs.

Work at the school walk therefore must follow and complement work at the trot, after the transformation of the latter into the School trot; the School walk must then be used as much to increase collection and lead the horse to the airs developed from the trot, passage and piaffer, as to embark on the study of the transitions to the canter.

The transitions to the canter can also be practised independently of the work of suppling the horse at this gait. The horse prepared for ordinary riding outside can strike into a canter on one lead or the other relatively easily and promptly and we can work him on both leads quite effectually before he is sufficiently sensitive to the aids to allow us to develop his agility in the transitions to the canter which subsequently determine perfection in the changes of the lead.

Thus, the rider disposes of many means of dispelling the monotony of his teaching and of varying the study matter offered to his pupil.

Furthermore, riding in the open will have offered the opportunity of giving the horse the exercise he needs, which must never be confused with the short periods of schooling, or with the lessons in deportment, which likewise should never be prolonged, and which by repetition, enable the horse to maintain his academic attitude with ease.

The work must be organised in a manner that ensures that the horse arrives at each lesson in the best state of receptivity. For example, a little "fresh" for a schooling session such as will make great demands on his energy, or, on the contrary, very relaxed for such another lesson when he might tend to become impatient.

In dressage, it is the frequent repetition of short lessons, rather than prolonged periods of schooling, that makes it easier for the horse to assimilate them. Persistent actions on the part of the rider are only required in cases of conflict when he encounters an obviously wilful resistance, and this will occur only very rarely if the trainer's demands are intelligently graduated. As regards suppling exercises, frequent repetition is even more imperative, as prolongation of the exercises is definitely harmful because it provokes painful muscular spasms, very similar to real cramp, which can persist for several days and provoke desperate resistances.

In broad outline then, the subsequent progression comprises a short revision, at the walk, of the conventions first established between rider and horse in the normal course of riding out of doors, and an adjustment of their execution if necessary.

THE TROT

Dressage proper can then start, with a long period of work at the trot, a gait that must be made perfectly regular before it can be developed to its maximum power with regularity, while the ability to change speed and direction will be developed simultaneously.

Symmetrically tensioned in his entire muscular system by this work, the horse must then be "adjusted" to the form of his course, so that equal lateral flexibility is obtained, which will help as much to straighten him in his entire length when moving on a straight line, as to bend him on a curved one.

This easily regulated flexibility then makes it possible to enter profitably on the work of two-track exercises, which develop agility with balance, promote progressively increased engagement of the hind legs and so prepare the "Rassembler".

From this stage of dressage onwards, appropriate action of the aids must gradually impart to the trot the elastic and lofty form of the School trot, the development of which will lead later on to the passage.

The School walk also will be developed from the School trot, and by practising both gaits alternately, two-track work is brought to its perfection in the pirouettes, which constitute the gymnastics "par excellence" of the loin.

Pirouettes, and especially those that are executed on the forehand, will be used to practise flexions of the jaw, for when the latter are executed in this manner, the dangers of immobility are avoided and the entire muscular system, particularly of the back, participates in the flexion. The horse, suppled in his neck and jaw as well as in the rest of his body by the overall gymnastics practised at the trot, will now be confirmed in the "Mise en Main" and the "Ramener" by these flexions.

His neck and poll will have then become sufficiently flexible to receive without ill-effects the extra thrust of the hind legs necessary to produce collection. With the increased energy the cadence of the trot will tend more and more towards the passage.

The rein-back, also obtained from the School walk, will further improve the longitudinal flexibility of the topline as well as the suppleness of the superior joints of the hind-quarters and allow the study of the piaffer to be embarked upon.

From the appearance of the first regular steps, and without any attempt being made at obtaining their elevation, the piaffer will be directed as soon as possible towards the passage; on the other hand, the latter, obtained from the school trot by the development of the action of each diagonal, and only in the moderately elevated form of the "doux passage" (soft passage) will be slowed down to lead to the piaffer.

It is the transition between the two airs that must remain the principal concern of the rider until the horse can execute it with the utmost facility and it is only then that the range and loftiness of both airs can be developed side by side and progressively.

THE CANTER

Work at the canter must be started concurrently with the work at the trot, and one should not worry at the beginning about achieving a perfect strike off.

This work, to start with, consists in confirming the horse in his balance, on both leads, regardless of the direction and figures of the course, and especially at the counter canter. These gymnastics must be practised during the whole period of the work at the trot and developed in parallel with it.

Later on, but not before the horse can execute the School walk without difficulty, striking off at the canter from the walk should be practised until it can be executed instantly on both leads. Striking off from the School walk having been brought to perfection in this manner, starts from the canter to a canter on the opposite lead, which constitute the change of leg, will be obtained without difficulty.

Once isolated changes of leg can be obtained distinctly from one beat to the next, without "blurs", truly "in the air", changes at close intervals can be considered without detriment.

With this in view, the rider must first ensure that the horse returns to the walk with as much precision and as instantly as he strikes off at the canter from a walk.

The horse must learn to pass from a flawless canter to a correct walk without any intermediate, regular or irregular stride of the trot and after a determined number of strides of the canter. As soon as he can start at the canter from the walk, on one lead or on the other, execute four perfectly regular strides of the canter, and immediately after the fourth stride return to a neat, energetic and regular walk, he will experience no difficulty in performing changes after every fifth stride. By progressively reducing the number of strides of the canter between the walk and the return to the walk, little by little the rider will get his horse accustomed to the changes at close intervals and finally to changes at every stride, "a tempo".

Work on two tracks at the canter can be started before or after the study of the changes of leg, but there is seldom any disadvantage in postponing it until later. Excessive lateral mobility of the croup at this gait is often present and entails the risk of the horse "traversing himself" (going crooked) in the changes of leg, a very serious fault of execution, which makes changes at every stride very difficult.

In reality, two track work presents no difficulty at all at the canter once the horse can execute it easily at the trot and at the walk.[1]

The pirouette at the canter is easily obtained from the pirouette at the walk followed by a strike off at a canter and a return to the walk as soon as the horse ceases to execute the pirouette. By starting another pirouette, again from the walk, we can easily get the horse to execute two, then three, then four cantering strides whilst remaining on a pirouette, which he will finally be able to perform without interrupting the canter. When the horse is able to execute a correct pirouette in these conditions, we can then easily link it, through the intermediary of a progressively smaller volte with the haunches in, to a canter on two-tracks on a straight line, and later on to a canter on a single track.

1. On the contrary, the duration of the moment of suspension of the body and the interval of time between the alternating upward thrusts of fore-hand and hind quarters make it easy for the horse to displace himself laterally without having to cross his limbs—which is the only real difficulty in work on two tracks.

PART TWO

Work at the Trot

Chapter 1 · DEVELOPING THE REGULARITY OF THE TROT AND PERFECTING THE GAIT

Books of Reference:
LA GUERINIERE
J. B. DUMAS
STEINBRECHT

The objects of the first period of the work at the trot will be:

(1) To increase the energy and the development of the gait to the limit compatible with maintenance of complete regularity;

(2) To improve the horse's mechanical ability to vary the speed of this gait, and also his sensitivity to the indications of the aids that command these variations.

As the horse selected for academic dressage must be already a perfectly confirmed outdoor ride, his elementary obedience to the aids is already assured, but the work for which he is destined in future demands a precision and a lightness in obedience which are usually lacking because they go beyond what is required of the saddle horse for normal use.

If, as is always advisable, the horse has already had the lessons on the lunge that are described in a later chapter, he will possess the mechanical ability to vary the speed without difficulty, but only within the limits imposed by the work on a circle.

The remaining task of the trainer will be to advance the gymnastic training of his pupil beyond this limit to one which permits maximum lengthening of the trot on straight lines; to develop the horse's sensitivity to the aids so that, on their indications, the variations of speed for which his mechanism has been prepared, can be executed with exactness.

Colonel Lesage on Taine   Thoroughbred for Racing

Madame Franke

This work must be practised out of doors, on good straight roads. In the manege, its results would be practically nil, and would remain negligible even in a very large outdoor school because of the insufficient length of the straight lines and the constant and marked changes of direction imposed upon the horse.

While he is developing the training, the trainer must endeavour to use the horse's instinct to the best advantage and, at least in the beginning, to act always in conformity with the horse's natural impulses. Subsequently, he will still avoid opposing these as much as possible, until the horse's increased sensitivity to his aids gives him the certainty of being capable of counteracting any natural, instinctive manifestations.

Thus, the first changes of speed will be demanded on the way back to the stable.

Lengthenings must then be executed "generously" in response to a minimum leg activity and, when slowing down, the horse's desire for a greater speed must still exist, as this constitutes the spirit of academic work and the key to its brilliancy.

In the same way, slopes of the ground will provide the trainer with favourable conditions for rectifying some of his pupil's shortcomings, developing his weak points, and correcting his balance. They will help to perfect his "locomotive system", so that a better output, in the form best suited to the work that is the object of his particular dressage, can be obtained.

On upward grades, the horse instinctively throws the whole of his mass forward to give it the best disposition for the economical use of the thrust of the hind legs. He loads his shoulders by unloading his hind quarters, thereby increasing the propulsive power of the latter. His neck lengthens. His forelegs are lifted in more rapid succession, they develop their elevation and augment their extension after touching the ground. The top is tensioned along the whole of its length, the loin becomes firmer so that it can transmit without waste the efforts of the hind legs, which for their part flex their joints better, extend more energetically and come to the ground in more rapid succession.

Lengthening of the trot, in these conditions, as long as it is obtained with prudent measure in progression and duration, and on carefully selected gradients, provokes a flexing and stretching of the locomotive system far superior to any that could be obtained from the horse, for an equivalent leg action, on level ground. Through the repetition and the judicious progression of these efforts, the horse will get into the *habit* of using more muscular energy in response to a set degree of impulsive action of the legs.

In similar conditions of sloping ground, the practice of slowing the pace on the upgrades, procures equally considerable advantages. Hollowing of the top, due to excessive elevation of the neck, becomes almost impossible to the horse, and the hind quarters are obliged to remain flexed and active, whilst their excessive loading can be avoided in great measure.

Going downhill, the horse instinctively balances himself in the opposite direction. He lifts the poll and the neck, compacting the latter between the shoulders in order to unload the front, and by hollowing his top along the whole of its length transfers to the rear the greater proportion of his weight. The forelegs delay their lifting, diminish their elevation, and are grounded more hurriedly so that they can better support the mass. The hind legs push off as little as they can help, hasten their lifting, engage as much as they can under the mass so that they can support it as quickly and as continuously as possible.

Lengthening of the stride should not therefore be demanded in these conditions until it has become easy to obtain and active on level ground and has been developed to start with on ascending slopes, and until the authority of the rider's legs is sufficient to prevail over the horse's instinct; however, careful progression of this exercise will increase the horse's confidence until he can project his mass boldly from one diagonal on to the other whilst reducing vertical projection to the utmost. This is not elementary work, but it is an exercise that teaches the horse to use his forces in the right manner, once these forces have been completely conquered by work on upward gradients. On the other hand, slowing down is considerably easier on downward slopes and is recommended, at the beginning, for horses who lack the ability to control their weight and to transfer it from front to rear.

The state of the ground will also influence the amount of muscular energy used by the horse and should be exploited by the trainer.

On level and firm, even rather hard going, the horse is more willing to go forward; on heavy, deep, sticky going he is obliged to increase the efforts of the elevating muscles of his limbs. The intelligent trainer will not fail to make good use of these circumstances.

In all this work, the influence of the rider's position is also considerable.

At the sitting trot, the backward or forward inclination of his upper body assists the shifting of the weight in both directions and must be taken advantage of.

The trainer must be especially conscious of the painful influence that the jolting of his seat cannot help but have on the horse's back. Going uphill, when the reactions of the pace are not strong, the rider need not hesitate to sit in the saddle, as close to the withers as possible, whilst frankly leaning forward with head and upper body. But going downhill, the violence of the reactions provokes abrupt returns to the saddle, and the trainer must take as much support as possible on the stirrups, and lighten his seat to spare the hollowed back, which is particularly badly disposed to bear the repeated jolts of the rider's weight. If the horse's reactions are particularly strong, the trainer will use the rising trot, rising as little as possible in order to limit the alternate upward and downward displacements of the centre of gravity of horse and rider combined.

The rising trot procures, besides this, other far greater advantages as it allows the rider to influence in different ways the alternating movements of the diagonals in order to achieve perfect symmetry of their development. The different attitudes of the upper body when the seat rises or descends cause displacements of weight which affect each pair of legs, and therefore the movement of one pair is developed under conditions of equilibrium different from those under which the opposite number works; it can be observed that the diagonal upon which one trots usually covers more ground than the other, and that its hind leg tends to step in the tracks of the fore-leg, thus to deviate to the side of this diagonal, causing the croup itself to move to the same side.[1]

The pace of the horse can also be influenced by the fact of his being ridden in the company of another horse, who acts as a school master, or of his being ridden alone; this is an extra aid that should not be neglected.

Therefore, the trainer disposes of several means of modifying his pupil's trot; the choice of direction, towards or away from the stable; the lie of the ground and its condition; the position of his own body; rising or sitting at the trot; company or isolation. Each of these means can also be used in very different degrees of intensity. Finally, several of them can be used simultaneously, and combined to serve the same purpose.

In order to obtain the best results from the natural or the acquired form of his pupil's trot, the trainer must study this carefully and methodically and note its peculiarities.

Already, work on the lunge, when it has been resorted to, will have enabled the trainer to form some opinion on this subject, despite the influence on the gait of the permanent curvature of the circle. Amongst other things, he will have been able to observe the general disposition of the horse and his balance, the ease or constraint of his whole attitude, the difference in the action either of front or hind pairs of legs, or of the diagonals, or of each leg of one diagonal.

But these observations, the scope of which is restricted owing to the constant curvature of the circle, and the margin of speeds possible on the lunge without disorder, must be verified on the straight. When the rider himself is in the saddle, he can feel only with the seat.[2] However, this sometimes discloses certain asymmetries of the gait which had escaped the notice of the eye and only become obvious to the latter when the rider has been made aware of them through the seat.

The trainer must therefore observe his horse ridden by an assistant, a competent one of course, who will obey his orders scrupulously, walk the

1. This is true only in the long run. If one starts trotting on the left diagonal on a horse which is used to being trotted on the right one only, he will certainly not develop immediately the range of his left diagonal. On the contrary, he will be surprised and upset, and will use it even less than usual and often attempt to throw his rider back onto the right diagonal by putting in false beats, rather as a marching soldier does when ordered to change his step. It is only by persevering, sometimes for very long, with the trot on the left diagonal that one overcomes the horse's resistance and gradually gets him to use this diagonal as willingly as the right one and finally, with practise, more powerfully than the latter.
2. Useful indications can be obtained by noting the tracks on the ground, and the sound produced by the steps.

horse towards him or in the opposite direction, trot, sitting or rising, on level, heavy or hard ground, up and down hills, at all speeds etc.

The same observations must be made with the horse viewed in profile and from all angles, as may be necessary to reveal clearly what might have escaped notice otherwise.

Thus informed about the peculiarities of his pupil's gaits, the rider will choose amongst the means at his disposal, those that are likely to correct the faults which he has noticed, and will combine those means when he decides on his working programme.

For example, in the case of a "cold" horse, with a trot lacking in energy and speed,[1] and with constricted gestures, particularly of the left diagonal, his first work will be done next to a companion who is more gifted at this gait, on ascending slopes, in heavy going, on the left diagonal, etc. etc.

Later on, when an obvious improvement in the development of the movements of the diagonals is noticed, the form of their action will have to be modified by work on descending slopes, alternating this with the previous work.

Needless to say, safeguarding the soundness of the limbs imposes certain limits on the use of these means and the progression of the work.

In the use of his aids, the trainer must avoid acting simultaneously with hands and legs.

For example, when lengthening:

The hand, passive but supple in its fixity, must give the horse a firm, elastic and continuous feel, without ever destroying impulsion.

The active legs give their indications by means of alternating or simultaneous taps, in rhythm with the pace, and care must be taken not to surprise the horse with the spurs.

The whip applied to the shoulder, to the less active one of course, will assist the legs, and sometimes be substituted for them with advantage, if the horse has had some schooling from the ground.[2]

The main difficulty in the work of developing the trot is the horse's propensity to break into the canter when asked to increase his speed, and this propensity can turn into a resistance if one does not take care.

In the first place one should avoid provoking a breaking into the canter due to abruptness when demanding increased speed, or to lack of firmness

1. Many ordinary riding horses are used to striking into the canter as soon as a certain speed is determined, and their trot is slow because of lack of practice at this pace. This habit of taking the canter as soon as a certain speed is reached is in any case beneficial for the preservation of the horse and the comfort of the rider.

2. "Because strokes of the whip chases better than pricks of the spur" (General L'Hotte), but the whip used behind the boot risks provoking the canter.

or suppleness of the seat, or in general to any asymmetries in the rider's position, movements or aids.[1]

If the horse does break into a canter, he must be stopped without brutality, but quickly and firmly so that he can associate this sort of reprimand with its object, i.e. breaking into the canter. Without raising his voice, the rider will thereupon utter the command: "trot", and will repeat this procedure every time the horse commits the same fault.

This serious fault often requires much time to correct, but correction must be tenaciously persevered with, until it is completely achieved.

It is only in this way that the development of the trot can be pursued and accomplished.

For it is not only the value of the ulterior school work at the trot that closely depends on it, but also that of the passage and the piaffer that is intimately related to it.

1. It may even be necessary to discontinue using the legs in alternate sequence.

A horse can turn regardless of the direction of the bend of the neck. The faster and shorter he turns, the more he tends to bend his neck in the direction opposite to that of the turn.

Chapter 2 · LATERAL SUPPLING OF THE BACK

In France, the practice of exercises on a circle to promote the lateral flexibility of the horse is often neglected.

Count d'Aure rejected it with good reason as unnecessary in the preparation of the ordinary riding horse, which was the sole object of his method.

Baucher, without discarding it altogether, reduced it almost to non-existence in his method, probably because he thought that his novel methods of dressage were sufficiently potent to replace it with advantage.

Without irreverance, we may think that he deceived himself on this score; the only fault that one could justifiably find with his horses was a lack of suppleness of the back, which was very noticeable in the case of his less successful pupils (read: "Baucher et son Ecole", by the same author).

There is no better procedure than bending work on the circle, as described at length and in great detail by La Gueriniere, to obtain and to develop the lateral suppleness of the back—which determines suppleness in the vertical plane.

Straightening the Spine and Lateral Flexions

The horse can change direction:

—by turning the fore-hand around the hind-quarters;

—conversely, by turning the hind-quarters around the forehand;

—by using both methods concurrently, executing fractions of one and of the other mode of turning.

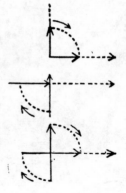

It is the latter procedure that the horse uses to execute wide turns when he is free and calm and when nothing happens to disturb him.

But to turn quickly and sharply, the horse increases the displacement of the fore-hand and reduces that of the hind-quarters: he tends to execute a pirouette.

Mechanically, it is not impossible for him to do the reverse, to immobilise somewhat his fore-legs and to move his hind legs around more quickly, in a kind of reversed pirouette, but he never uses this procedure when he is at liberty, nor when the rider, whilst indicating a new direction, gives the horse freedom to choose a way of taking it. Structurally, lateral mobility of the hind-quarters is not as great as that of the forehand.

In the schooling of the horse intended for ordinary riding in the open, there is little point in attempting to modify his natural inclination to turn by "successive tangents" of the curve that links the new direction to the preceding one. It will be enough to develop his agility by methodical and progressive exercises.

But this is not the case with academic equitation, which requires greater precision and lightness.

"From head to haunches, says General L'Hotte, the horse must be straight when travelling along straight lines, and curved when he follows a curved line."

The purpose of work on curved lines is to satisfy those demands.

However, all horses have a spinal curvature.[1] The spinal column forming the axis from head to tail, in a vertical plane, is not exactly in the middle of the body. One part only of this axis, approximately half-way along its length, is centrally situated. Its extremities are more or less deflected and *always to the same side.*

1. This remark applies also to human beings. According to observations of a whole class of recruits, straightness of the spine exists only in the proportion of 3/1,000.

Whether standing or in movement, the horse finds it difficult to alter this attitude, either to straighten himself or to bend in the opposite direction.

If the curvature is pronounced, and when the skeletal development of the horse is complete, this fault which is incompatible with academic correctness is extremely difficult to rectify adequately and above all with long lasting results.

However, if the curvature is not too pronounced and if the horse is still young, it is possible to straighten the spine to a partial extent by holding it flexed in the opposite direction more or less frequently and for varying periods of time; above all, appropriate gymnastics can provoke an asymmetric development of the muscular system which favours an opposite flexion. This asymmetric development of the muscular system, opposed to the skeletal asymmetry, will partly counteract the latter and enable us to obtain a "relatively straight position".

Straightening the horse

To straighten a horse that is naturally flexed to the right, General Faverot de Kerbrech[1] recommends the use, whenever possible without the legs, of an effect of the left indirect rein, which bends the neck to the left and moves the shoulders towards the right, in front of the hips.

This result is certainly easy to obtain when the horse is going to the left hand on the track, because the wall is there to prevent the quarters from moving as far, or further, towards the right as the shoulders do under the influence of the rein effect.

Away from the wall, the left rein continues to push the shoulders towards the right, but the horse is free to move his quarters that way also, if the rider's heels do not oppose this. The horse thus evades the straightening action attempted by the rider.

Instead of continuing to progress in the original direction, the horse will move forward and towards the right, in a half-pass—concerning which General Faverot de Kerbrech writes precisely:[2] "the indirect rein must be used as often as possible instead of the leg on the same side."

These effects of the indirect rein, the one driving the shoulders *only*, and the other driving shoulders and haunches *together* to one side, are not of course identical, but are sufficiently similar to make the subtle shade of difference elude the rider sometimes and even more the horse who has no real wish to understand; if the rider then persists in using this rein effect only,

1. "Dressage methodique du cheval de selle". III Part: "Assembler"—Chapter One: Striking off and work at the canter.—Means of straightening the horse.
2. Ibid. part II: Preparation—Chapter Two: At the walk.—Side steps, the head, then the tail to the wall.

he runs the risk of assisting a more extensive turning out of these haunches which the horse is not inclined to surrender.

It is prudent therefore to hold the use of the heels in reserve, if not to prevent, at least to correct this escaping of the haunches. General Faverot de Kerbrech makes no mention of this, but General L'Hotte specifies it after having explained how the pressure of one heel, "absolutely in one place", produces an effect similar to the one used by a dancer when she presses her hand against her flank on the side to which she wants her body to flex.

It is this curving, or arching effect, which General L'Hotte recommended and which he says must be obtained by a pressure of the heel on the same side as the indirect rein, while the opposite heel, which only comes into action if necessary, exerts its own particular action in a backwards direction, without however having to change its position. If we assume, furthermore, that the right rein can sometimes exceed its purpose and thereby oblige the rider to counteract with the left rein the excessive bend he has produced with the

The horse 'adjusted' to the curve of the circle[1]

Commandant Lesage,
Chief Instructor at the Cavalry School
(Saumur) on TAINE

German school

1. The German horse is circling at the trot on the right rein (he is slightly overbent). Taine is circling at the canter on the left rein. Both riders are using a lightly adjusted curb rein. Note the temporary drawing back of the outside heel of the riders, particularly obvious on Taine (compare this with the position of the same rider on the same horse, P. 105). (Note to 2nd edition.)

right one, we are finally led to admit that the rider needs no less than both his hands and both his legs to straighten the horse, though he must avoid, as often as possible, using them simultaneously.

Lateral flexions of the Spine
Getting the horse to adapt his curvature to the curves of a course is as difficult as straightening him on a straight line.

On his concave side, the horse is often excessively flexible, and his bend tends to exceed that of the figure described.

On his convex side, his flexibility if often insufficient and his curvature tends to remain short of the required degree.

It will be by progressively suppling the horse by work on circles that the rider will be able to obtain an almost equal flexibility of both sides.

To prescribe the use of the aids that serve best the purposes of work on circles, we must specify what the trainer wants to alter, and which modifications he wants to obtain.

If the horse which has not been suppled is represented—approximately— by the imprints of his median longitudinal plane on the ground, his turn is executed more or less as is shown in Fig. i below:

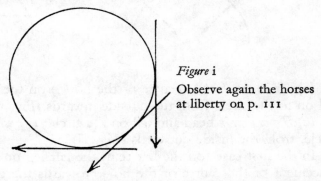

Figure i
Observe again the horses at liberty on p. 111

Once the horse has been suppled, he will have to regulate his movements so that the imprints of the hooves of each lateral pair of legs are situated on either side of the circle upon which he is moving, on two circles concentric with the first, and equally distant from it, as is shown in Fig. ii below.

Figure ii

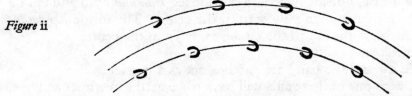

The outline of his spine corresponding to the circumference of the circle

A.E.—9

To the transformation in the movement of the limbs corresponds a transformation in the attitude of the body, which was more or less inclined towards the centre before suppling and is held more or less vertical after this.

The horse which turns as in Figs. i and iii is said to "keel over on the volte" ("couché dans sa volte" as the old masters used to say). The one which turns as in Figs. ii and iv can be said to be "upright on the volte".

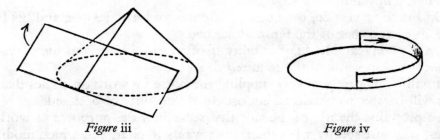

Figure iii   *Figure iv*

Theoretically, there are two ways of laterally curving the horse:

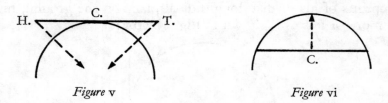

Figure v   *Figure vi*

(1) *To maintain* (c) (centre of the horse) on the circle; *to push* head and tail on to the circle from the outside inwards (Fig. v)

(2) *To maintain* head and tail on the circle; *to push* the centre (c) on to the circle, from the inside outwards (Fig. vi).

In the first case (on the left rein) the left leg on the girth opposes a displacement of the centre of the horse towards the centre of the circle. The hand draws the head and the forehand to the left on to the circle. The right leg brings the hind-quarters in on to the circle by pushing them to the left.

The inside leg (left) is passive, acts as a barrier. The outside hand and leg are active.

In the second case, outside hand and outside leg *maintain* head and tail on the circle, oppose their moving away from the centre. The inside leg *pushes* the centre of the body out on to the circle, away from the centre.

The left, inside leg is active.

The outside leg and the hand are passive, act as a barrier.

In practice, each one of these aids will have to be used sometimes actively, sometimes passively, and their combinations will have to be adapted, in mode and intensity, to the nature and the force of the resistances the horse will set against this bending.

When circling to the left, the left rein will act by moving slightly to the left, with the hand held rather low, because the neck is more flexible when it is low. The trainer will also use the aid of the right rein if the horse, as he usually does, attempts to localise the flexion in his neck by "breaking" it in front of the withers instead of allowing the flexion to extend from one end of his body to the other.

It will usually be found that the most effective way of counteracting the "break" that allows the horse to escape total flexion from withers to tail, is to oppose it with the right rein held against the base of the neck. It should however be noted that lateral flexibility of the neck is much diminished when the latter is high, and to limit its incurvation and force the spine to participate in the flexion it is sometimes more effective to lift the right hand to a greater or less extent and not to hold the left hand quite so low, rather than merely to use the right indirect rein against the base of the neck.

The position of the legs can also be modified so that each heel is able to fulfil its role exactly.

As always, therefore, it is only by trial and error that the rider will be able to discover the correct use of his aids, and to modify them according to the various resistances of his pupil.

At the beginning of the work on circles, it is usually profitable to exercise the horse only on turns that are contrary to his natural curvature until he achieves and keeps without resistance an equal degree of opposite curvature.

The basic circle, selected by trial and error, will have to be of a large radius. Correct curvature will be demanded only for a few strides, and the trainer must stop demanding it before constraint and fatigue compel the horse to put up an open resistance.

In the intervals between the demands, the trainer will allow the horse to move on straight lines, with complete freedom of attitude.

The demands can become more frequent and prolonged as the horse's limit of tolerance widens.

As soon as the unresisting horse can remain properly flexed for a few circuits of the basic circle, the rider can lead him into a spiral towards the interior of the circle, by gradually increasing the curvature, as the head, the shoulders, and the rest of the body in turn, engage on the new circuit.

As soon as the rider feels a resistance, and if possible before it occurs, he must yield with all his aids, starting with the inside rein, which by its contact with the mouth, gives him the most valuable indications on the general state of suppleness of his pupil, and allow his horse to relax on straight lines.

These, (the information provided by the softness of the feel on the inside rein, and the instantaneousness of the yielding of the hand), are the points to which the rider must pay particular attention.

Complete obedience is nearly always accompanied by a slight yielding of the jaw, and especially of the tongue. This is precisely the moment to yield, to let the horse straighten, and to extend rather than to slow. Some horses with a numb mouth will not relax it completely until they have been enticed to do so by the practice of flexions of the jaw, and it is not advisable for the time being to seek this relaxation, still less to obtain it by force. It is enough merely to endeavour to seize the moment when the feel on the rein becomes as light as possible, but still trusting, and to reward this immediately.

The trainer must also take into account the fact that absolute continuity of curvature of the whole length of the spine can be only apparent, as the latter is not equally flexible in its different parts. The neck, the hindermost part of the back, and the anterior part of the loin are more flexible than the other parts. A continuous geometrical curvature therefore can never be achieved, but rather an adjustment of the *whole* constituted by the different regions of the spine, to the curve followed by the horse. The muscular masses that bind the various skeletal parts together dispose themselves in such a way as to bend the horse and to adjust him as accurately as possible to the desired curve.

The attitude of the rider, his position, and the resulting distribution of his weight play an important part in this work, particularly as regards correcting the inward inclination of the horse on the curve.

To place himself also accurately on the circle, the rider must be careful not to leave that half of his body behind which is on the outside of the curve. He must constantly face in the same direction as the horse. His shoulders and hips must be in a line with the centre of the circle, instead of the shoulders remaining behind, as is so often seen.

He must, with the utmost care and the greatest suppleness possible, adjust his own inclination towards the centre of the circle to that of his horse. An excessive inclination on the part of the rider would provoke a reaction in the opposite direction on the part of the horse and upset the latter in the pursuit of his balance.

As soon as this work has made the horse sufficiently flexible to enable him to maintain without pain a curvature of his convex side equal to that of the other, the rider may start working on the latter side.

The main difficulties that the rider will encounter here will arise from the horse's tendency to bend more than in the measure required by the curve of the circle, at least when this is of a wide radius, and to go more or less with "both ends turned in". It is therefore more of an "unfolding" than a "folding" that is wanted, and the rider will have to modify his aids accordingly.

The actions of the aids may have to be transformed or even reversed, but their transformation must always be proportionate to the resistances encountered by the rider. To the left hand, in order to keep the horse out on the circle, the right rein, instead of acting against the base of the neck to limit the bend, may have to move outwards with more of an opening effect, while the left rein will yield and be brought closer to the neck. The left leg may have to slide further backwards, so that it can be used to produce a bending effect opposed to the curve of the circle.

As the basic circle corresponds now to the natural bend of the horse, and it becomes easier to straighten the horse by the influence of the aids, the rider must gradually enlarge the circle on an outward spiral, straighten him completely on a straight line, and finally bend him again on a circle in the opposite direction.[1]

Increasing the curvature of the originally concave side should only be undertaken at the end of this work, and never beyond the results obtained in the other direction, which must always be achieved first.

To confirm the results obtained in equalising lateral flexibility, the horse should be ridden sometimes on serpentines, sometimes on figures of eight, and in the intervals, on straight lines.

On serpentines, the loops should be unequal most of the time: tight to the side opposed to the natural bend, and wide to the other one. The same applies to figures of eight, and to the spirals which may be described within or outside these.

Thus the trainer can impart infinite variety to his work, as much by varying the degree of curving imposed upon his pupil, as by the time devoted to each side, until the deliberately unequal exercising of one side as opposed to the other establishes equal flexibility of both.

The rising trot will also be profitably made use of, as the asymmetry which it provokes in the horse's movements can be set against those which the rider is counteracting. It is prudent, however, to ascertain that the horse's reactions to the rising trot are the same as the rider expects, for it seems that they are not identical always in the case of all horses and in all circumstances.

When the series of exercises that have been explained above has been practised without omissions, and for a long enough period of time, the horse's habitual position is usually notably modified and approaches perfect straightness.

The slight curvature that persists is in any case easily overcome by invisible aid effects which allow the rider to keep his horse straight on straight

1. To summarise: on the left rein, horse bent on the circle; enlarge by a spiral; straighten and progress along the diagonal; circle on the right rein, bending the horse; tighten by a spiral and so on. (Note: second edition.)

lines, and correctly bent on curved ones. The indirect rein effect, advocated by General Faverot de Kerbrech will often be sufficient. For their part, either of both heels will have acquired sufficient authority to prevent the hind leg on the same side from turning out instead of engaging under the centre of the mass.

The horse is then ready for two track work.

The beneficial effects of these gymnastics do not stop here. Each lateral pair of legs has been alternately exercised in "flexion" on the inside of the circle, and in "extension" on the outside. In each of the diagonal pairs, the more extensive movement of the outside shoulder has been associated with the flexion of the hind leg working on the inside of the circle.

The development of the gestures, and their greater suppleness will have imparted more rhythm, expression and amplitude to the horse's trot. It will have modified its form and will more closely resemble a "School" trot.

Two track work will complete the transformation.

Chapter 3 · TWO-TRACK WORK

Books of Reference:
LA GUERINIERE
DU PATY DE CLAM
STEINBRECHT
BAUCHER
GENERAL FAVEROT DE KERBRECH
GERHARDT

Sideways progression is not natural to the horse. In a state of freedom, he only accidentally uses it, and then in leaps, to get away from a sudden cause of fright.

His locomotive mechanism, though it is not completely unadapted to continuous lateral progression, only allows it in an oblique forward direction.

Lack of natural practice makes this mode of lateral progression difficult for the horse, both as regards the disposition of his body as a whole and the movement of his limbs.

The practice of "side-steps"[1] will eradicate his awkwardness, and will improve the horse's ability to preserve or modify his balance, or to recover it rapidly if necessary. It will improve his agility and his ease of movement.

The play of his entire muscular system will be modified because he will be required to use his energy to produce an "oblique" direction, instead of a straightforward one parallel to the long axis of his body as in single track progression. The muscles of the topline, especially in the region of the loin, are particularly stimulated, suppled and strengthened.

With regard to the limbs, the stimulation of the adductor and abductor muscles commanding lateral movements, which are practically inoperative in straightforward progression, will have to be co-ordinated with the simultaneous efforts in flexion and extension of those which determine forward movement in the direction of the long axis of the body.

The resulting modifications in the activity of the locomotive system are

1. We will call "side-steps" all modes of lateral displacement, regardless of the direction of the long axis of the horse.

very favourable to the development of the gaits required by academic equitation, which is the purpose of the dressage contemplated in this work.

Especially, in the crossing of the legs, the outside fore is obliged[1] more than it is in straightforward movements and even on circles, to lift at the shoulder and the knee to avoid striking the inside fore when it moves ahead of it, and the outside hind must also increase the lifting and lengthening of its stride for the same reason.

In two-track movements, each leg in turn therefore, depending on the bend and the direction of lateral displacement, is obliged to increase the efforts of its extensor and adductor, flexor and abductor muscles. The resulting improvement in overall mobility is particularly noticeable in the flexion which facilitates collection (Rassembler) and determines the elevation of the movements.

The horse, however, disposes of one means of avoiding this effort and it is seldom that he does not have recourse to it.

When crossing from left to right, for example, he will avoid as much as possible *advancing* his right hind and instead will carry it towards the right and ground it behind the position it should assume, thereby avoiding in part the necessity of engaging forward with the left hind to avoid striking the right hind as it crosses in front of the latter.[2]

If the rider, in previous work, has not secured the means of obliging the right hind to engage as far forward as it should and of preventing it from escaping to the side, the advantages of two-track work are limited to the development of lateral mobility and to the detriment of engagement of the hind limbs.

This is the reason why side-stepping often produces such small results from the point of view of dressage as a whole, and especially of the pursuit of collection when it has not been prepared by work on a circle, which provides the rider precisely with the means of controlling the movements of the inside hind, of preventing its sideways evasion, and of enforcing its engagement in the direction of the centre.

1. We will designate as *inside* legs those on the concave side, *outside* legs, those on the convex side, *regardless of* the direction of movement of the body. If the horse is not bent, we will indicate the direction of the movement and refer to the "right and left" legs, thus avoiding confusion.

2. The gait (walk or trot) must be bold and energetic. The forward reach of the hind limbs matters more than obliquity of direction in the half-pass, which must remain *very* moderate for a long time. The same recommendation applies to the orientation of the horse's body in the "Head-to-the-wall" or the "Tail-to-the-wall". (Although The Old Masters executed full-passes at an angle of ninety degrees, perpendicular to the side of the "manege square"; La Gueriniere.) (Note: 2nd edition).

To preserve the rider's ascendancy over the inside hind, as obtained on the circle, the half-pass must be prepared by two other exercises: the "shoulder-in" and the "haunches-in", and, if necessary, complemented by the exercise of "both-ends in" (see footnote 1, p. 126).

RIGHT SHOULDER-IN
Spanish Riding School

In the shoulder-in, the horse—having been properly bent on a circle—leaves the circle at a tangent; the tangential point being that at which his hindquarters find themselves at that precise moment. Whilst maintaining the bend which has been achieved, the body of the horse remains in a position parallel to that which it had on leaving the circle. The hind-quarters proceed along the tangential line, and the forehand follows a track parallel to the tangent, but between the latter and the circle, due to the bend previously obtained.

The movement is of no use unless the forehand and the hind-quarters remain exactly on their respective tracks.

At the beginning, the bend must be one corresponding to a very large circle, i.e. very slight, and the imprints of the inside hind and those of the outside fore follow the same track. (The horse moves on three tracks.)

Steinbrecht's 'Schulter vor'
(shoulder fore).

The bend and the crossing
of the legs are
extremely slight.

In the left shoulder-in, the right—or outside hind—which is not subject to much stress, does not usually try to evade this, but not so the left or inside hind which is obliged to move further under the centre of the mass and is therefore greatly loaded by the mass (and consequently flexed). It will therefore almost invariably attempt to evade the flexion and the loading by "escaping" towards the inside, i.e. towards the left.

The rider must then drive the horse forward on to a new circle and continue on this circle until he has restored the correct bend and normal engagement of the escaping hind leg, and having obtained this result, he may proceed again along the tangent.

Gradually, the degree of curvature and the distance between inside and outside track must be increased. A point is then reached beyond which the rider will feel that the outside hind in its turn tries to escape from the track and to turn out instead of advancing forwards.

This is the time to start the opposite exercise, the "haunches-in".

In the haunches-in, the horse correctly bent on the circle leaves it at a tangent at the moment when the *forehand* touches the tangential point and then continues moving in a direction parallel to his body, while maintaining the same bend.

The forehand follows the tangent, whilst the hind-quarters follow a line parallel to the tangent, between the latter and the circle.

SHOULDER-IN

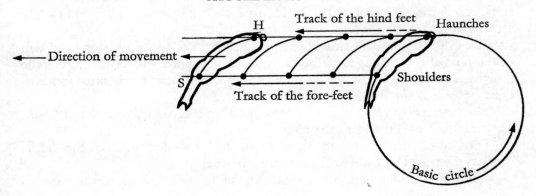

In the above diagram, the obliquity and bend of the horse are *purposely* exaggerated. In the early stages, they should be infinitely less, and the inside hind should follow the track of the outside fore; the exercise was called 'Shulter vor' by Steinbrecht and is thus known in the German School: shoulder-fore.

HAUNCHES-IN (Travers)

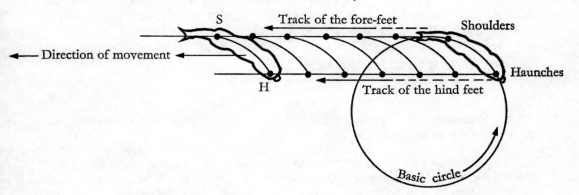

In the first stage of this work, the distance between inside and outside track must remain as narrow as when starting the shoulder-in; it will be sufficient if the imprints of the inside fore and the outside hind follow the same track.

The outside hind will thus lose its tendency to outward evasion, and will develop its ability to engage in its turn under the centre of the mass, until the limit is reached when the inside hind, under this thrust, tends once more to escape towards the inside.

The rider again resorts to progression on a circle, then to the shoulder-in, to come back eventually to the haunches-in.

Thus alternately between shoulder-in and haunches-in, by the intermediary of the circle, the horse acquires gradually:

—the ability to position his shoulders in relation to his haunches, and reciprocally,

—the ability to displace his limbs sideways, bringing his hind legs back to their position of engagement, and his forelegs back to their supporting position.

Use of the Aids

In both these movements, the aids play much the same role as they do when controlling the bend on the circle.

However, in the shoulder-in, the inside heel must accentuate its forward action, to promote the displacement of the mass in the direction of the outside shoulder, and the outside rein must likewise "lead" the forehand along the track.

In the haunches-in, the outside heel must transform the passive role of acting as a barrier which it had during work on the circle, into an active role, controlling the outside hind, whilst the inside rein, in addition to its duty of ensuring the bend, must "lead" the fore-hand along the track.

Once the results of the work at the shoulder-in and the haunches-in are secured, the horse is ready for the half-pass.[1]

THE HALF-PASS

In the half-pass, the horse displaces his shoulders and his haunches simultaneously towards the same side.

---

1. The simultaneous execution of the shoulder-in and the haunches-in places the horse in the attitude called "both ends-in". The resulting very pronounced bend makes it a rather tricky exercise. It must be avoided towards the naturally concave side, and on the other side should be practised only with discernment, as it provokes a tendency to make the horse lead with the haunches at the half-pass. La Gueriniere also points out that it can produce overbending, but advises using it if necessary to prepare the Passage.

If the lateral extension of the limbs is equal in front and behind, the horse moves in a direction parallel to himself. His limbs follow straight, parallel tracks, at an angle with the direction in which he faces. This is a half-pass on a straight line.

If the lateral extension of the shoulders is greater than that of the haunches, the limbs describe concentric circles. It is the half-pass on a circle, the haunches-in, and its limit is the pirouette.

In the opposite case, it is the half-pass on a circle, the haunches-out, the limit of which is the reversed pirouette.

In the half-pass on a straight line, the horse can be straight in his long axis, from head to tail.

However, says General L'Hotte, in side steps, there is a good reason for demanding a slight flexion ("le placer trouve sa place"). It compels the horse to look in the direction of the movement and *it helps in bringing forward the outside shoulder* which has the harder task.[1]

1. The General adds: "For all that, it (the flexion) must be very slight so that the action of the rein producing the flexion does not react on the haunches". It is difficult to imagine that a bend imposed on one extremity of the spine will not be communicated to the other end. However, the flexion can be so slight that it is unnoticeable, or it can even be reduced to a mere tendency.

This tendency of itself can even be favourable to the desired movement, for when a horse is inflexed in the "Mise en Main" his haunches always tend to displace themselves in the same direction as his head, which is the object of the half-pass. What we must avoid is an excessive bend on the side of the half-pass which would react on the shoulders by pushing them towards the other side.

The degree of flexion must be proportionate to the degree of the half-pass. The old masters used to say: "For a half-hip, the rider must see the corner of the horse's eye; for a whole hip (45 degrees and more) he must be able to see the ball of the eye scintillating".

What matters mostly is that the rider should be able to regulate the action of the rein producing the flexion so that it achieves the required effect and not the opposite one. For example, if to produce a right flexion, the rider draws the right rein towards the left hip, by pressing it somewhat against the neck, he transfers the weight of the neck onto the left shoulder, thereby hindering it instead of assisting it.

Therefore, when demanding flexion, the hand must act in its normal position, or even *outwards*, but never *inwards*—unless the rider needs to moderate the displacement of the left shoulder towards the right which happens rarely.

Influence of flexion on the movements of the limbs in the half-pass
We should note that the lateral inflexion of the horse influences the movements of the limbs in two-track work.

The legs on the concave side come closer to one another, and those on the convex side extend further apart from one another.

Consequently, the inside fore is relatively behind the outside fore, and the inside hind is relatively in front of the outside hind.

The effort of stepping across is therefore less for the limb which is forward, and greater for the one which is behind. Thus, in the shoulder-in, in which the horse moves in a direction opposed to his inflexion, the hind legs exert less effort in crossing themselves, and the forelegs have to make a greater effort.[1]

It is the contrary that happens in the half-pass.

1. Which justifies the use of the shoulder-in as the first exercise in side-stepping, as it is usually more difficult for the hind-quarters to cross over than for the forelegs.

INFLUENCE OF THE STRAIGHTNESS OR CURVATURE OF A COURSE
ON THE MOVEMENTS OF THE LIMBS IN THE HALF-PASS

We should note also that in two-track work on the circle, the movements of the limbs are influenced by their position in relation to the direction of the movement.

When the hind-quarters are inside the circle, as in the haunches-in, the displacement of the hind limbs is smaller than that of the fore-limbs; the latter have to reach out more.

In the half-pass on the circle with the haunches-out, the opposite obtains.

EXECUTION OF THE HALF-PASS

The horse that is already proficient at the shoulder-in and at the haunches-in will usually experience no difficulty in executing the first half-passes demanded of him, though of course on a very slight oblique.

However, in most cases, he will tend to slow his pace considerably.

The trainer will, therefore, have to pay particular attention to the maintenance, or rather to the restoration of impulsion. To start with, he will resort to the convention established between himself and the horse from the beginning of dressage: "When the rider rises at the trot, the horse must go into a more extended trot", and he will ensure the observance of this convention by the use, if necessary, of legs and whip.

But whether to rise on one or on the other leg is not an indifferent matter.

In theory, it would appear logical to rise on the diagonal which is on the side of the direction of the half-pass; as the hind leg of this diagonal tends to be drawn towards this side,[1] this procedure should facilitate the effort of crossing.

It happens sometimes, however, that a horse restricts the movement of the outside diagonal[2] because, as was explained at the beginning of the present chapter, he does not engage the inside hind; in such a case we should trot on the outside diagonal.[3]

Here again, despite the most attentive observation and the most clever arguments, experience is the only thing that counts. It is by trial and error that the trainer must discover which diagonal gives the better results, and it is on this one that he must rise.

1. General L'Hotte.
2. Note that the diagonal is named according to its foreleg. The inside diagonal, therefore, is made up of the inside fore and outside hind, and conversely.
3. This almost always happens when the lateral flexion is excessive. It is therefore a warning to verify the use of the inside rein.

Finally, he can also resort to trotting uphill to re-establish impulsion, a task which must be pursued until complete success is achieved.

The same applies to the use of the aids.

Theoretically, a slight flexion in the direction of the half-pass should draw the outside shoulder in this direction and "facilitate" the movement. Practically, this is not invariably so at the outset. The horse frequently finds it easier to obey if he is not flexed, or even if he is flexed very slightly in the opposite direction.

There is no reason why we should deprive ourselves of a means of achieving the most immediate aim, which is to make our intention clear. Once the horse has overcome his initial clumsiness, he will obey the aids instead of distorting their effects by resistances the origin of which eludes us, and we will then have no difficulty in returning gradually to the normal use of the aids which assures utmost regularity of the movements when the horse is completely unconstrained.

The same method of trial and error must be applied to the use of the heels, and we should not be too hidebound to modify their point of application if experience shows that this yields certain advantages at the beginning in producing the movement; as suppleness improves, we will gradually be able to return to a normal use.

Once it is effective, in a half-pass to the right for example, the right rein leads the horse and gives him a suitable flexion with a direct or slight opening action; the left rein must be ready to limit the bend if necessary, and also acts as an indirect rein, pushing the shoulders towards the right. The left heel acts in the direction of the half-pass to push the whole mass in that direction. With an action from back to front, the right heel firmly sustains the impulsion and prevents the inside hind (right hind) from escaping. However, perfection and consequently perfect lightness in the half-pass can only be entirely achieved once the indirect rein on its own suffices to produce the movement. It is with this ultimate aim in view that the rider must strive to improve the use of the aids.

We gradually increase the periods of exercise in the half-pass, always only very slightly oblique, until the horse can execute it with the utmost facility, resume a straight line (or a circular one if he is inflexed), and half-pass once again, without ever altering the pace or the rhythm and even lengthening the stride if his rider demands.

It is unnecessary and even detrimental to attempt to obtain too soon a half-pass exceeding 25 to 30 degrees in inclination.

The practice of the half-pass on the circle, with a slight degree of inclination enables the trainer to develop separately the capacity for lateral movement of the haunches and the shoulders.

In the haunches-out on the circle, the haunches have to make a greater lateral effort than the shoulders as they have to cover a greater distance; as the hind-quarters are usually the least mobile part of the horse in sideways movements, this exercise is the most useful one at the beginning, and is succeeded by the exercise of the haunches-in at a later stage. In the opposite case (when the forehand is least mobile) the haunches-in on the circle would come first.

When the horse can execute both these exercises on a circle easily, at an angle of 25 degrees for example, he is ready to half-pass at an angle of 30 degrees on a straight line, and so on.

The half-pass must be frequently alternated with the shoulder-in[1] which is not just a preparatory exercise for the half-pass, but of itself is an excellent way of suppling and developing the muscles.

Assuming an equal degree of inclination in either exercise, the play of the limbs will be very different as the inflexion of the horse modifies the distribution of his weight, loads the limbs on the concave side and thus unburdens the others.

For example, if the movement is executed from left to right, the thrust of the left hind determines the direction of march in both cases, but this leg will be loaded in the shoulder-in, and unloaded in the half-pass. The right shoulder, which supports more weight in the half-pass when it is on the concave side, is lightened in the shoulder-in. Its forward extension towards the right will necessarily be affected differently by each exercise.

Thus the trainer can adapt the exercise to the peculiarities of the play of the locomotive system of his pupil.

If, for example, the horse's right diagonal is awkward, the left hind failing to engage and the right fore to extend properly, the trainer corrects this:

—by resorting to the *left shoulder-in*, on straight lines and also and especially on circles to the *right* (sometimes called the counter shoulder-in);

—by practising the *half-pass to the right*, on straight lines and also and especially on circles to the right hand with the haunches-in.

During all these exercises, the use of the rising trot will contribute its own particular effects, and the practice of riding uphill on straight lines should also be resorted to.

At the beginning, side-stepping, if it has been done without inflexion, must finish with a few straight strides in a straight line, but if done with inflexion, then must be completed by single track movement on a large circle corresponding to the inflexion. In the latter case, the alternations must be

1. Not excluding, obviously, work on straight lines, on circles, and all the previous dressage lessons.

separated and connected by a few straight strides before the opposite bend is demanded.

Later on, when the horse has become proficient at counter-changes on two-tracks, the transition from one form of side-stepping to the other can be executed directly. For example, without altering the direction of movement, we can change from the left shoulder-in to the right half-pass, first without flexion, then with flexion. By altering the direction of movement, we can change from the left shoulder-in to the *left* half-pass, and conversely.

All these exercises considerably improve the horse's agility and his submissiveness to an extent where we get the feeling of being able almost to "knead" him with the aids.

It should be noted finally that, in the half-pass, the indirect rein on the side opposite to the direction of movement must be gradually substituted for the action of the leg on that side, until it even completely replaces it (Du Paty du Clam, and Faverot de Kerbrech).

Perfecting two-track work by the use of the walk
In side-stepping, the efforts of the limbs to cross in front of one another can only be entirely exploited at the walk, because at the trot the moment of suspension enables the horse to avoid to some extent making this effort.

At the trot, instead of lifting the leg that is to be crossed only after the leg which must cross in front of it has touched down, the horse springs from one leg to the other, and thus avoids a true crossing by "disengaging" prematurely the leg to be crossed.

At the walk, on the other hand, the crossing is complete, and consequently the suppling effect on the adductor and abductor muscles of all four limbs and (especially) of the back produced by the crossing of the hind legs is much greater and more effective than at the trot.

It is useful therefore to start all over again, and to perfect at the walk, where greater effort is required, the work on two-tracks which was started at the trot because the moments of suspension made the task easier for the horse.

Furthermore at the trot, in the exercises of the haunches-in and the haunches-out on a circle we cannot complete the gradual reduction of the radius which leads to the pirouette or to the reversed pirouette, as it is not possible for the horse to continue to trot on one spot with the forelegs or with the hind legs before he can execute a piaffer.

It is therefore at the walk also, and especially at the School walk, that we must seek to perfect the movements of haunches-in and haunches-out, and that we will be able to exploit to the full the very important advantages of the pirouettes.

Chapter 4 · SCHOOL WALK, PIROUETTES, COUNTER CHANGES

A perfectly correct collected walk, performed quite spontaneously by a
horse of good conformation under the influence of excitement
(Drawing by Lt. Col. Margot, from a photograph)

SCHOOL WALK

During the course of the work at the trot, this gait has acquired cadence and
lightness. It has become the "School trot". Changes of speed, practised
concurrently with inflexions on curved lines and with side-steps have made
it increasingly easy to slow the gait.

By continuing the slowing down until the horse comes to the walk,
without allowing the head to change its position, or the horse to alter the

attitude he has acquired at the trot, the rider effects the transition from the trot to the School walk, which is loftier than the natural walk.

The trainer must remain aware of the fact that the School walk, as all other forms of the walk, is a four-time pace, and he must not allow the horse to continue progressing at a two-time diagonal pace, which Raabe baptized "petit trot marche" (jog-trot).[1]

It is absolutely essential that the horse should break up his diagonals and make distinctly audible the four clearly distinguishable beats of his hooves. If the horse does not do it of his own accord the trainer will have to increase slightly the load on the hindquarters by exaggerating the elevation of his hands in successive requests to slow the cadence of the forelegs. He will achieve the same result more easily if he demands the transition from the trot to the walk at the summit of a downhill gradient, as this slope always tends to provoke the breaking up of the constituent diagonals.

Periods of the School walk must be short to start with, and must end with a return to the trot, without a transition to a natural walk, in order properly to confirm the horse in the School gait required. Later on, halts should be demanded from the trot, with the fewest possible intermediate strides at the ordinary walk, and the rider should only yield after the halt.

When the School walk is properly established, the trainer will continue the work on inflexion and ride his horse at the walk on curved lines as he did at the trot, then later in the shoulder-in and the haunches-in, and finally in side-steps.

PIROUETTES

Properly engaged in a left shoulder-in, on a circle to the left, for example, the horse is gradually led away from the circumference on a diminishing spiral and brought gradually closer to the centre. The circle described by the forelegs continues to decrease to a limit where the left foreleg can only move upwards and downwards, to be grounded each time on the same spot on the centre of the circle, whilst the other three limbs revolve around it. The

1. We must draw attention to the mistake made commonly by present day riders of confusing the "School walk" with the "extended walk" which is its opposite. The extended walk, in the form of the "Pas de conscrit" or the "Pas de Biche" which develops in elevation to become the Spanish walk, tends towards diagonalisation, i.e. the four-time beat broken up more or less into two groups of two beats. Furthermore, because of the necessary adjustment of balance it produces a braking effect, sometimes sufficiently extensive to cause compression of the joints of the hind legs. For this reason, academic equitation rejects the Spanish airs, which it puts in the category of artificial equitation under the title of fanciful gaits. (Note: 2nd edition).

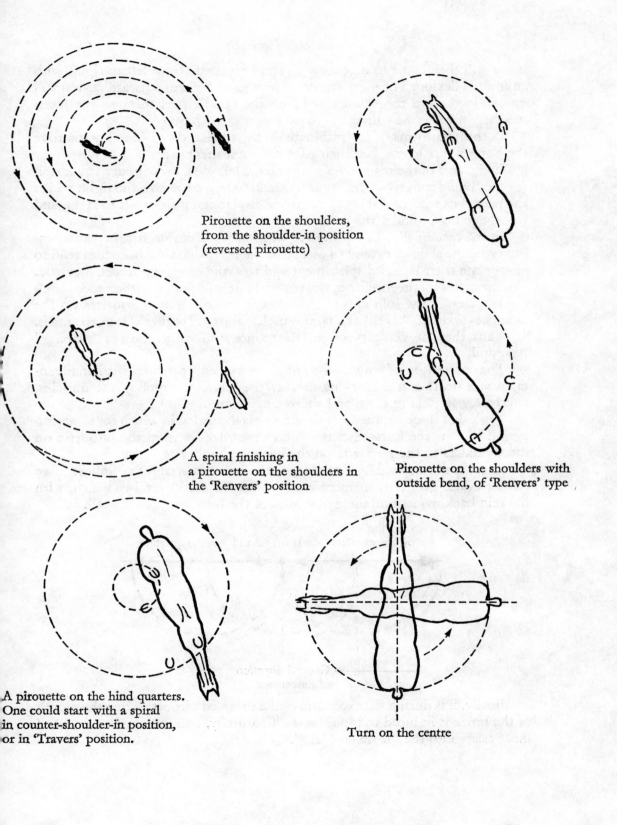

Pirouette on the shoulders,
from the shoulder-in position
(reversed pirouette)

A spiral finishing in
a pirouette on the shoulders in
the 'Renvers' position

Pirouette on the shoulders with
outside bend, of 'Renvers' type

A pirouette on the hind quarters.
One could start with a spiral
in counter-shoulder-in position,
or in 'Travers' position.

Turn on the centre

horse will then come to execute a reversed pirouette from left to right, with an inward flexion. The same (reversed pirouette) with an outward flexion will be obtained from the haunches-out on the same circle, through the intermediary of the same spiral.

Both these forms of the pirouette on the forehand considerably improve the horse's suppleness, but their effects are not identical.

In the case of the reversed pirouette from left to right, with inward flexion (of the shoulder-in type) the shoulders tend to move towards the right, whilst the haunches tend to restrict their lateral displacement from left to right, and to engage better under the mass.

In the case of the same pirouette with outward flexion (of the haunches-out type) the shoulders tend to escape to the left, whilst the haunches tend to exaggerate their lateral displacement and to avoid engaging under the mass.

Pirouettes on the forehand, with or without inflexion, lengthen and stretch the muscles of the loin and tend to lower or hollow it. Pirouettes on the haunches shorten, "swell" the same muscles, and tend to lift the loin, to arch it.

Thus, these movements provide the trainer with many means of "shaping" his pupil.

The connection of sequences of these movements procures further advantages still, in that it enables us to vary the work of suppling the muscles, alternately stretching them and shortening them.

Typical of these alternating movements is the waltz, in which for a varying period of time the horse executes successive changes from the pirouette on the shoulders to the pirouette on the haunches, and vice versa.

Then again, depending on whether the horse is straight or inflexed, we can introduce greater refinement in the variety of these exercises which, with the rein back, constitute the gymnastics of the loin "par excellence".

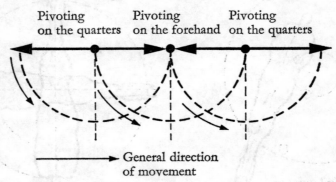

Pivoting on the quarters   Pivoting on the forehand   Pivoting on the quarters

General direction of movement

Finally, it is during the execution of the reversed pirouettes that the mouth of the horse is induced to mobilize itself naturally, and that the horse "falls" most easily into the "Mise en Main".

We must therefore take advantage of the favourable conditions which they create to start the work of flexions of the jaw, using at the beginning the bridoon with which the horse has been bitted up to now and later the curb which should be used in conjunction with it from then on.

This work will be the subject of the following chapter.

COUNTER-CHANGES OF HAND ON TWO-TRACKS (AT THE TROT)

When the body is in the air, during the moment of suspension of the trot, and both diagonals are off the ground, it is impossible for the horse to change the direction of his movement. He can only land where his hind-quarters have propelled him.

However, in the oblique propulsion of two-track movement the role of the hind legs is different.

The left hind, for example, can thrust the mass forwards, towards the right, but it is impossible for it to thrust it towards the left, or at any rate, it can only do so in a very restricted measure, and only when the mass, already propelled in this direction, has moved sufficiently far towards the left.

To enable the horse to push his body resolutely to one side, it is absolutely necessary that the hind leg on the opposite side be in support.

To enable the horse moving in side steps towards the right to change his direction and move towards the left, his right hind must be in support.

The counter-change of hand from right to left is therefore only possible when the left diagonal (left fore, right hind) is in support.

The right diagonal, in suspension at that moment, will therefore be the first to change direction, and the right foreleg, crossing in front of the left one, will be observed by the rider to mark the first step of the change, from right to left.

However, at the trot, when the left diagonal touches the ground the right one is already in suspension and it must necessarily make the change of direction as quickly as possible as the gait would become defective and irregular if the duration of the moment of suspension were altered by the counter-change.

The left hind could have moved to the left as soon as it was taken off the ground, as the right hind is not obstructing. But the right fore cannot start changing direction before it has come into line with the left fore, in front of which it must cross to move to the left.

Even the greatest precision in the use of the aids cannot secure this result immediately. The horse himself, once he has understood what is required and developed the necessary agility, must gradually and instinctively discover the way to achieve it.

Usually in the case of a horse responsive to the aids as the one who has received all the preceding lessons should be, the right diagonal will have time to alter the direction of its movement if the new indications are given at the moment the left diagonal touches the ground.

To give his new indications, the rider is advised to continue to guide himself on the grounding of the left diagonal, even if the horse does not succeed at first in achieving the change of direction in time. He must allow the horse to feel his way in calmness and he should on no account attempt to hurry a response to his indications by giving these before the grounding of the left diagonal. This would be most likely to spoil the regularity of the pace and to increase confusion. On the contrary, the rider should learn to wait until the horse's increasing agility gradually enables him to reduce the delay of execution to the duration of a normal beat.

As usual, however, it will be found helpful to split the movement up in the following manner:

To start with, the horse, trotting perfectly straight on a single track, should be asked to incline to the left (on a single track), the rider acting on the shoulders only and deliberately avoiding any action of the legs on the haunches; the horse should next be made to incline to the right by a displacement of his haunches to the left, the rider avoiding any action of the reins on the forehand.

The rider need not worry if the haunches deviate in the opposite direction from the shoulders in the first exercise, or the shoulders in the opposite direction from the haunches in the second one.

The movement should be repeated until the first oblique step of the forehand, marked by the foreleg on the opposite side of the movement, and the first oblique step of the quarters, marked by the hind leg on the same side as the movement, are distinctly obtained.

Once the shoulders make the change quite clearly, the rider can start opposing the turning out of the haunches to the opposite side, and conversely.

Finally, he can increase the action of the leg and the hand which oppose the turning-out, and drive both ends of the horse simultaneously in the same direction.

Once shoulders and haunches are easily displaced independently, he can start connecting both movements, but always with more attention to the shoulders. There are two reasons why a little turning-out of the haunches is unimportant to begin with; in the first place, this outward deviation of the haunches facilitates the movement of the mass of the horse in the new direction ; in the second place, the change of direction is much easier behind, because the hind leg that changes direction first does not have to cross in front of the other to do so.

Chapter 5 · PRACTICE OF SUPPLING EXERCISES
(See Appendix I: Flexions from the ground)

SUPPLING OF THE JAW

Some procedures are applied to the mouth itself, while others activate certain groups of muscles which by their reaction on those of the jaw and the tongue produce the mobilisation of the latter.

Ever since Baucher, the first procedures have been called flexions and in current equestrian language this expression has taken the place of "teasing with the reins" ("badinage des renes") of the old school.

The second procedures include:

—The stimulation of certain muscles of the thoracic region by a special use of the spur, which induces by reaction the mobilisation of the muscles of the mouth.

—The stimulation, by the use of the whip, of the muscles in the region of the loin, which has a similar reaction on the muscles of the mouth as the previous action.

—The production of energetic activity of the same muscles of the loin by special movements of the whole of the body which react in a similar manner on the mouth.

The first could be called "direct" flexions, and the second "indirect" flexions of the mouth.

DIRECT FLEXIONS OF THE MOUTH

In Baucher's first manner, these flexions were mainly actions practised on both jaws simultaneously, but in opposite directions, to induce an opening of the mouth.

A typical flexion consisted of tilting the curb bit in the mouth by pulling forward on one of the reins and drawing backward on the other, so that one end of the mouthpiece pushed the upper jaw forward and the other drew the lower jaw backward.

Mobilisation of the tongue is not specially induced in this manner, but is obtained as a side effect. No effort is made to preserve the immobility of the head in the vertical plane. On the contrary, mobility of the poll is associated as early as possible with the mobility of the mouth and exploited from the first to obtain the "Ramener" by drawing the head back towards the body, the chin being brought gradually closer to the chest by tractions operating on the lower jaw.

In Baucher's second manner, the principal purpose of the flexions of the mouth is to obtain the mobilisation of the tongue without movement of the head and neck. Flexions of the neck are extremely reduced and all those which aimed at bringing the chin closer to the chest are eliminated. The Ramener, instead of being sought at the beginning of dressage by pulling the head towards the body is now achieved by the reverse procedure, i.e. by progressively pushing the body towards the head during the entire course of dressage, by means of a whole series of suppling exercises.[1]

In Baucher's second manner, as in his first, these flexions are executed at the halt. Now, when the horse stands at the halt, unless his hind legs are perfectly vertical, he can lean on the rider's hands and supports this resistance by propping himself on one hind leg or the other, or both, and this he never fails to do.

Even when the halt is correct, the immobility of the hind legs is not favourable to the achievement of lightness. It is attended by a certain "atony" of the muscles of the topline, usually communicated to those of the mouth because of the close connection existing between them.

In these conditions, it is not easy to obtain relaxation. When it does happen it has a tendency to remain limited to the mouth, instead of extending as it should to the whole muscular system. Furthermore, relaxation obtained in this manner is lost almost as soon as the horse moves on.

All these difficulties and drawbacks are easily overcome by an experienced trainer. They could, however, have been readily avoided if the flexions had been executed with the horse in movement, as was Fillis' practice for example, but the nature of the movement is of some importance. This will be discussed further on with the indirect flexions of the mouth.

Besides the flexions, certain bits designed to induce mobilisation of the mouth can be ranked as direct means of flexing the jaws. Bits with high ports, such as the Arab bit, produce the same result as the previously described Baucher flexion. As the bit tilts in the mouth, the upper extremity of the port

1. There is no doubt that the essential difference between both manners and the advantage of the second manner over the first reside in this fundamental change in the way of obtaining the Ramener. In the second manner, the "philosophy" of dressage returns identically to the conception of the classical school: the body of the horse is gradually driven towards the mouth. However, if the mouth has been previously prepared and educated, many of the difficulties encountered by Baucher's predecessors are eliminated or considerably reduced.

presses against the vault of the palate, whilst the arms press on the bars of the lower jaw.

The jaws are compelled to open, but mobilisation of the tongue is not directly induced.

To obtain the latter, a mouthing bit, provided with "keys" has been used from the earliest times.

These special bits may sometimes be useful, but their utility is almost invariably counterbalanced by their disadvantages. The roof of the mouth is very sensitive, and to avoid pressure upon it by the high port, the horse gets into the habit of constantly keeping his mouth open. This fault can be partly cured—but only partly—on the one hand by regulating the adjustment of the curb chain in a manner that limits the tilting of the port and prevents it from assuming a disposition at a right angle to the bars or, on the other hand, by tightening the nose band to prevent the opening of the mouth. We may, in this manner, be able to obviate the effects of a new resistance, which has been substituted for the first, but without eliminating the causes of either.

As regards the pendant "keys" with which a mouthing bit is provided, the movements of the tongue which they induce have nothing in common with the correct "mouthing" of the bit which is a "swallowing" movement. All that the horse does is to fidget with the point of his tongue to move the pendant laterally, as he cannot lift it, and this habit soon becomes an almost incurable "tic" called "snaky tongue". It seems therefore that we should almost invariably reject the mouthing bit, but that the bit with a high port may be used with great precautions and circumspection to ride in some fashion or other a horse that is only occasionally being used rather than one which is being schooled.

In schooling, the use of this bit can give some good results with certain horses that "bore" strongly on the bit, clamp their teeth violently or over-bend, as the pressure of the port against the palate pushes the head forward.

It is therefore before academic dressage is started that the use of this type of bit is temporarily justifiable, but only to prepare the way for a return to a normal mouthpiece.

INDIRECT FLEXIONS OF THE MOUTH

1. *Use of the spur*

The simultaneous pressure of both spurs in the region of the girth nearly always results in an opening of the mouth, and frequently in the mobilisation of the tongue.

In the latter case, the result of this pressure of the spur presents many similarities with the relaxation of the mouth described earlier.

But frequently the opening of the mouth obtained in this manner is jerky and excessive, and the movement of the tongue is fugitive and insufficient. The horse opens his mouth wide and closes it suddenly with a clacking of the teeth. The bits are either not lifted at all by the tongue, or are lifted so little that their characteristic tinkling cannot be heard. The movements of the mouth on the whole resemble more those made by the horse when chewing (or biting) than those made when he swallows. The mouth never gives the elastic feel of yielding, either spontaneously or by the persuasive effect of good hands, which testifies to overall relaxation.

As this grudging concession can be wrung from the horse by the painful prick of the rowels of the spurs, even if his attitude and the distributions of his forces are faulty, its value as a proof of lightness is practically nil. For the same reason its reciprocal influence on the balance of the body is doubtful. It can act as much to its detriment as to its advantage and in an unpredictable manner because it is independent of the previous state of perfection or imperfection of balance.

Furthermore, the sole result of this continued pressure of the spurs in the region of the girth is not merely an opening of the mouth. Wherever it is applied, the spur used with a continuous pressure does not foster forward movement as well as it does when it is used in successive touches. When the pressure is exerted close to the girth, the impulsive effect of the spur is nullified and can even be transformed into a retarding effect, sometimes strong enough to cause a halt or a backward movement.

It would be a great imprudence to tolerate that the horse should cease to respond by an increase of impulsion to any action of the spur. This often leads to nappiness and at best turns the horse into an unreliable character and invariably deprives him of much of his keenness.

The opening of the mouth obtained by a pressure of the spurs is therefore of little benefit and this use of the spurs is fraught with the greatest dangers as regards the preservation of that foremost quality of the horse, his impulsion. It is a practice which should be unquestionably rejected by the novice in academic dressage.[1]

---

1. The use of the spur to obtain the "Mise en Main" is characteristic of Raabe's method, but he only uses it after he has first induced the mouth to yield by a series of flexions, which differ from Baucher's only in the way the whip adds its effects to those of the hand. He specifies also that with a horse trained according to his own method, it is the threat of the spur that should be used to hasten a tardy obedience, and not the use of the spur as an habitual and normal means of obtaining the "Mise en Main".

Two riders, Bonnal and Barroil, who faithfully practised Raabe's method, have kept to his way. Only Doctor Lebon, an amateur and a rather artless and extreme admirer of Raabe's method, advocated the outright use of the spur to obtain the Mise en Main.

2. *Use of the whip*

Light taps of the whip over the loins, close to the top of the croup, induce an opening of the mouth and mobilisation of the tongue.

The opening obtained in this manner is slow and discreet and the movements of the tongue are those made in the act of swallowing; the clinking of the bits is clearly audible. This kind of mobilisation of the mouth, therefore, is very similar to the spontaneous one executed by the horse who has found his balance; produced by the whip above the loins, it is far less dangerous than the kind obtained by the spurs near the girth, because it cannot impair the impulsive authority of the legs.

But it also has some disadvantages which can be partly obviated by an exact knowledge of the effects of the whip on the different parts of the body to which it is applied, and by a judicious choice of the part to be touched according to each special case.

These effects are the following:

1. As a rule it is at the junction of the loin and the croup that the whip acts most effectively in producing the mobilisation of the mouth;

2. Almost along the whole length of the loin the whip produces a lifting of this part, which can even become a very marked arching;

3. Used on the summit of the croup, the whip tends to produce a lifting of this part also, caused by a lengthening of the hind limbs which occurs through the opening of the angles in their joints. This lifting of the croup can be strong enough to cause the horse to buck. As they return to the ground the hind legs tend to alight in front of the vertical, to "engage" better, even if the horse has not bucked;

4. Mobilisation of the mouth is nearly always accompanied by some degree of lowering of the neck and some degree of flexion of the poll which brings the chin closer to the chest.

It must therefore be noticed that although this yielding in the mouth in response to the action of the whip on the loins is very similar to a correct Mise en Main, it differs from it in the general attitude of the horse at the moment it is produced. It is possible to modify and correct this attitude at least to some extent. The lowering of the neck can be reduced gradually by a skilled hand, opposing it with an upward movement, but this entails a slow progression and considerable adroitness because the mobilisation of the mouth tends to stop when the horse can no longer lower his head. When it can be obtained then the raising of the head opposes that of the croup and loin. The general attitude is therefore improved, though it still falls short of the one produced by the correct Mise en Main which, on the contrary, prepares a lowering of the haunches and leads to it.

The results obtainable by this use of the whip can be helpful, especially in the case of horses that are too high in front, that sit on their hocks or that hollow the back, but those horses are not really suited to academic equitation if their faults are at all pronounced.

Furthermore, it is neither convenient nor correct for the rider to use the whip in this manner, and the practice could not be adhered to indefinitely. By the usual method of gradual substitution, it is possible to replace the whip by the invitation of the hands alone. This amounts to a return in a roundabout manner to the practice of "flexions" or "badinage" which certainly makes them easier, but is a rather slow procedure.

It would be quicker to substitute the spurs near the girth for the whip on the croup. It is in fact what Raabe used to do, but the very serious disadvantages of this use of the spur would still exist.

To sum up, the use of the whip over the loins can be of some benefit, mainly because it can be combined with other means and used in conjunction with them. This method, like the use of the spur in the region of the girth, should not be rejected on principle, but must be held in reserve as an auxiliary aid in some special cases, and particularly to raise the back of a horse which has a tendency to hollow it, or on some horses which sit on their hocks.

3. *Use of General Suppling Exercises*

Forward movement, on straight lines, on a single track, is already more favourable for the mobilisation of the mouth than the stationary position, so long as the pace, which should be the walk or a slow trot, does not require considerable muscular effort.

Curved courses on a single track increase the willingness of the mouth to yield, and this willingness becomes a tendency as soon as the horse can move laterally on two-tracks. Once the hind legs are able to cross themselves properly, the activity of the mucles of the loin is considerably increased and their reaction on the muscles of the mouth, similar to the one obtained by the use of the whip above the loins, induces mobilisation of the mouth. This tendency increases with the improved mobility of the haunches in relation to the shoulders, and reaches its maximum in the reversed pirouette which, if practised for long enough, unfailingly induces a "natural" Mise en Main, if such a thing exists.[1]

And thus, in the course of dressage, the tension of the reins by the horse

---

1. As early as 1870, Rul, the "beloved disciple of Baucher" advocated the use of the reversed pirouette to obtain a relaxation of the mouth. He called this kind of flexion "the Baucheriste". (Methodical Progression of Dressage on the Bridoon, Baudoin, 1870)—This pamphlet, therefore, preceded by two years the "Traite des Resistances" of Gerhardt, and by three, the 13th edition of Baucher, the one of his "Final Manner".

has become positive, then steadier, and gradually lighter as he acquired "poise" and "composure" under the weight of the rider. Occasionally, in the course of a movement which has been specially well executed owing to the activity of "the useful forces alone" and the perfect adjustment of balance in the movement, the horse has lightened the tension even more. The rider feels that the bit hardly touches the tongue, as the latter, under the hint of a pressure, makes the first attempt at lifting the bit which constitutes the beginning of relaxation; this the rider, as soon as he has sensed it, has not failed to reward.

However, the frequency of these attempts and their extent will vary considerably depending on the nature of the movement being executed. The rotation of the haunches about the shoulders—which latter we should not compel to remain fixed on one spot, but on the contrary, should keep moving on a small circle—provides an almost unfailing means of inducing a suggestion of mobilisation of the mouth, which, if it is fostered and regularised, becomes the proper "Mise en Main".

This method eliminates most of the difficulties and drawbacks encountered in the others. The horse maintains a regular and uniform movement. The sustained activity of the hind legs, associated with a slight overloading of the shoulders, irresistibly draws the horse on as soon as the rider's hands deliver the "Laissez-passer", and this should be granted at the first sign of relaxation of the mouth. It is therefore the method which we will unfailingly adopt, because it is in accordance with the principle that prescribes that the horse should always be placed in such conditions as will make it easy for him to understand and to obey his rider's commands.

The details of execution of this procedure will be explained in the next chapter, for which we have kept the title "Flexions", although the methods used are not quite the same as those to which Baucher's school applied the name.

FLEXIONS
Books of Reference:
GENERAL FAVEROT DE KERBRECH. RAABE GERHARDT
DE MONTIGNY FILLIS BEUDANT RUL

The horse is in a double bridle.

We let the curb reins lie on the neck and take the bridoon reins in both hands.

We slowly describe a volte with the haunches out, making sure that the hind legs step sideways as evenly as possible, as regards both extension and rhythm.

We must keep the horse straight in the whole length of his body, without any bend at all.

Impelled by the action of the left leg, the horse's hind legs move from left to right for example: the left hand should be raised without increasing the tension on the rein, which should remain exactly the same; the left arm is stretched out so that the rein can act directly on the corners of the mouth, as vertically as possible. The rider *waits*, and slightly relaxes the fingers on the right rein.

As soon as mobility of the tongue is felt upon a tension of the left rein, the left hand must be lowered, the right leg must close quietly against the horse's side, in the same position as the left one and with the same amount of pressure, and the horse must be driven forward, the rider rewarding him with a yielding hand and caresses.

The work is then repeated, but the rider should yield a little less and a little later when the horse goes forward, to try to preserve the mobility for a few strides on the straight.

The horse must be worked alternately to the right and the left though obviously more frequently on his stiff side.

Work on straight lines

Well away from the wall, on a straight line, and at a rather slow walk, lift the left hand and wait. If a relaxation is felt, lower the hand, yield, pat the horse, and proceed in the same manner with the other side. If relaxation is not manifested sufficiently promptly, close the left leg and make the horse execute a volte on the forehand, then drive him forward and reward him when he obeys.

Request the relaxation of the right and the left sides alternately, but always work the stiff side more than the other.

This procedure has the advantage of associating from the beginning a yielding of the jaw to the action of one rein with an increased activity of the hind leg on the same side.

Once the relaxation can be obtained most of the time without recourse to the intervention of the leg, the flexion should be requested by the hand alone and the action of the leg should be kept in reserve.

Lift the left rein as before and keep it softly fixed and, on the other rein, execute half-halts or vibrations as needs be (See Part II, Chapter I, The Hand).

If a horse has been conducted in his dressage in the manner described up to now, resistances of weight usually will be slight and infrequent, and half-halts will not often have to be resorted to.

The half-halt consists in a firm upward action on taut reins, with the fingers closed, followed quickly by a progressive relaxation of the fingers and a yielding with the hand.

The vibration, a quivering of the *fingers* on the reins, rather like the "vibrato" of the violinist on the strings of his instrument, must be executed without appreciably moving the hand or the wrist and must be skilfully graded. It is the perfection of touch that produces the "insinuating hand" (Beaudant).[1]

Should the tongue not mobilise itself sufficiently promptly in answer to this quivering of the right rein, the left leg will have to be brought into action again. The procedure must then be repeated until relaxation can be obtained quickly and easily, solely by a tension of the left rein without the intervention either of the right rein or of the left leg.

As soon as a yielding can be obtained readily on either of the two reins separately, we should try to obtain relaxation of one side and then of the other, alternately, and with such increasing rapidity that the yielding of one side is hardly completed before the other side starts yielding in its turn.

It should gradually become possible to induce relaxation on equally taut reins by a slight raising of the hands, which should not come closer to the body, and if necessary by a slight quivering of the fingers.

Should the horse resist unduly, a simultaneous pressure of both legs should not be resorted to, although it would in all probability induce a relaxation; but it would also produce a certain degree of engagement of the hind legs— and we want to obtain relaxation of the mouth without having to collect the horse—outside this attitude. Instead we should go back to the use of one rein only coupled with vibrations on the other, and even to the intervention of the leg on the side from which a yielding is demanded.

Thereafter, the simultaneous use of both reins to obtain relaxation should be practised in all changes of direction and on circles on one or two tracks.

The same work must then be repeated on the curb rein, the half-halts and vibrations being executed at first on the opposite bridoon rein and finally on the opposite curb rein.

An excessive and permanent mobilisation of the tongue must not be sought. What is required is a permanently light tension and the faculty of readily obtaining mobilisation of the tongue by a mere closing of the fingers.

The opening of the mouth must remain as slight as possible, only just sufficient to permit the movement of the tongue.

Lateral flexions of the poll
These are of two kinds:
  —The direct lateral flexion (Fig. i) which bends the poll and the top part of the neck laterally and leaves the base of the latter straight, or with a very slight bend in the same direction.

1. You may endlessly twiddle a key in a jammed lock without success. The skilful locksmith opens the lock with the same key. His hand is not only skilful, but also insinuating.

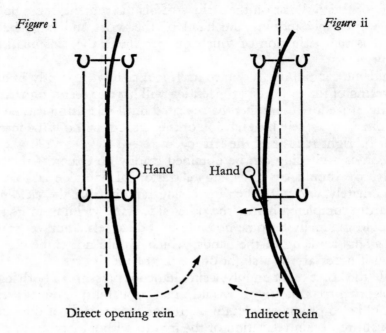

Figure i   *Figure* ii

Hand   Hand

Direct opening rein   Indirect Rein

 —The indirect lateral flexion (Fig. ii) which also bends the poll and the
top part of the neck to one side, but reacts on the base of the neck by
pushing it in the opposite direction.

The first is obtained by a direct opening rein and tends to load the
shoulder which is on the side of the flexion.

The second is obtained by an indirect rein which bears against the neck
to a varying extent and tends to load the shoulder which is on the opposite
side of the flexion.

Work on circles will already have developed the lateral flexibility of the
neck and the suppleness of the body as a whole. The bend is much the same
as the one required for correct guiding of the horse and for a flexed position
when this is wanted.

Lateral flexions should not therefore be considered as a means of steering
the horse but rather as a means of facilitating subsequently the vertical flexion
of the poll in the "Ramener" by developing separately the play of each parotid
gland in its own groove.

The direct lateral flexion is particularly suited to this purpose; the indirect
rein effect being only fully effective once the horse has already achieved a
certain degree of Ramener. We will therefore postpone a discussion of the
latter rein effect until we have dealt with the Ramener.

Direct Lateral Flexion

We return to the circle on the forehand on two tracks.

The horse having been previously kept straight from head to tail and softened on the left rein is gradually flexed and put into the position corresponding to the pirouette of the "shoulder-in type" by a lowering and an opening of the left rein; simultaneously, the inside leg acts close to the girth, from back to front, as it does in the shoulder-in.

When we are satisfied with the horse's position and the softness of the mouth, we drive the horse forwards on a circle corresponding to the flexion, and straighten him out gradually.

THE RAMENER

As a result of these suppling exercises, the head, poll and neck as a unit will have become more flexible, and the horse of his own accord will have given a somewhat more vertical position to his head in answer to the resistance of the rider's fingers. Now, by advancing *the body towards the head* while opposing the forward movement with the hands, a better bend of the poll can then be obtained. This is achieved gradually by delaying a little the freedom allowed by opening the fingers whilst driving the horse forward; the degree of "Ramener" obviously improves as the resistance of the poll to the flexion diminishes.

However, the pliability of the poll must always remain a consequence of the softening of the mouth which must always come first, as otherwise the horse comes behind the bit.

Owing to its design, the curb bit produces effects which favour the transmission to the poll of the flexing of the mouth. It is therefore the bit which is principally employed when inducing the "Ramener" and the combination of one curb rein together with the opposite bridoon rein is the one that best prepares and ensures the transmission to the poll of the suppleness obtained in the mouth.

The rider frequently passes from one of these effects to the other, taking the opportunity of the moment when the horse yields to operate the change and gradually arrives at a simultaneous use of both curb reins alternating with a simultaneous use of both bridoon reins.

It is at the trot that the work will be most beneficial because of the natural steadiness of the neck at this pace, in contrast with the walk where the oscillation of the neck is quite considerable.

The rider should frequently drive the horse on energetically without any opposition of the hand, and use his legs vigorously should the impulsion become insufficient.

Indirect Lateral Flexion

When the horse is confirmed in the "Ramener" he must be educated to the indirect lateral flexion which, as the previous flexions, should be practised in motion and preferably at the trot.

To obtain it, the rider requests lightness on one rein and having obained it then carries his hand somewhat towards the opposite side, so that the rein bears against the base of the neck. Most horses will move in the direction thus indicated by the hand. In the rare instance of a horse hesitating to comply, the corners of the manege, which automatically enforce the turn, would assist the rider to get the horse to understand him, and to make his intention quite clear to the horse; he can also resort, if necessary, to the usual method of gradual substitution of one effect for another by using a discreet and *momentary* opening rein on the other side.

Alternately using the direct and the indirect effects of the same rein, he then steers the horse on serpentines of gradually tighter loops and on figures of eight of gradually decreasing size.

This work must be practised with each of the four reins separately, with the occasional assistance of the opposite rein of the other bit[1] and finally only with the curb reins held in one hand.

The importance of the indirect flexion does not reside in the lateral bend of the head towards the side of the rein which is being used, but in the reaction to the pressure of the rein on the neck which pushes the shoulders in the opposite direction. As the horse becomes more proficient, this second effect becomes preponderant and the lateral bend of the head diminishes, to the extent of disappearing completely when relaxation and Ramener reach perfection (Faverot de Kerbrech, p. 80).

It is essential that the rider himself should remain completely relaxed in every part of his body if he wants to obtain relaxation from the horse in the practice of the flexions. The slightest stiffening of the fingers would be transmitted by the reins to the mouth, just as electricity along a wire, and this would delay or prevent the flexing.

It is obvious that a traction, however slight, should never be exerted. The rein that "asks" must be only sufficiently taut to allow the contact to be clearly felt by the horse. Fixed in this position, it *politely* requests and must then patiently wait; the other rein, which is used to produce the half-halts or vibrations must be used most delicately as the intensity of its action must never be greater than the horse's resistance.

1. i.e. Bridoon with opposite curb rein and conversely.

Chapter 6 · THE REIN BACK

Books of Reference:
GENERAL FAVEROT DE KERBRECH
RABBE
STEINBRECHT

It is needless to repeat that the horse which is to receive the higher education which leads to academic equitation must already be a good outdoor ride, well confirmed in this sphere. Therefore, he already knows how to rein back.

His new destination, however, requires that his backward mobility be regularised and perfected to the same extent as his forward and lateral mobility.

Furthermore, the rein back, providing it is executed regularly and correctly, is an excellent means of suppling the loin and the hind quarters, but it is harmful to the development of flexibility when it is badly executed.

It is therefore necesssry to define the correct and "useful" form of the rein back, and to point out the most common distortions and malpractices.

In the correct form, the hind legs are compelled to step back by the previous backward movement of the trunk—because it is weight that impells the limbs to move—and every joint in the hind leg must participate in the flexion produced by this temporary additional load and its resulting compression. It is at the moment when, during the backward movement of the trunk, the point of the hip comes vertically above the corresponding foot that the flexion of the limb as a whole is equally distributed over all the joints. If the horse lifts his hind leg at that precise moment he remains in control of the movement of his body. His general attitude does not alter. His limbs move at the same speed as his body, and remain in suspension for the same length of time as they remain in support.[1] He reins back with long strides, and perfectly diagonal steps.[2] His feet are lifted off the ground to the same extent as

---

[1]. This speed is, however, always much greater than that of the body, for the latter continues to progress backwards while the leg is in support.

[2]. i.e. the foreleg and the hind leg of each diagonal must be lifted and grounded exactly at the same time.

in forward movement. He is able to arrest the backward movement at any moment and to move forward without difficulty.

This is the rein back in balance, the one which is "useful" from the point of view of the gymnastic development of the whole body.

If the horse fails to lift his hind leg precisely at that fleeting moment, but only later when the point of the hip has moved behind the vertical line down through the foot, he will find himself suddenly forced to prop up his body which is in danger of collapsing backwards. He must then rapidly put his foot down to prevent himself from "sitting down".

He will then rein back in short, hurried steps, and drag his feet to gain time. By lowering and lengthening the neck he tries to preserve his balance as he feels it being dragged to the rear. This hurried grounding of the hind legs causes a breaking up of the diagonal stride.

It is an incorrect form of rein back which is difficult to check and from which a return to forward progression is difficult without a pause at the halt of varying length.

This fault is usually due to a previously incorrect attitude of the horse, in which the neck was excessively low or overbent.

More often, however, it is the opposite fault that is observed in the incorrect rein back; the horse lifts his hind legs too soon, before the hips come vertically above the foot.

This happens when the rein back is demanded too early, before the right kind of gymnastics has restored suppleness to the joints of the hind quarters, stiffened by the weight of the rider and by the young horse's apprehension of the unfamilair action of the hands. The worst form is observed when the rein back is demanded from the halt, especially with a forced elevation of the neck without flexion of the poll.

In this case, the back is hollowed behind the withers by the downward pressure of the neck and head. To alleviate this pressure, the horse straightens the coxo-femoral joint. This compresses the gaskin downward and overflexes the hock, and so the horse continues to escape backwards with spread out hind legs, lifting his hocks in snatching jerks.

He runs backwards and drops the contact, and this sometimes gives a false impression of lightness.

The best way of obtaining regularity in the rein back in most cases, is to start again from the beginning with attention to the following points:

In ordinary equitation outside, the rein back is only occasionally executed, on a straight line, and more often than not is started and terminated from the halt. It is seldom necessary to request more than a few steps.

But as a means of gymnastics, exercise at the rein back may have to be prolonged. In addition, alternating forward movement and backward movement without a pause is of capital importance in the development of the general suppleness of the horse.

And the halt can be obtained from the rein back without difficulty once the horse is able to move forwards as soon as he has finished stepping backwards; equally, it will be easy for the horse to rein back from the halt as soon as he is able to reverse from forward movement into backward movement without a pause.

On the contrary, if the horse was first taught to rein back from the halt, it will be difficult afterwards to get him instantaneously to change forward movement into backward movement, and conversely. It will always be awkward, and almost always impossible to prevent an intervening pause.

Finally, as a gymnastic exercise to correct certain deficiencies of the locomotory system, the rein back can be used not only on straight lines, but also on curved lines.

The rein back used as a suppling exercise requires therefore more thorough schooling than is necessary for its simple and normal practice in outdoor equitation.

Teaching of the Rein Back
It is almost invariably much more difficult for the horse to displace his mass backward from a standstill than it is to transform his forward movement, though obviously a very slow one, into a backward movement.

To achieve this transformation, we must slow him down more than would be required to produce a halt, i.e. passed the point where forward movement stops and so utilise the remaining momentum of the mass to pass over the neutral point and to prevent the horse from stabilising his halt.

Position of the Horse
The horse should be placed on the track close to the wall of the riding school, in a direction opposed to his natural inflexion. A turning out of the haunches in the rein back is more likely to occur towards the side of the natural inflexion. Thus, if the horse is concave on the left side, he should be placed on the track on the right rein, with the wall on his left.

Furthermore, and for the same reason, the first step of the rein back must be made with the right diagonal, because the left hind leg will then be close to the wall.

Gait and Attitude of the Horse
The horse should be perfectly light and flexed at the poll, and ridden at a very slow School walk, but not too collected.

As the actions of the hand for slowing the pace must necessarily produce a certain lifting of the neck, the horse should be allowed a rather low head carriage to start with so that the maximum degree of lifting does not exceed an amount of elevation which allows the spine complete suppleness and freedom of flexion in a vertical plane.

Action of the Hand

To slow the walk, the trainer should not use a continuous action of the hand, he should instead try to shorten the stride by intermittent actions, based on the movements of the forelegs.

As the right fore is lifted, the rider loads the right shoulder in order to make the limb on that side come down sooner and take a shorter step. He continues with this action, alternately on either side, thus obliging the horse to shorten his steps until a stage is reached where forward progression is reduced to a few centimeters, the horse continuing to move but gaining hardly any ground. The action of the hand best suited for this purpose is the indirect rein of opposition acting on the shoulder which we want to load, a rein effect which has already been developed and confirmed by the indirect lateral flexion.

The rider holding his hands close together carries them alternately up and to the right, and up and to the left, to shorten the step on the corresponding side.

These actions must be very carefully graded and executed in a faultless "Mise en Main".

Progression

The horse must be gradually trained to transform the very slow walk into a walk almost on the spot after a given number of indications of the hand—three for example which, on the right rein, influence successively the left fore, the right fore, the left fore. After the third movement, the hands should yield sufficiently to prevent the horse from halting, for at that moment, instead of pausing, he should move forward into a more active walk.

Once the horse is completely familiarised with this exercise, the rider must then, after the third indication, give a somewhat quicker and stronger fourth one, and again yield as soon as the horse executes, however slightly, a backward movement of the right fore, which he will do quite readily in most cases.

Having achieved such an initial and even tentative backward step, instead of concentrating on developing and perfecting it, the trainer must first of all develop the immediate resumption of forward movement as soon as the first attempts at a backward step have been achieved. To this end the rider can use the legs, the whip and a clicking of the tongue, but *discreetly* and with *moderation* as he must be careful not to confuse the horse by indications so vigorous and rough that they can be mistaken for a punishment, or even a "censure" of his attempt at reining back; it is here that the rider's tact will be put to the test. He must not demand perfection from the beginning and must be tolerant of progressive improvement. We should not forget that the length of the first forward step can never be greater than that of the first preceding backward one, which necessarily must be short.

When the resumption of forward movement becomes as positive as the preceding backward one, but only then, the trainer must endeavour to develop both at the same time, until the horse can execute five movements at an even, slow rhythm: 1, 2, 3 ,slow down, 4, backward step, and 5, forward step; the hand then yields and the horse is allowed to relax and is rewarded.

It should also be noted that the first forward step cannot be quite identical to the preceding backward one. This is because in the rein back the right fore and the left hind come into support at the same time as soon as the horse can execute the movement with a measure of facility. On the contrary, the first forward stride is at *the walk*, which is a *four time* pace, in which the legs of a diagonal pair do not move simultaneously, but one after the other.

The preceding exercise should be practised alternately on either rein, until equal results are obtained from the right and from the left diagonal.

Two successive strides of the rein back can now be requested by executing a fifth indication with the hands, rather quicker than the preceding ones, and again driving the horse forward immediately after the execution of the second backward stride, and so on.

When the execution of the rein back is easy, the lateral displacement of the hands is no longer necessary. It should be replaced by a mere closing of the fingers on the reins, with the hand in its normal place, in the longitudinal axis of the horse.

Later, the movement must be practised away from the wall and if the hind legs show a tendency to deviate to one side this will have to be corrected by a bend to the opposite side, obtained with the indirect rein, thus placing the shoulders in front of the haunches; the legs should only be used as a last resort because the regularity of the movement must not be disturbed.

Finally, the horse will have to be taught to move from the rein back to the halt, and from the halt to the rein back.

To halt the rein back, the legs must act as if to urge the horse forward and the hands oppose the forward movement immediately. However, the legs should not act as forcefully as in a reversal of direction of movement, for the horse would then collect himself excessively; and the hands acting very soon after the legs should not however act at exactly the same moment as we do not want to "lock" the horse.

To rein back from a balanced halt, the legs must not act with more energy than necessary to produce the motion which the hands convert into a backward one.[1]

Execution of the Rein Back

If reining back is used for the sole purpose of displacing the horse towards a point situated behind him without turning him round, it should still be done with regularity and only for a few strides unless circumstances, like finding oneself in a narrow, sunken path, should prevent a half-turn.

If reining back is solely to verify or to demonstrate backward mobility, the movement should never be prolonged beyond absolute necessity.

In a presentation, a little "coquetterie" or stylishness should be displayed, and the horse should be collected previously to a suitable degree in order to produce elevation and a moment of suspension between the movement of the legs of both diagonals.

Reining Back as a Gymnastic Exercise

As an exercise to supple the hind-quarters, the rein back may be prolonged, but progressively and in moderation because this prolongation which produces great strain demands careful preparatory training.

The rein back can be practised on slopes to take advantage of their influence on the attitude of the horse. When the horse is reined back up a slope, it is much easier for him to lift his hind legs which will be relatively longer at that moment, but as they will touch down sooner than if the ground were level, their stride will be shorter. Furthermore, the horse tends to lift the head and the neck tends to sink down between the shoulder.

When the horse is reined back down a slope, the joints of his hind legs will be more heavily compressed at the beginning of the movement, the backward stride will be longer and the neck will show a tendency to stretch downwards.

Therefore, the trainer, by utilising this work on slopes has at his disposal suitable means of correcting the detrimental tendencies of his horse and of developing the good ones.

Finally, the rein back can be practised on circles. This exercise could be used to produce greater flexion of the joints of the hind leg situated on the inside of the curve. It can only be advised in a case of persistent stiffness of a particular leg, and only to that side. The circle can be tightened into a spiral

---

1. The very light leg action should be only in the nature of a warning signal that mobilisation is required. It must cease before the hand comes into action: "Always legs without hands. . . . " (Note of the 2nd edition.)

ending with a pirouette while still reining back, with the inside hind as the pivot. But this is a rather drastic remedy and if not a kill or cure one, at least medicine which is tricky to dose accurately; for the abnormal stiffness of a hind leg may be due to a physical cause, to an injury which would be aggravated by this enforced exercise.

Alternating forward and backward movement is however a more useful form of gymnastics than the rein back of itself. It develops especially the suppleness of the back and immediately influences the functioning of the whole locomotive system.

With this procedure, it is the frequency of the alternation that is beneficial and the length of the progression forward or backward must therefore be limited.

If practised without a pause on a single diagonal, it produces quite rapidly a "diagonalisation" of the forward stride, because of the simultaneous grounding of fore and hind legs. This makes it easy to obtain a start from the rein back to the trot by using a slightly stronger leg action and, especially if the horse has been given the lessons from the ground described further on, by tapping with the whip on the summit of the croup or on the haunch of the particular diagonal involved.

Causing each diagonal to move alternately backward and forward, a procedure much advocated by Raabe, is an effectual way of preparing the Piaffer, and will often obtain this air from horses that have undue difficulty in finding a rhythm when they must move on one spot.

It would appear that an inclination of the rider's body in the direction of the movement would help to start the latter. In point of fact, the reverse is often the case, because when the horse is still hesitant and worried by the rider's demands, he reacts in the opposite direction.

The rider therefore is advised to maintain a vertical position above the horse's centre of gravity and to remain as supple as possible; he should be able to accompany the horse in all movements, and should not try to initiate them by displacements of his own body.

Finally, the trainer must be always aware of the dangers of reining back and of its most common pitfalls, i.e. a loss of impulsion and a horse coming behind the bit, unless the greatest precautions are taken to avoid them.

As General Detroyat so truly used to say: "The first thing which we must teach the horse is not to rein back."

Chapter 7 · THE TURNING OF CORNERS

Book of Reference:
LA GUERINIERE

It is frequently thought that the rules laid down by the old masters regarding the turning of corners were just arbitrary matters of form.

But although they may be matters of form, they are not arbitrary for they necessarily follow from the whole conception of Academic Equitation.

The rule which must be adhered to when turning corners is:

"In the corners, the horse must turn by describing a quarter of an Academic volte, from wall to wall." Now the dimensions of the Academic volte are not arbitrarily defined. They are the dimensions of the smallest circle that it is possible for a horse to describe, *whether on two tracks* or on one.

When the horse circles with, for example, the haunches in, the forelegs move on the circumference of the circle while the hind legs step on another circle inside the first, around the same centre. The smallest circle possible is described when the horse steps with one hind leg on one spot exactly in the centre, while the other hind leg treads around it: this is a Pirouette, and it is impossible, on two tracks, haunches in or haunches out to describe a smaller circle.[1]

This smallest possible circle is the one which precisely defines the size of the academic volte. Whatever the dimensions of the manege, the radius of the volte is equal to the length of a horse.

This rational convention of what constitutes a volte is equally applicable to the manner of turning corners, as this must also be done on two tracks in a presentation.

[1]. It is obvious that voltes of all sizes, and particularly some smaller than the Academic one, can be described, but only on a single track. Two-track voltes of smaller size are also possible, but only if the hind-quarters and the forehand move in opposite directions, instead of in the same one. The smallest limit is then the pirouette "on the centre", in which the shoulders move towards the right and the haunches to the left, or vice-versa. This exercise is not executed often in Academic Equitation, but it can be of some utility when preparing for the piaffer with horses that are heavy and insufficiently mobile in all directions.

From one wall to the next at a corner, the horse must be incurved along the whole of his length on a quarter of a conventional volte, the radius of which is "the length of a horse".[1]

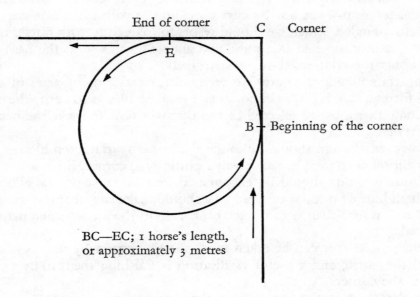

BC—EC; 1 horse's length, or approximately 3 metres

It follows that the horse must leave the first wall at a distance of "one length" from the corner, and that every point of the outside of his body in turn must move away from the track parallel to the wall which it was following, and then come back to the next wall at a distance of one length from the corner to continue on the track in the same conditions as before.

The horse must be absolutely straight until the beginning of the turn, incurved during the turn, and then gradually straightened from head to tail as the different parts of his body complete the turn.

Obviously, we could drive the horse further into the corner, at least on a single track, thus bending him on a smaller circle still. This way of turning corners, of "forcing" them, could be used to develop greater suppleness of the horse but would not be executed in a presentation which prescribes only "correct turns" and not "forced" ones.

1. The length of a horse nowadays is estimated to be 3 meters approximately. The old masters reckoned it to be 8 feet, i.e. a little less than 2m. 70. This is no doubt because the horses which they rode in a manege were of Bearn, Andalusian, "Limousin" or of Oriental stock, shorter than present-day horses, and probably made even more compact by the degree of collection demanded at that time, as pictured in old prints.

USING CORNERS FOR SUPPLING EXERCISES

1. *Volte in a corner*[1]

The more or less frequently repeated execution of the volte in a corner enables the rider to control the horse's curvature, and to adjust it if necessary. This is a useful practice, which we should resort to frequently with horses that are laterally, usually on one side only, and almost always so at the base of the neck, either too contracted or too stretched.

But straightening the horse after the volte, or after the quarter of a volte which forms a turn is just as important; it both enables us to verify the change of attitude that must be effected and to discover how to make the necessary correction.

However, the aim should be to get the horse to straighten himself of his own volition as soon as he has finished turning the corner. If he does it of his own initiative, this should be encouraged, but he must not be allowed to straighten himself out too early and we should make sure that the straightening is real rather than a camouflage of a faulty bend, whether natural or acquired.

Later, the corner can be taken more sharply, especially towards the stiff side of the horse, and a useful verification is finishing the turn by a smaller volte in the corner.

2. *The shoulder-in, started from a corner* (the corner taken on a single track)

If a fraction of a volte in a corner is carried on until the haunches reach the end of the turn (Fig. 1), the horse will be placed, in relation to the second wall, exactly in the position of the shoulder-in.

Then, to execute the shoulder-in, we drive the horse along the wall while maintaining the bend and modifying as necessary the aids required for turning the corner (Fig. 1).

In the example of a corner turned on the left rein by the executing of a fraction of a volte which brings the haunches to the end of the turn, the left rein which had been used previously as an opening rein should come closer to the neck, and limit its action to preserving the bend. Simultaneously, the right rein may have to leave its position close to the neck and assume, if necessary, a more open position to direct the horse to the right. The left leg continues to demand the bend, but at the same time must drive the horse forward, while the right leg limits its action to keeping the hind-quarters on the track, and preventing them from moving closer to the wall.

3. *Haunches-in, started from a corner* (the corner being turned on a single track.
(Fig. 2)

[1]. One corner, at least, of the school must be clear of heaps of wood shavings.

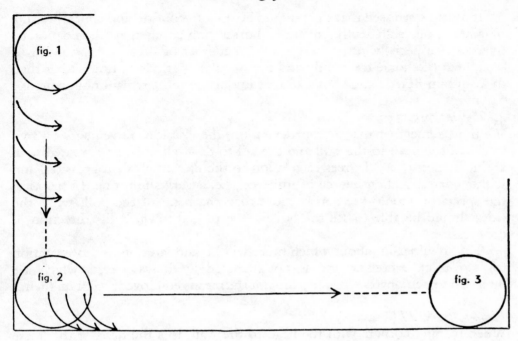

At the moment the shoulders have reached the end of the turn in the corner, when the haunches have just moved past the beginning of the turn, and providing the bend is correct, the horse is in the position of the haunches-in in relation to the second wall (Fig. 2). The aids must then be modified to drive the horse along the wall while maintaining the bend.

Then, as the horse in the position of the haunches-in arrives at the next corner, which he meets with the shoulders first, a volte is executed by a further modification of the aids (Fig. 3). This enables the rider to check on the bend in the volte, and to correct it if necessary.

The alternate execution, between the corners of the riding school, of the shoulder-in, followed by a straightening of the horse, and the haunches-in, also followed by straight forward movement is excellent gymnastics for obtaining lateral flexibility.

This series of exercises enables one to concentrate on flexing the horse's stiff side; as the play of the limbs is constantly modified, although the same bend is maintained, it does not cause muscular fatigue and cramp which should never be mistaken for wilful resistance.

But it must be noted that the shoulder-in and the haunches-in executed in these conditions impose a much greater bend than the one that should be demanded in the suppling exercises practised at the beginning of schooling.

It must be stressed that they should be used to confirm and control results obtained from sufficiently advanced horses only; that they should not be overdone, especially on the soft side; that it is of greater importance to straighten the horse frequently and for sufficient periods of time rather than to keep him flexed; and above all that impulsion must remain unimpaired.

4. *Turning corners on two tracks*

We must remember that, in a presentation, the classical movements on two tracks of the head-to-the-wall and the tail-to-the-wall must be executed with an inclination of 45 degrees in relation to the direction of progression, and with a corresponding degree of inflexion, i.e. a very slight one. In practice, the spectator should see hardly more than the bend of the poll, while the rider should be able to see the horse's eye turned towards the direction of progression.

The shoulder-in, about which more will be said later on, is a preparation for two-track exercises, and is not included in dressage tests which are intended to demonstrate results, and not the means employed to obtain them.[1]

Head-to-the-Wall (Travers)

When turning corners with the head to the wall, it is the head of the horse which follows the section of the volte that is inscribed in the corner; the forelegs move on a smaller circle within the first, and the hind legs on a smaller one still (Fig. 4). The rider's legs must therefore limit the lateral displacement

Figure 4

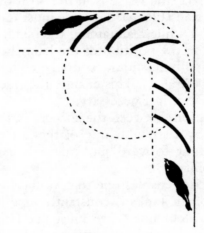

of the hind legs at each stride, and at the same time the inside leg especially must maintain the activity and the regular cadence of the movements. For

1. However the Spanish Riding School of Vienna shows the shoulder-in in its "Quadrilles".

their part, the hands, and especially the indirect outside rein must amplify the lateral displacement of the forelegs.

Turning corners with the haunches-in constitutes a quarter of a volte and is therefore a preparation for the volte on two tracks but, needless to say, should not be practised before the horse has been prepared by exercises with the haunches-in on large circles to start with and then on progressively smaller ones.

Haunches out (Renvers)

Turning corners with the tail to the wall is done in the opposite direction, with an appropriate modification in the application of the aids.

This exercise has its uses in dressage, but although it is not absolutely excluded from dressage tests it is usually avoided, as are all movements in which the lateral displacement of the hind-quarters exceeds that of the forelegs, for they tend to put more weight on the forehand.

In dressage tests, the movement of the haunches-out is executed off the track, with the forelegs at a distance of two horse's lengths approximately from the wall, to enable the horse, when he arrives at a corner, to execute three-quarters of a Pirouette on the haunches, from the inside-out, in order to resume the movement of the haunches-out along the next wall, and at the same distance from it as before. (Fig. 5.)

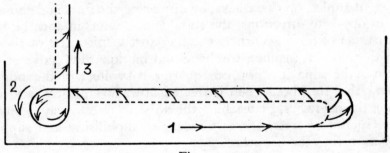

Figure 5

Turning corners in the position of the shoulder-in complements the lesson of the shoulder-in. It increases the lateral mobility of the hind-quarters, which is but one form of their "industry".

Nowadays, turning corners with the shoulder-in is done, as in side-stepping with the haunches-out, by reducing the lateral displacement of the forehand and increasing that of the haunches. But it seems that this was not La Gueriniere's conception and that his execution was quite different.

A.E.—12

Turning Corners with the Shoulders-in
from La Gueriniere

(His Text): "To this effect, at every corner, i.e. at the end of every straight line, make the shoulders go into the corner. . . ."

(Note: "The text seems to indicate that La Gueriniere continued to move forward on two tracks until he came to the second wall. . . .")

Text: "And as one engages the forehand on the other track, make the haunches in their turn pass over the spot where the shoulders previously passed."

(Note: ". . . and that the hindquarters were then displaced until they reached the furthest point previously reached by the forehand, near the second wall. . . .")

(Text): "But when one brings the forehand onto the other track, it must be done with the outside rein, by moving the hand to the inside . . . so that the outside shoulder can move in front of the inside one. . . ."

(Note: "While the rider brings the shoulders from the outside to the inside, to resume the position of the shoulder-in in relation to the second wall.")

Thus, while in the modern procedure on the one hand, the horse executes a quarter of a volte with the shoulder-in, it appears from the text, despite its vagueness, that, on the other hand, La Gueriniere, to turn the corner, drives his horse in the same original direction, (and position in relation to this direction, without modification), as close as possible to the second wall, and then turns at right angles, on two tracks, by displacing the forehand and the hindquarters in opposite directions, the shoulders moving in and the haunches out. His manner of turning corners was therefore a "pirouette on the centre", whilst in the modern manner, forehand and hindquarters move at different speeds, but in the same direction, on a quarter of a volte, with the shoulders-in.

It seems that the shoulder-in is treated nowadays mostly as a means of controlling the haunches, by teaching the horse to move away from the legs, while La Gueriniere treated it as a means of mobilising and suppling the shoulders as well as the haunches.

Chapter 8 · PIAFFER — PASSAGE

Books of Reference:
GENERAL FAVEROT DE KERBRECH
RAABE
GERHARDT
J. B. DUMAS
STEINBRECHT

In the elevated gaits, the thrust of each hind leg displaces the horse's body simultaneously forward and upward. An effort of horizontal propulsion, and one of vertical projection can be distinguished in this thrust.

If the effort of vertical projection is increased, and the moment of suspension of the horse's body lengthened, the trot starts showing the form of the Passage.

If the vertical projection is developed to the detriment of the forward progression, the length of the stride diminishes. However a greater output of energy from the hind legs enables the horse to increase the effort of projection without reducing the forward progression, sometimes even improving the latter, and to preserve the length of his stride, or to amplify it while also elevating it.

The characteristic of the "Passage" is the heightening and prolongation of the moment of suspension of the mass, regardless of the length of the stride.

The form of the Passage can vary infinitely, and so can the height of the steps proportionately to their length.[1]

In the school trot, which can be regarded as a stage towards the Passage, the lengthening of the moment of suspension is barely perceptible, and the heightening of the gait is almost solely due to the play of the limbs, which step higher than in the ordinary trot.

In the form which the old masters called "le doux Passage", (the soft

---

1. One form will be more natural to a horse than another, depending on his conformation. He can be taught other forms which with practice will become familiar to him, but they will never reach the degree of perfection that can be attained by the original one. Every horse has his own particular Passage.

Passage), the suspension increases to the detriment of the length of the stride. While acquiring more cadence, the gait becomes shorter.

In the form of the "Trot-Passagé", the greater energy delivered by the hind legs enables the horse to heighten his steps without shortening them (and even to lengthen them).

The Passage proper is situated somewhere between the "doux Passage" and the "Trot-Passagé", but it would be impossible to assign precise limits to these *varieties of the same air* which are so closely linked one with another.

As the length of the stride of the Passage diminishes, it becomes the "Piaffer", which is nothing else but a Passage on the spot.

Finally, it is possible for a horse to execute a Passage in a backward direction by stepping back with each successive stride.

Form of the Passage—The precepts of the old masters regarding the form of the classical Passage were the following:

—The length of the stride should be approximately one foot (cm.33).

—The toe of the forefoot in suspension must be lifted to a height level with the middle of the cannon bone of the other foreleg. That of the hind foot, to the height of the top of the fetlock.

—In the Piaffer, the elevation of the limbs must be considerably more pronounced: the height of the knee for the foreleg, and of the middle of the cannon bone for the hind leg.

We must note that these precepts were applied to a type of horse favoured by the old masters for manege work—Bearn, Andalusian, Limousin, which were all built "uphill", and had a naturally high carriage. Furthermore, they liked them to have a high and rounded knee action. This had some influence on the form of their Passage; the preparation between pillars must also have

Passage and Piaffer (drawn by Parroceal, who
illustrated de la Gueriniere's 'Ecole de Cavalerie)

Passage executed spontaneously by an excited thorough-bred.

had an influence to the same effect, and their horses were made to "sit" on their hocks to a greater extent than in the modern Passage.

Most of the horses used nowadays are of a very different type.

The introduction of English blood, and selection for speed have thoroughly modified their conformation. The overall height of the topline is lower in front. The pursuit of a sweeping action suited to fast paces has lengthened the fore-arm and lowered the knee. The natural action is longer and lower.

This important modification of the natural gaits cannot fail to influence the airs evolved from them, and the standards established by the old masters for their horses cannot be exactly applied to ours.

The precepts formulated earlier seem to show that the old masters' horses had a higher action in the Piaffer than in the Passage because, no doubt, of the disposition of their joints. Nowadays, the opposite is the case with the majority of our horses.

Old prints also show that the angle of the knee was then well under 90 degrees in most cases. With our horses, even in the best developed Passage, where the forearm assumes a horizontal position, it is extremely rare to find the cannon bone coming behind the vertical; more often than not, it will be seen to remain in front of it, even in the Piaffer.

Baucher, in his first manner, in which he laid down as a principle that a horse should be absolutely horizontal, demanded that the hind legs be lifted as high as the forelegs in the Piaffer and in the Passage. It is astonishing that he continued to stipulate this equal lifting of the limbs even after he had prescribed, in his last manner, a lifting of the forehand and a general disposition of the horse's body much like the attitude given to their horses by the old masters. It is only logical that the relative lifting of fore and hind legs should correspond to that of the forehand and of the hindquarters, and that the movement of the forelegs should exceed that of the hind legs if the elevation of the forehand in relation to that of the hindquarters is also greater.

All the preceding remarks might lead us to surmise that the rider ought to be able to use his aids to transform the trot into the Passage by compelling the horse to produce a certain degree of energy in the thrust of the hind legs and to adopt a general attitude which causes the output of energy to be directed upward rather than forward.

In reality, however, the rider's indications will rarely obtain this result straight away.

The lifting of the mass, resulting in the moment of suspension in the Passage on the one hand depends on a vertical position of the hind leg when it delivers its thrust, and on the other hand on the simultaneous advance of the haunches towards the centre of gravity. (See 1st Part, Chapter on the Rassembler.)

A horse which has conscientiously been put through all the exercises prescribed in the progression set out up to here will be supple in his spine and in his joints, and confirmed in the Mise en Main and the Ramener; he can easily adopt and maintain a general attitude which ought to produce the Passage.

His inability to do so is usually due to his awkwardness at extending each hind leg in support when it is close to the vertical and flexed to its utmost.[1]

In all the natural gaits the hind legs finish delivering their thrust once they have passed behind the vertical, and the more so as the speed increases. The horse's natural way of slowing down is to diminish the energy of the thrust, and not the inclination of the hind leg that is about to leave the ground.

If the rider tries to oblige the horse to deliver the same thrust, or even an increased one, earlier than at the normal moment, the horse hesitates and fumbles and experiences all those difficulties which are, for any living creature, inherent in the execution of an unaccustomed movement.

He will often succeed quite quickly in *freeing*, or *lifting* a hind leg before the normal moment, but only by more or less completely losing the effect of thrust—a slower pace may result, but one lacking in cadence.

To develop the Passage from the trot, we must first restore, and then develop, the thrust by anticipating the moment the hind leg is about to leave the ground. If this anticipation can cause the hind leg to thrust off at the moment when it is perfectly vertical, we will have succeeded in transforming the Passage into a Piaffer.

We can also obtain the Piaffer directly, without using the Passage, from

1. Note that when he is being groomed the horse readily surrenders the hind leg which is further back, and the other one only with difficulty.

the halt, with the horse collected so that his hind legs are vertical, by teaching him first to lift each of his hind legs, and next to project his mass upward each time, until it is clearly lifted between the alternated thrusts of the hind legs.

Once this result is achieved, the Piaffer can be transformed into the Passage by advancing the centre of gravity, with the effect of not only displacing the mass in an upward direction, but simultaneously upward and forward.

Thus, this "conventionalisation" of the trot which is the basis of all the airs derived from this gait, can be undertaken from "both ends" as one might say.

Either method has its advantages and its draw-backs, and one of them will be more suited to the preparation of each particular horse than the other.

Horses trained to the Passage to start with will usually show greater amplitude of movement, but the transition to the Piaffer will have to be done with punctilious regard to a gradual progression in order to avoid causing an irregular gait when the slowing down is accentuated, and a "Saut de Pie" (magpie hop) as soon as the horse stops moving forward altogether.

On the other hand, these horses usually change easily and energetically from the Piaffer to the Passage.

Horses trained first to the Piaffer usually show more cadence ("tride") than the others, but have greater difficulty in developing forward movement in the Passage. They readily come back to the Piaffer from the Passage, and are more reluctant to "accelerate" from the Piaffer to the Passage.

As a rule, the direct pursuit of the Passage before the Piaffer is more particularly advisable in the case of those horses which have a natural disposition to a marked suspension in the trot, a lightly mobile croup, naturally elevated gaits, and an aptitude to movement on the spot.

On the contrary, the direct pursuit of the Piaffer from the halt is more suitable for horses endowed with a low, sweeping action, and with hindquarters that thrust forward better than they lift, who find mobility on the spot difficult.

In whichever order the Passage and the Piaffer are obtained, the trainer's big difficulty will always be the transition from the one to the other, the perfect "blending" of the two which is the major part of the artistic value of these movements as a whole.

For this reason, it is better in most cases to start "conventionalizing" the trot at both ends simultaneously, i.e. to start on the Passage and on the Piaffer at the same time, even if more time and care must be devoted to one of the two depending on the horse that is being schooled, and to attempt from the beginning to make them "tend" towards one another.

As soon as a measure of cadence starts appearing in the Piaffer, the horse must frequently be ridden forward without losing this cadence, at least not altogether. As soon as the upward thrust in the trot is sufficiently vigorous to approximate a Passage, the pace can start to be shortened, in the same rhythm—but with caution.

For quite a long time, the stress should be on the "blending" of both airs rather than on their development in height.

Capitaine J. B. Dumas
Passage produced by slowing the trot.
(It should be noted that the horse was first schooled
to a diagonal walk with prolonged moments of suspension).

Direct pursuit of the Passage from the trot

The increased activity imparted by the rider's legs to one hind leg, combined with an unloading of its diagonal shoulder should, theoretically, enable us to prolong the suspension of this diagonal, and a symmetrical reversal of the aids should obtain the same result from the other diagonal.

A lengthening of the period between the application of these combined aids should produce the longer interval of time between strides which differentiates the Passage from the trot.

In reality, the horse thus placed "between hands and legs" can gradually find a rhythm, but will take a long time to do so, and the final result often remains limited.

The *attention* of the horse is too distracted by these successively and too closely repeated opposite indications to give him time to start obeying the one before he receives the other.

He will remain hesitant for a long time, and his eventual compliance will be rendered timid by his perplexity.

The trainer disposes of an easy remedy to these difficulties if he breaks up his demands, by applying them only to one diagonal at a time.

The horse's attention at the beginning is more easily fixed by this procedure and the reiterated single indication is easier for him to understand. He has more time to discover the muscular and articular adaptation to make in order to obey the indication, as he is not worried by a sudden reversal of the aids. It is thus easier for the rider to make himself understood and it enbles the horse to obey more readily.

At a later stage, when perfection is being sought the same procedure will enable us for the same reasons to obtain quicker and better results in *developing* the movements.

This breaking-up has a further and capital advantage: it enables us to counteract the very usual asymmetry in the play of the diagonals and to obtain perfect symmetry between the movements of the two.

However, the rider must beware of persisting for too long in this unilateral localisation of these gymnastics, and must endeavour to "marry" as early as possible the progress obtained from each diagonal singly.

To exercise one diagonal alone, we could, while maintaining the horse in a straight position, activate the hind leg of this diagonal with successive leg actions and execute equally successive half-halts on the shoulder on the same side, in order to unload the other shoulder.

But we can produce an even more localised effect if, instead of insisting on the straight position, we give a bend adapted to our objective. The inflexed horse has a natural tendency to engage his inside hind leg and to unload his outside shoulder. In his practice of the Passage, La Gueriniere advises an average bend corresponding to the "demi-pli" (half-bend), i.e. very much the same bend as in the shoulder-in, but he goes on to say that it may be necessary to demand a more pronounced bend, with both ends in.

The rider must of course stop using this incurvation as soon as it becomes unnecessary, and gradually reduce it until he can obtain from his straightened horse, from each diagonal separately, one or two well developed steps—and one preferably to two.

A closer succession of alternate demands will then enable the rider to obtain two consecutive beats alternately, each one of which will have been developed by a different diagonal, and this is how he will start obtaining cadence.

Practice will help him to maintain this cadence over an increasing number of strides, and he should gradually reduce the use of the aids, particularly of the hands, until alternative pressures of the foot on the stirrup are sufficient to keep the cadence for approximately twenty strides, without intervention from the hands.

At this moment it is not only unnecessary, but inadvisable, to attempt to increase the height of the Passage, but it is on the contrary essential to try to maintain rhythm in changes of speed, especially when slowing down, in order to prepare the Piaffer from the very beginning of the Passage.

Execution

At the end of an energetic lesson at the trot, with the horse in perfect balance in the "Mise en Main", and going either on one or on two tracks, and after the specially careful execution of *marked* changes of speed, the rider puts his horse into an energetic School trot, on, for example, a circle to the left of a diameter of 10 metres.

Incurved to the left on the circle, the horse is obliged to take longer strides with his right fore than with the left one, and to engage the left hind more than the right. The bend to the left on the circle is, as can be seen, already favourable to the greater development of the right diagonal.

Gradually the rider increases the bend by a suspicion of left shoulder-in.[1]

A very slight opening of the left rein must then increase the bend to the left, and bring the left fore towards the inside of the circle, thus causing it to tread a few centimetres further to the left than previously.

The right rein, enveloping the neck, acts by bearing from right to left to bring the weight of the forehand onto the left shoulder.

The left leg firmly on the girth takes care of the bend and of the engagement of the left hind, while the right leg, in its normal position, guards the quarters and is prepared to prevent any attempt of the right hind to escape.

When the horse is firmly established in this attitude, the rider can gradually start acting intermittently instead of continuously with his aids, guiding himself on the grounding of the left diagonal.

He simultaneously breaks up the synchronism of his indications and dissociates their combination according to the reactions of the horse. If the latter is naturally energetic and spirited and valiantly maintains his impulsion, the legs must become passive, although without modifying their respective positions, and the hands alone must be active. But the actions of the latter must also be dissociated. If, for example, the horse yields readily to the left rein and shows no difficulty in bringing his left fore closer to the centre of the circle, the effect of the left rein must be progressively reduced, while the indirect effect of the right rein on the left shoulder must be more clearly

1. The degree of useful inflexion varies with each horse, and even with the same horse depending on his temporary reactions. The rider may be obliged to increase the bend to bring "both ends" in if the horse persists in escaping with his outside hind. However, such a degree of inflexion is detrimental to impulsion and should only be resorted to for a short while to destroy a resistance, which should not occur for more than a fraction of a moment if the horse is sufficiently prepared by his previous dressage to be ready to start learning the Passage.

stressed with intermittent actions that weigh on the left shoulder every time the left fore comes down and are prolonged as long as it is in support, or even, if necessary, for an imperceptible fraction of a moment longer.

This procedure causes sooner or later an asymmetrical action of the fore-legs, which shows first in a shortening of the stride of the left fore rather than in a lengthening of that of the right one, while the left hind often loses some activity.

Then the action, or the preponderance of action, passes to the legs. If the general impulsion of the horse diminishes, the legs acting in concert must re-establish it. If the left hind especially is the inactive one the rider's left leg will assume the major role, which would have been taken by his right leg if the horse's right hind had lost its energy or attempted to step off the circle.

To make himself more clearly understood the rider will always find it helpful to use the whip on the right shoulder every time the left fore comes down—or even a little earlier—especially if the horse has been schooled in hand, and also to rise at the trot on the right diagonal.

Under the simultaneous or alternate influence of these various actions of the aids, the horse will gradually develop the play of his right diagonal, sooner or later, and in a greater or smaller measure, depending on his natural aptitudes—and on the tact and skill of his trainer.

Any appreciable tentative attempt to obey, however slight, must be immediately encouraged, but the rider must always restrict the immediate succession of beats to two or three at the most, later to one or two, and preferably one for the same diagonal. For it is of the utmost importance that the horse should not be allowed to get into the habit of this asymmetry, which would cause serious difficulties when the time arrives to obtain the association of two successive alternate beats of both diagonals.

Consequently, once the rider is able to obtain one or two clearly marked elevations from the right diagonal, he must stop circling to the left and start circling to the right to do the same work on the left diagonal.

Alternately exercising the right and left diagonal, he must regulate and apportion the work in a manner that will produce as much symmetry as possible between both sides, and it will always be better to start with the weaker diagonal, to counteract from the very beginning any congenital, or acquired, asymmetry, and not to worsen it but on the contrary to reduce it.

When the rider can easily obtain the elevation of the outside diagonal on both circles, described tangentially to one long side of the riding school, he takes the track at a tangent and on the straight demands the elevation of the same diagonal, while maintaining, to start with, the bend which the horse had on the circle. He must gradually reduce the bend until the horse is perfectly straight and executes, as soon as requested, one or two beats—one always preferably to two—of the diagonal nearer to the wall, on either rein.[1]

We should then leave the track on straight lines in various directions, and to start with at not too closely spaced intervals of time, solicit each diagonal alternately and separately. This work must be persevered with and gradually the actions of the hands must be limited to an opportune closing of the fingers on one rein or the other, depending on the horse's disposition, until the elevation of a diagonal can be obtained solely by an action of the opposite leg (of the rider), the hand remaining still and passive.

Afterwards, by using the legs in more rapid succession, we can fairly easily obtain two alternate and successive elevations of each diagonal, but it is then advisable to resort once more to the circle as this considerably helps the horse to develop his outside diagonal (inside hind and outside fore).

To this effect, the rider sets the horse forward on a track parallel to the wall, at some distance from it, for example on the left rein, and solicits the left diagonal only at every third or fourth beat. With the assistance of the corners of the manege, he gradually curves his course while still insisting on the elevation of the left diagonal, until he can finally keep his horse on the circle when he (the horse) will very soon be able to "offer" this diagonal quite easily.

As the horse is already proficient at "offering" the outside right diagonal on a circle to the left, the alternate succession of an elevated step of the left and of the right diagonal will be quite easy to obtain without the use of brusque aids.

Once the horse can easily execute alternately two elevated steps, starting with the inside diagonal—the most difficult one—the rider solicits three, starting with the outside one.

This minutely detailed progression is essential in the case of nervous and scatty horses, but not always with other types. Quite often, when the horse has been taught to lift *first* his outside diagonal, and *next*, the inside one, he will alternate several elevated steps of his own initiative, and will launch himself in a beginning of a Passage, a rather uneven one to start with, but one which will be easy to regularise by using a serpentine and gradually coming back to a straight line by "flattening" the loops.

In any case, as soon as the horse can execute three successive alternate

1. If, at the ordinary trot, the rider continues to insist on obtaining several successive beats of the same diagonal, he will get the horse, once the latter has understood, to produce several successive elevated steps of this diagonal. We should not scold him, as he might then refuse in future to produce any at all on this particular diagonal, but he should not be rewarded either. We should yield as soon as possible after the first one, and disregard the others, which will gradually disappear.

high steps, starting with one diagonal or with the other, he is "virtually" doing a Passage. To bring him to do it "practically" the rider must, first and solely, insist on the perfect regularisation of the air on straight lines and on all sorts of curved ones, and on two tracks.

What we must avoid with the greatest care during this period is to attempt to increase the *height* of the steps, as the movement should be executed as effortlessly as possible, in the form of the "Soft Passage".

As soon as the horse can easily maintain his cadence in work on two tracks, in which the hands almost solely should produce lateral displacement (see chapter concerning two track work at the trot), we must start to slow the Passage progressively, to get it to tend gradually towards the Piaffer.

The rider will have to be extremely moderate in his demands and most carefully observant as he will have to avoid at the same time *precipitating* the steps (proximity in time) and diminishing their *height*.

The hand alone must obtain the slower rhythm, by means of light half-halts applied to each foreleg just before it touches the ground, and which must cease if the cadence or the elevation diminish, to be immediately replaced by the action of the legs alone.

We will spare ourselves illusions if we use markers and then count the exact number of strides at the original speed between them—10 strides for example. If, at the end of two or three lessons in slowing down, the horse can do the same distance in 11 or 12 strides with exactly the same elevation as previously and with the same interval of time between each step, we should be very satisfied with the results obtained.

This work should be conducted simultaneously with work on two tracks. Progress achieved in the gradual development of obliquity in the half-pass on straight lines or, better still, on circles with the haunches-in, greatly facilitates the task of slowing the Passage.

PIAFFER

If the horse has received the lessons from the ground explained later on, he should be able to trot, though not necessarily to do a Passage, on one spot in hand and without a rider, before the work is tackled by the trainer mounted.

To teach the Piaffer, if the trainer has an able assistant, he can get him to sit on the horse passively at first, and later on to substitute his own indications for those of the trainer.

In all cases, and even in the latter, once the trainer gets on the horse himself he will be well advised to start all over again from the beginning and to follow the progression detailed hereafter, which is particularly essential if the horse has not had any training from the ground.

N.B.—The progression of dressage to the Piaffer which I set out in a

Piaffer produced by slowing the Passage
Capt. de Saint-Phalle

pamphlet published eighteen years ago is not essentially different from the present one, but for the following reason is not absolutely identical:

The first was intended for a group of French horses which were being prepared at that time for international dressage tests, and it was designed to be suited to the stage and form of this preparation once work on the Piaffer could be undertaken by their riders.

The present progression is destined for those horses which have been thoroughly prepared in the manner outlined in the previous chapters of this book, and is designed to avoid or to reduce difficulties inherent in the work on the School airs derived from the trot.

In order to obtain the Piaffer, we must produce:

—a mobilisation of the limbs, in diagonal pairs, without forward progression;

—a suspension of the mass between the beats of the diagonals.

We can pursue both results at the same time, by trying to produce a regular trot, while simultaneously preventing forward movement, but this is a delicate procedure, fraught with considerable difficulty in the case of some horses and which often produces mediocre results.

We could almost certainly achieve better ones, and no doubt avoid the major difficulties by resorting first to appropriate gymnastic exercises.

An immediate transition to the trot from the halt is difficult enough to obtain from some horses, even when no opposition is made to forward movement, but is always extremely difficult if the rider opposes forward movement while demanding the trot.

If a motion of the limbs can be obtained, more often than not it will be a kind of irregular prancing which has nothing in common with the trot. But forward progression from the rein back to the trot, providing of course that the reining back is correct and easy, can be achieved easily without breaking-up the diagonals which are as perfectly synchronized in a correct rein back as they are in the trot.

At the moment of reversal of direction of the movement, when haste must of course be avoided, the alteration of the diagonals, so difficult to obtain from the halt, continues quite naturally from the backward movement into the forward one, even at the moment of "neutral gear".

This is also the case as regards the moments of suspension of the mass, which anyhow can only be obtained once the gait is perfectly diagonal.

If we attempt to obtain these periods of suspension directly and without any preparation, we will nearly always find that the alternate efforts of the hind legs are unequal, thereby causing unequalness of the successive suspensions of the body, serious enough sometimes to result in hops ("Sauts de Pie") which are difficult to eradicate later on.

What is however more often than not the case, is that the efforts of the hind legs affect only the hind quarters without being transmitted to the whole of the body. The croup is lifted, but not the forehand. This will not only vitiate the form of the future Piaffer, but will also make the eventual transition from the Piaffer to the Passage extremely difficult. But the horse that can move smoothly from a slow trot to a rein back will find it much easier to preserve, and to preserve for longer, the moments of suspension of the mass in this transition than in the transition from the trot to the halt, in which upward thrust disappears well before the halt is complete.

In the first transition, although suspension may be feeble, it remains equal in front and behind and persists easily until a neutral point is reached between forward and backward progression, or even beyond this point into the first backward steps. The horse himself acquires the habit of rhythmically projecting his mass upward, without any forward movement at all, at "no speed".

Preparative gymnastics favourable to this spontaneous automatic creation of the elements of the Piaffer will therefore consist in alternating the slow trot with reining back, and conversely. The speed, in both directions, should of course be as slow as possible and sufficiently limited to preserve perfect diagonal action in the rein back, and of the moments of suspension in the trot.

With the same purpose in mind, the distance covered in both directions must be quite short as it is the frequency of those moments when the horse passes into "neutral gear", between the changes of direction, which will develop his cadence in movement on the spot. When the cadence on the spot becomes markedly even in the region of this "neutral gear", we must try not to step backwards beyond this point, and to resort less and less to reining back, thus transforming the preceding exercise into one which constitutes the basis of the Piaffer: i.e., "to move from the halt to the trot, and from the trot to the halt", while maintaining motion at the halt and regularity of the diagonal movements.

These lessons must always end with energetic forward movement before the horse is allowed to rest. We must conduct this work in such a manner that the horse will come to realize that motion on one spot is always temporary and invariably followed by a marked forward progression, with or without cadence depending on the extent and the way the rider yields with his hands.

When the horse can easily execute a few regular trotting strides on the spot while maintaining the whole time an urgent desire to trot forward as soon as the rider opens the barrier, we can try to obtain the true Piaffer, which is not a *trot*, but rather a *Passage* on the spot. We must produce the loftiness of movement and the longer moments of suspension required in the Piaffer as much as in the Passage.

However, before going on to studying the means which we will use to this effect, we should note that the moment chosen in the execution of these airs for obtaining their development is far from being unimportant. Experience is there to prove that it is during the transition from the Piaffer to the Passage, or conversely, that a marked lowering of the movement occurs and an appreciable diminution of the moments of suspension. The higher the movement in the Piaffer or in the Passage, the lower it will become during the transition from the one to the other. Therefore, it is not advisable to try to *heighten* the motions of the Piaffer while it is stabilised; we would only increase a difference which we must on the contrary reduce.

What we should do on the contrary is to provoke the opposite tendency: for example, to get the horse to start from a low but steady Piaffer and then to obtain simultaneously the transition forward and a heightening of the steps.

It is during the moments of transition from one air to the other that we must try to develop the movements, at least at the beginning of this work.

The development in height of a diagonal will depend partly on the development of thrust in the hind quarters, and partly on the unloading of the shoulder of this same diagonal. Once the latter has left the ground, its hind leg is no longer in a position to influence the development of the movement, but the other hind leg, on the contrary, is then able to propel the mass and to magnify the gesture of the diagonal suspension.

The rider's leg opposite to the diagonal (i.e. the left leg for the right diagonal) is the one that starts the beginning of the movement, as it has a direct action on the lifting and flexing of the hind leg (of this diagonal) but once the diagonal is projected the action of the rider's direct leg (i.e. right leg for the right diagonal) must magnify its trajectory. Therefore the use of both legs is necessary to the development of the movement but with variations depending on the immediate purpose of the rider. If both legs are used simultaneously, with the same intensity, the development of the movement as a whole will be influenced.

The predominating use of the left leg (for the right diagonal) influences especially the flexion of the left hind, and the resulting elevation. A predominating action of the right leg, for the same diagonal, will cause a lengthening in time and length of the movement.

This predominant use of one leg may, if necessary, become an isolated action, depending on circumstances, and taking into consideration the fact that the left leg to be effective should act before the lifting of the diagonal, and the right leg after, during the time of suspension of the right diagonal.

The left leg elevates the movement, the right leg prolongs it and lengthens it.

As regards lightening the shoulder of the same diagonal, this is produced by an action of the hands which causes the weight of the forehand to weigh more heavily on the opposite shoulder.

For example, the indirect right rein loads the left shoulder somewhat, and to the same extent unloads the right shoulder, providing of course that the horse responds to this action and obeys the indications of his rider.

The extent and form of this reaction to the indirect rein will vary depending on the position of the neck. The higher the elevation of the neck and the better the degree of Ramener the greater the shifting of the weight.

The straightness or the bend of the neck will also have a very marked effect on the nature of the resulting effect.

When the neck is concave on the same side as the rein bearing against it, and the horse, for example, is bent to the right, the shifting of the weight to the left resulting from the action of the right indirect rein will be greatest, and sometimes is even communicated to the left hind. It will be less if the neck is straight (without incurvation) and lesser still if the neck and the horse are bent to the left.

But the effect of the indirect rein is not limited to this shifting of the weight; it influences to a marked degree the form of the gesture of the unloaded foreleg.

If the neck is bent to the right by the indirect rein, all the muscles of the right side will be shortened to a certain extent, and this applies especially to the mastoido-humeral.

The horse's tendency will then be *to lift* the knee, rather than to reach out with his shoulder.

If, on the contrary, the horse is flexed to the left, the neck being convex on the right side, the muscles of the right side will be more or less stretched.

The knee is not lifted as high, but the shoulder and the foreleg extend more.

The bend of the neck therefore gives the rider the means of either lifting or of extending the movement of the foreleg of the diagonal which he wishes to develop; however the effectiveness of this means is linked to the perfection of the Mise en Main, the yielding of the jaw and the degree of Ramener and diminishes to the extent of disappearing altogether if these are lost.

Thus, to lead the horse progressively from the Passage to the Piaffer without restricting the gestures or the time of suspension, the dominant aids, for the right diagonal will be the left leg and the right indirect rein, the horse being flexed to the right.

On the contrary, to drive the horse from the Piaffer to the Passage, for the same diagonal, the dominant aids will be the right leg and the right indirect rein, with the horse flexed to the left. The transition from the Piaffer to the Passage is much facilitated by this intervention of the aids, if they are given clearly, decisively but without roughness.

BAUCHER

FRENCH EQUITATION
General Wattel, at that time
Chief Instructor at Saumur,
performing the Passage and the Piaffer
on "Clough-Bank" and "Rempart."

Passage (Repart)

Passage (Clough-Bank)

Piaffer (Rempart)

Piaffer (Clough-Bank)

Comte de REGENTHAL

Passage (Obr.-Br. Gebhart)   Passage (Obr.-Br. Lindenbauer)

Piaffer (Obr.-Br. Lindenbauer)   Piaffer (Obr.-Br. Meixner)

STEINBRECHT

GERMAN EQUITATION

Passage (Prof. Lörke)

Passage (Lt.-Cl. Gherhardt)

Piaffer (Prof. Lörke)

Piaffer (Général von Holzing)

PART THREE

Work at the Canter

Chapter 1 · THE WORK OF CONSOLIDATING
THE CANTER

Book of Reference:
GENERAL FAVEROT DE KERBRECH

This work is not a continuation of the preceding lessons, as the horse will have had exercise at the canter every day from the very beginning of dressage, except during the period devoted to obtaining extension at the trot, during which it might have been necessary to stop the use of the canter for a while.

However, the purpose of this work will have been to perfect the canter in its form and not to improve on the transitions from another gait to the canter or the strike off at the canter, and we would be well-advised to postpone this education until the horse is confirmed in his dressage at the trot and at the walk.

As the horse is an experienced outdoor ride before his academic dressage starts, he can canter from the walk or from the trot, or from both gaits. This he will be able to do with greater or less facility depending on his nature and the skill of his first trainer. There will usually be a certain lapse of time between the moment of the breaking up of the first pace and the beginning of the canter. The work of obtaining a correct strike-off will consist in reducing this interval of time to a minimum and of finally obtaining instantaneousness.

Previously, the horse will have been quietly urged to canter by whatever means were formerly employed in his outdoor work and he should be given all the time necessary to achieve this without precipitation and be allowed to canter in the manner which he finds easy as regards position and speed.

CONSOLIDATING THE CANTER

The first end to pursue in the gymnastics of the canter is its consolidation on both leads, i.e. maintenance of order and rhythm in the supporting phases of the limbs, regardless of the changes of direction.

The space chosen for this purpose must be as spacious as possible, so that the trainer is not faced with the necessity of having to change direction inopportunely when practising a particular exercise.

A typical figure for this work is the serpentine in which many variations of bends are possible, from the faintest undulation of the course to figures of eight on a small radius.

We must be very careful never to punish—or even to scold—the horse if he changes the lead or becomes disunited, but must bring him back to the original lead with unflagging perseverence and without roughness.

The easiest way to succeed, if, for example, the horse is cantering on a straight line on the right lead, is gradually to lead the horse on to a very wide circle to the left, of a sufficient radius to avoid an immediate disturbance of the gait. As soon as the canter loses its regularity, the rider guides the horse on a large circle to the right, outside the first circle, and continues on this circle until the canter on the right lead is re-established and has once again become quite regular. We should try to detect the very first symptoms of an alteration of the canter and, as far as possible, start circling to the right *before* the horse goes disunited or changes lead. However, if we have not succeeded in catching this moment and the horse has changed lead or becomes disunited, it will usually be sufficient to put him on a circle in the *same* direction as the original lead, which will then be restored after a few incorrect strides. The rider must endeavour to interfere as little as possible, to remain supple and upright, and to preserve the steadiness of his aids. If he finds that a return to the original lead is unduly delayed, he should slow down and progressively go back to the gait which preceded the canter, walk or trot, and while remaining on the same circle to the right, *quietly* strike off on the correct lead, again take a straight course, and then proceed as indicated previously.

It is most important that the horse should never be made to feel that a change of lead or going disunited are "punishable faults", be it even by too sudden a slowing down of the canter, as it would then be very difficult later on to obtain changes of lead and to eradicate from the horse's memory the punishment which he would expect to receive.

As time goes on, it will be found unnecessary to describe the whole of the outward circle corresponding to the leading leg. To re-establish the regularity of the original canter, it will be sufficient to demand a few strides on this circle, and eventually just to orientate the horse in that direction. Furthermore, the disturbance of the gait caused by the counter-canter will gradually diminish and it will be possible to execute a serpentine of progressively more pronounced loops, controllable on both sides at the will of the rider.

The exercise must be continued for a long time until absolute regularity is obtained, before the circle at the counter-canter can be made smaller by the execution of a spiral towards the centre. However, we must never describe a circle smaller than the actual speed of the canter permits (which we must avoid slowing down at this stage, because we could only do this by losing impulsion instead of transforming the output of impulsion, which is what is required.)

These results are not usually difficult to obtain on one lead, but much more difficult on the other. The latter is evidently the one which we should work upon more frequently, until the counter-canter on a circle on this lead become entirely familiar to the horse, and perfect symmetry is established in both canters.

In the whole of this work, the correctness of the rider's position and his suppleness play an especially important part. He must strive to face exactly in the same direction as the horse and must avoid bringing forward the side of his body on the side of the horse's leading leg, or leaving the other half behind. He must lean in to the same extent as the horse, neither forcing or refusing the latter's inclination. The pressure of the ischia on the saddle and of the feet on the stirrups must remain as equal as possible. The legs must remain at exactly the same distance from the girth, symmetrically close to the horse's body which they must embrace with the same pressure and as often as possible.

All movements, all gestures, all modifications in the distribution of his weight must be avoided. "Supple passivity" and a minimum of interference are the aims to achieve.

The same principles apply to guidance, which must be limited to the absolute minimum necessary to produce changes of direction, as the *influence* of the direction of the figures rather than the aids of the rider must be used to obtain consolidation of the canter.

Most of the time, the legs should be passive, and only come into action if necessary to ensure continuous impulsion. They must then act simultaneously and symmetrically.

The reins should provide the horse with a frame which is at the same time steady and light. A turn to the same side as the leading leg must always be asked by the indirect rein on the opposite side, which places the shoulders in front of the haunches, and a turn to the opposite side by the direct rein, opened as little as possible, to avoid provoking by reaction a turning out of the haunches.

We must try not to "force" the horse to remain on the same lead but, by our insistence must make him understand what he is expected to do, and then, without "hustling", which would provoke disunitedness or a change of lead, allow him to "sort things out" until he succeeds.

STRAIGHTENING THE CANTER

Once the canter is properly consolidated, we can start straightening it, but we should remember that absolute straightness is only obtainable if a marked Ramener already exists, requiring a much slower pace than the canter used out of doors up to now which demanded, on the contrary, great freedom of head carriage and an open angle of the poll.

Straightening and slowing the canter are therefore aims that cannot be pursued independently of one another, or only to a very limited extent. They must on the contrary be pursued simultaneously, and the progress achieved towards either end must be exploited alternately. Furthermore, the Ramener should be completely established in the trot and the walk before it can be obtained in the canter.

In this gait, the horse is not naturally straight, and his obliqueness in relation to the direction of his progress is seldom the same on both leads.[1]

Usually, the horse which is naturally inflexed to *the left*, for example, canters in a relatively *straight* position on the right lead. The legs of his *right* diagonal will *both* be placed more or less on the line of the course. Those of the other diagonal will be placed on either side of this line, but with the hind leg further away from it than the foreleg. In this case, the natural bend of the horse counteracts the crookedness peculiar to the canter on the right lead, and therefore produces relative straightness.

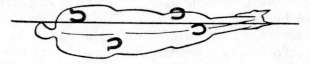

A horse with a natural bend to the left, cantering on the right lead.

On the contrary, on the left lead, the two deviations add up, and the horse is seen to go markedly crookedly as well as bent.

Absolute straightness in the whole length of the body is never natural to the horse at any pace, because of congenital asymmetry, but it is at the canter that the bend is most pronounced, and the task of straightening him at this gait is especially difficult.

1. This obliqueness diminishes with an increase in the speed of the canter, and at a racing gallop all four legs are placed practically on the same straight line corresponding to the direction of progress. It increases if the horse is held to a speed slower than the one to which he is accustomed and he has not been previously prepared for this by gymnastics.

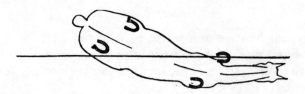

A horse with a natural bend to the left, cantering on the left lead.

It can only be achieved by prolonged exercise, by using the influence of the loops of the figures and partly by the aids of the rider.[1]

On a circle, beyond a certain speed which increases with the radius of the circle, the haunches show a tendency to deviate outwards, and this deviation is accompanied by a more or less marked *outward* inflexion of the horse.

The rider, by judiciously regulating in relation to one another the degree of curvature of the course and the rate of the horse's speed, has thus at his disposal a means of provoking a deviation of the hind-quarters and an inflexion of the horse towards one side or the other, and therefore of counter-acting any opposite tendencies.

For example, the easiest way of straightening a horse inflexed to the left, is to use a circle to the left, which will provoke at the same time a turning out of the haunches to the right and a concave bend of the horse to the right. On this circle, the speed will have to be greater on the left lead than on the right one, upon which the horse is already less incurved naturally.

On a circle to the right, with the same horse, the speed will have to be relatively slower, especially on the left lead, and circles to the left will have to be practised for shorter periods and less frequently to the right than to the left.

On the other hand, certain actions of the hands also tend to straighten the flexed and crooked horse.

—Opposition of the left direct rein to the thrust of the hind quarters will cause the latter to turn out to the right, while "locking" the shoulders in their own directions. This effect will be all the more pronounced the more the neck is rigid laterally, i.e. held higher.

—The right indirect rein brings to bear upon the shoulders a pressure which at every stride pushes them over to the left in front of the haunches, which latter are relatively fixed in their own direction, and this effect tends to bend the horse to the right.

The effects of the circular track and those of the hands can, and must be, judiciously combined to co-operate in straightening the horse.

1. The old masters were less concerned with straightness than we are, as they hardly prac-tised flying changes of leg, and never practised close changes. It is especially with these in view that it is absolutely necessary to make the horse familiar with a straight position in the canter on both leads.

For example, in the case of a horse bent to the left:

—On a left hand circle, of unchanging radius, *lengthen* the gait and guide the horse with the left *direct* rein, the hand rather high to prevent a bend of the neck.

—At a certain *set* unchanging speed, and certainly not at a slower one, reduce the circle with the right indirect rein.

The legs could also be used to straighten the horse, but any asymmetry in their use entails a risk of provoking disunitedness or a change of lead. It is better to dispense with this and to utilise their action symmetrically to maintain impulsion if necessary.

The effects of the curvature of the track and of the hands, either singly or in combination, must be practised alternately, and the horse submitted to one effect and to the other in frequent alternation. Leaving the circle at a tangent, the trainer will endeavour to preserve for some time on a straight course the straightness obtained by work on the circle, and come back to the circular track when it is lost, and so on.

The results of this work can only be secured by long persistent practice and only if the trainer can avoid hustling the horse in a manner which could spoil the regularity of the canter.

SLOWING THE CANTER

At the same time as the rider endeavours to straighten the canter, he must also strive to slow it down.

He first drives the horse at a speed greater than the one normally employed out of doors, and once regularity, balance and calm are secured at this greater speed he imperceptibly brings the horse back to his usual average speed.

The influence of a slightly declining slope is very favourable to this slowing down. Instinctively, the horse takes an attitude that lightens the load on the fore-hand, while the slope prevents a shortening of the strides of the hind legs.

The hands must be used in successive upward actions at every stride and not in one continuous one. The rider must try to shorten the stride of the forelegs, while avoiding as much as possible hastening the placing of the hind legs. At the same time he must direct his efforts towards systematically placing the shoulders in front of the haunches, as the tendency of the horse to "traverse" himself and to inflex is always considerably increased by the slowing down of the canter.

In all this work, the position, the seat of the rider and his suppleness play an especially important part. He must remain closely united with the horse, and lean forward only to the extent essential to counteract the effects of inertia, and inwards, if necessary, only in the very restricted measure required to fight the centrifugal force, while he must avoid overloading the horse's hindquarters. His weight should be supported rather more on the stirrups than on the saddle, in order to give complete freedom to the back and loins of the horse. His legs must remain still, symmetrically placed, rather forward than backward, in order to bring the hindlegs further under the mass instead of precipitating their extension.

Once a return from the faster speed to the normal one can easily be obtained on slightly declining terrain, then on even terrain, and finally on slightly ascending terrain, the trainer gradually endeavours to prolong the slowing down to reach a speed *inferior* to the normal one, and to this effect will follow the same progression and make the same use of slopes.

The minimum speed which we should obtain and maintain easily is one at which, on the *outside* lead the horse can canter in perfect balance on a circle of the same diameter as the width of our manege, so that we can continue there the gymnastics of the canter without fear of the restricted size of the riding school causing any disorder in the counter-canter.

The horse must be exercised alternately at changes of speed and changes of direction and incurvation. The work of slowing down and of straightening must progress along parallel lines and support one another. They will easily be completed in the manege by the Mise en Main and Ramener, which alone permits absolute rectitude in the canter.

In the latter part of the gymnastics of the canter, the trainer will utilise the same procedures as those he had already employed at the trot and at the walk, taking into account the fact that the canter, unlike the latter two gaits is not a symmetrical one, and that not only the limbs, but the whole body of the horse are affected by the asymmetry peculiar to the canter, which sometimes adds to, and sometimes opposes, the natural and permanent end of the horse.

Yielding of the mouth will be sought as previously on each rein separately, then, on all possible combinations,[1] until the mouth yields softly and immediately to any pressure of the fingers on the reins.

Afterwards, as he has done at the walk and at the trot, the trainer will proceed to obtain the Ramener by "filtering" the impulsion in the changes of speed.

The basic canter should be relatively slow but only to the extent which the horse can sustain easily in all manege exercises, whether cantering true or in counter-canter.

---

1. There are 11 combinations: one bridoon rein alone (2); one curb rein alone (2); both bridoon reins only (1); both curb reins only (1); one bridoon rein on one side with one curb rein on the other (2); (This combination being much liked by the General); one bridoon rein and the curb rein on the same side(2); all four reins evenly (1). This effectively amounts to 11. (Note 2nd edition.)

When the Ramener is well secured, and also the slowing down of the canter, the trainer can put the finishing touch to the complete straightening of the horse at this gait.

In this work he will persist in avoiding as much as possible any interference of the legs, besides their symmetrical action which must sustain the impulsion.

—The *"traversing"* of the horse will be counteracted as much as possible by making use of the presence of the wall on the same side, and consequently by using the counter-canter on the track. If absolutely necessary, the influence of the wall can be reinforced by a few half-halts in an upward direction on the rein which is on the side of the leading leg, and these half-halts will often be necessary when, dispensing with the wall, the trainer will gradually start working his pupil away from it.

—The "inflexion" of the horse will also be counteracted initially by the wall for the same reason, and by the influence of the neck rein on the opposite side of the leading leg at the canter.

Once complete straightness on the track is secured, the trainer will gradually come closer to the centre of the manege, and to start with he will try to hold his horse perfectly straight along straight lines.

Later on, with cautious progression, he will "adjust" the horse on curved lines, making sure that the hind legs tread exactly in the tracks of the forelegs, without any lateral deviation.

To obtain this result in the counter-canter, it may sometimes be necessary to increase the inflexion beyond what it should be and even to enforce a wrong bend, for example by asking a horse cantering on a circle to the right, on the left lead, to bend momentarily very slightly to the right.

Finally, *of his own accord*, without any interference from the rider's aids, the horse must remain perfectly adjusted to the tracks of his direction, confirmed on the determined lead, in a rhythmical, unhurried canter, and always willing to lengthen as soon as the hands open the barrier which orders the temporary slowing down.

Chapter 2 · STRIKING OFF AT THE CANTER

From the time of Xenophon, the problem of striking off at the canter has been solved in the most diverse manners—and this leads us to reflect that it is not a simple one.

It does appear that the famous principle of "position and action" is insufficient to solve it, no doubt because no "position" can *impose* the canter on the horse; some may only be "*favourable*", and none are "*compulsive*".

Usually, on the lead favoured by the horse—and there is always one—the central diagonal is oriented in the direction of progression and the horse consequently traverses himself more or less. However, in this position he is perfectly capable of remaining at the walk or at the trot without striking into the canter, and he can also strike off and stay at the canter in positions which are very different from that one. Furthermore, this position will vary in the case of each horse, and even in the case of one particular horse will vary considerably in degree depending on whether the horse, on a straight line, is cantering on one lead or on the other.

Until the cinema was invented, the imperfection of the human eye and ear led the most observant and the most knowledgeable onlookers to errors concerning the action of the canter which were only corrected by the camera. It is not useless to point out some of these.

—The three-time canter, which is more or less considered to be the typical canter, in which the two limbs of the central diagonal alight and lift simultaneously, is so rare that one could almost say that *it does not exist*. In reality, in for example the canter on the right lead, the left fore leg and the right hind lift and alight at intervals so short that they are imperceptible, but the absolute simultaneity of their alighting and lifting *hardly ever* occurs. Therefore, the horse almost always canters in four time.

When the horse is on the forehand, the foreleg of the central diagonal alights first; when he is on the haunches, the hind leg does. Each of both limbs of each *lateral* pair reaches out in turn beyond its opposite number of the other pair.

It is therefore incorrect to say, as we often hear and as we sometimes read, that in the canter on the right lead, the right limbs are constantly ahead of the left, or even that they alight further forward than the left—for the left limbs *always* reach out in front of the right at every stride of the canter on the right lead, and they also alight in front of the right limbs.

The truth, revealed by the camera,[1] is that the leading leg is ahead for a *longer period of time* than the other, and stretches further out. The same applies to the hind leg on the same side.

Not at any moment of the canter does the highermost point of the withers or of the croup rise above the height of either when the horse is standing square. On the contrary, each is alternately *lowered* to a greater or lesser extent beneath this height.[2]

Thus there is in truth a rocking motion in the canter, but due to the alternating *lowering*, and not lifting, of the forehand and the quarters. The horse does not "lift" himself into a canter and neither does his rider lift him.

It is the lowering of the quarters which gives the rider the illusion of a lifting of the forehand, an illusion strengthened by the lifting of the horse's head, which actually *does* occur.

These false premises, and others equally false, have often been used to justify the means advocated by riding masters to obtain the strike off at the canter.

And it is undeniable that their horses did canter off perfectly despite the use of methods that make little mechanical sense.

We must draw the conclusions that it is to the understanding of the horse that the rider must address himself and even if to this end he has to act more or less correctly on the *mechanics* (of the horse), he should not either be unaware of all the extraneous circumstances that can enlighten the horse about the rider's intentions.

We must not try to "trigger" off the mechanism by infallible means, but must try to make ourselves *understood*, and let the horse *execute*, whilst we make use as best we can of what seems certain about the motion of the canter as revealed by the cinema.

In all the films which have been made, without exception, we can observe the following:

The transition to the canter from another gait is more or less prolonged and during this transition the original gait undergoes a series of successive changes.

For instance, to go from the walk into the canter on the right lead, the horse will *always* start by hurrying the *lifting* of the right hind. Similarly, the

1. See: Colonel Gossart: "Les allures du cheval".
2. This error was demonstrated, even before the invention of the cinema, by M. Le Noble du Teil, Ecuyer at the Ecole des Haras, by the means of a registering device of his own invention.

camera shows only those movements which are peculiar to the canter from the moment when the right fore is prematurely lifted before the alighting of the left fore.

We are therefore led to thinking that the period of transition between the *walk* and the canter right *starts* with the hurried lifting of the right hind and *finishes* with the hurried lifting of the right fore.

However, this hurried lifting is not sufficient to establish a regular canter, but must be such that the right hind succeeds in leaving the ground *before* the left hind alights, and the right fore to lift *before* the left fore alights.

The horse does not always succeed at the first attempt, nor even at the second, and as a result there will be an interval of groping attempts during which the horse, no longer at the walk, is not yet at the canter.

When, on the contrary, he succeeds at the first attempt, within the interval of time of a complete walking stride, the strike off *appears* to be instantaneous and can be deemed to be perfect.

From the trot, the transition *always* starts by a hurried *alighting* of the right fore, and finishes when the equally precipitated alighting of the right hind occurs *before* the lifting of the left hind—with an intermediate period of varying length.[1]

All actions of hands and of legs prescribed by various masters to determine the strike off to the canter thus have as their first effect a precipitation of the lifting of the right hind, if the transition is from the walk, or of the alighting of the right fore, if the transition is from the trot.

None of these actions is capable of *unfailingly* hastening this lifting or this alighting in a measure sufficient to establish immediately the canter. The rider may well be able to provoke the beginning of the evolution that leads from one gait to the other; he may also no doubt be able to shorten the duration of this evolution, but he could only impose an immediate canter by using an effect of force or surprise which the horse would soon resist and which would therefore soon also become ineffective.

With a horse that has received no more than the indispensable dressage, the pushing of the croup towards the right resulting from the action of the left heel behind the girth may provoke the lifting of the right hind, rapidly moved by the horse to come to the support of this side of the quarters which by moving to the right impair his balance. The evolution which leads to the canter is thus started, but the horse grounds his hind leg undeniably to the right rather than forward: he "traverses".

1. From the walk the horse can start to canter either with the fore pair of legs (with a certain Rassembler), or with the hind pair (the ordinary case). From the trot, the same applies: either the front pair (ordinary case); or the hind pair (from an extended trot). (Note: 2nd edition.)

With a horse schooled to the effect of the right heel in its normal place, near the girth, which draws the hind leg forward, a precipitation of the lifting of the right hind is also obtained, but with a greatly reduced lateral displacement, if any. The horse will not traverse much, if at all.

Similarly, the infinite variety of rein actions can hasten the evolution of the right hind to initiate (or commence) the transition period from the walk (or the trot) to the canter.. It is therefore logical that we should be able, as experience demonstrates, to obtain the strike off on the same lead by the most varied methods. Our preference for one of them must be founded on the rider's skill in using it, on the previous dressage of the horse, and on the use the latter is intended for.

However, in the case of academic equitation, the longitudinal straightness of the horse's position is of capital importance, because only this makes the changes of lead "a tempo" possible.

We must therefore avoid all methods which cause the traversing of the horse, and adopt the one which best serves his straight position.

To strike off on the right lead, it will obviously be the right leg (of the rider) which will least drive the right hind to the right, and the right rein will be the most effective in preventing any turning out in this direction.

The strike off obtained with "direct leg and hand", as prescribed by Baucher in his last manner, is thus the one which is most suited to the demands of academic equitation.

However, though the aids are used in very close succession, they are not used absolutely simultaneously.

To change from the *walk* to the canter, the leg must precede the hand, because besides the possible necessity of increasing the impulsion, the horse starts the transition with the hind-leg. The right hand must act immediately *later* to lighten the right fore leg by a "soupçon" of bend to this side or, if necessary, to prevent the possibility of the horse traversing from left to right and to draw the shoulders in front of the haunches.

At the trot, where the evolution commences with the fore legs, the rein must precede the leg, and its action which is the strongest, may even have to be in the nature of a half-halt to precipitate the grounding of the right fore; the leg will act only later, but *immediately* later and then only in the measure necessary to activate the right hind and re-establish the impulsion if need be.

Practice of the strike off at the canter
While trying to produce the *mechanical* effects which may produce the canter, the trainer must first of all attempt to place the horse in a whole set of extraneous circumstances which help to provoke a strike off on the lead selected, and proceeding as in everything up to now, *progressively substitute*

indications still unknown to the horse to the indications which he already understands.

If the horse has received, as is always advisable, the schooling on the lunge described further on, it is a good thing to put him back on the lunge for a few days before starting to practice the strike off at the canter from the saddle and to remind him of the strike off at the canter at the command *of the voice* until he executes this faultlessly.

When this has become again easy and smooth, the trainer gets an assistant to take the lunge and he mounts and gradually substitutes his own verbal command "canter on" to his assistant's, according to the usual method: simultaneity to start with, then substitution.

When the horse strikes off easily at the command of the rider's *voice* without *any intervention* of the aids of the latter, the lunge is discarded, and the horse, still on the same circle, is given practice at striking off at the command *of the voice*, always *at the same spot* on the circle.

If the impulsion is insufficient, the voice can be accompanied by a touch of the whip on the right hip, (in the case of striking off on the right lead from the walk), firstly without the intervention of the aids, later with the intervention of the right leg, and finally with the leg and the rein on the same side.

Gradually, the indication given by the voice is given less frequently and then ceases, and so does the one given by the whip. We do not resort to these any more unless the actions of the right leg and hand take too long to produce the canter, but we remain very tolerant towards the promptness of the evolution from the walk to the canter, and carefully avoid hurrying it. On the contrary, we must allow the horse to find out for himself the means of achieving, in the space of time of one complete walking stride, the changes of balance and locomotion which produce the canter.

When he has succeeded, the horse must be trained to strike off at different places on the circle, then on the track, and then on the inside of the riding school.

As soon as the horse strikes off easily on straight lines, he must be worked preferably along the track, and on the *outside lead*, the proximity of the wall being wisely exploited by the rider to counteract any turning out and flexion at the moment of striking off, and subsequently in all strides.

If the horse has not been trained on the lunge, and if the rider is in the regrettable necessity of having to renounce this method, he will use, *on the same circle*, the same method of substitution. The horse will first be put into the canter by the means to which he has become accustomed to when ridden outside, accompanied by the indication of the voice, "canter", until he strikes off at the command of the voice alone. In this case the final substitution of the direct effect of leg-and-hand for the voice will be usually more difficult, because of the horse's confusion at the beginning between the old and the new indications. Much patience, and a slower progression will be needed.

We should always try to start from the walk to *begin with*, and only *later on* from the trot, particularly with horses bred from trotting stock. The ultimate transition from the canter to the canter, i.e. the flying change of lead, is always much more difficult to obtain if the horse has started with the transition to the canter from the trot, and often assumes a faulty form, consisting in a kind of intermediate trotting stride which makes the changes "a tempo" impossible later on.

Chapter 3 · CHANGES OF LEAD AT THE CANTER

When the horse executes a change of lead at the canter, the cinema shows that each of his fore and hind pairs of limbs alights twice consecutively on the leg upon which he was originally cantering, while the other leg remains in suspension, without touching the ground.

Thus, to change from canter right to canter left, each of both pairs, fore and hind, alights twice on the right leg, or, rather, springs from the right leg onto the right leg, or again, ends the moment of suspension by alighting with the right leg first instead of the left, as the horse did previously.

The cinema also shows that the changes of lead of both pairs of legs are *never* simultaneous. For the change of lead of the *horse* to be correct, i.e. *executed* in front and behind during the same stride, the *hind pair* must always change first. If the fore legs change first, the next stride will always be *dis-united*, the horse "cantering left in front and right behind".

Many riding masters have indicated precisely the moment when, during the last stride of the original canter, the indication for the change of lead should be given to the horse. The moment indicated by each one of them is not always the same. It is therefore appropriate to examine this problem.

To solve it completely, we would have to be able to determine exactly the limits of time during which the change of lead, in front and behind, is *possible*, and outside of which it is *impossible*. The possibilities of animal mechanics are not well known enough to allow ourselves to be as categorical as this, and it is prudent to stick to the probability of the following facts:

(1) The reversal of the movement of the limbs, in both fore and hind pairs is made easier during the moment of suspension if both limbs are at approximately the same distance from the ground[1] i.e. more or less half-way through this period of suspension.

(2) With the hind legs, which must change first, the reversal is difficult

---

1. This is not rigorously certain, because, when both feet are at the same distance from the ground, the position of the legs is not identical and, consequently, the speed with which they can return to the ground is not necessarily identical either.

at the first time of the canter, because the hind leg in support bears all the weight of the body and consequently is not very mobile and cannot easily execute the kind of "entrechat" that is necessary in the change. The facility of the change increases after the second time, when both hind legs are in suspension, and decreases again progressively as the hind legs come down again.

(3) With the fore legs, the change is easy at the first time, as they are both off the ground, but it must be rejected because it causes disunitedness at the canter (see above).

The change becomes difficult from the moment when the forehand starts coming down, i.e. at the second and third time, and afterwards becomes easy again up to the second time of the next cantering stride.

Therefore, to enable the horse to change lead easily it would appear to be sufficient that he should *want to do so* a short while before the third time, and during the phase of suspension. All riding masters are more or less in agreement on this point.

However, if he is to *want to* effectively, he must have first felt his rider's indication and had time to start executing it—provided his understanding and obedience are perfect.

To achieve this result, the indication which must cause the beginning of the execution by the horse must first originate in the rider's brain and travel to the latter's aids, the sensation produced by them (the aids) on the horse's body must travel to his brain, and the latter must provoke the start of the mechanism of reversal of movements.

Physiologists have discovered that the duration of the transmission to and from the brain between a sensation and the reaction it provokes is in the order of 1/10 second, with, however, an "index of conductivity" which varies considerably from one individual to another, man or horse, and which can be modified by practice and habit.

The moment indicated by the different masters as the one most favourable to provoke a beginning of execution of their indication must be influenced necessarily by the "personal index of conductivity" of each of them, and also by that which they obtained from the average of the horses which they schooled.

If Raabe, therefore, requested the change of lead on the second time of the last stride, and Fillis, between the second and the third time, no doubt this is due to the difference which must have existed between their own "index" and also between that of the horses which they trained.

We may also wonder whether they did not partly deceive themselves in indicating the precise moment when they *thought* that they were giving the signal to the horse.

According to what we have already seen, the duration of the transmission from the brain of the rider to the horse's legs lasts not very much longer than 1/10 second, and the duration of one stride of the school canter is in the order of 6/10 to 7/10 second, two of these approximately for the moment of projection.

However skilful the riding master may be, can he, in the interval of time of 5/10 second which is contained between the first time and the end of the third, be certain of "situating" his indication in that split-second which he *believes* to be the most favourable?

This we may doubt, even if we admit that the transition from the conscious to the sub-conscious, the transformation of the voluntary action into a reflex considerably augments its rapidity.

In any case, it is not open to doubt that if this localisation is possible, it can only be so at the cost of a precipitation akin to abruptness and abruptness of orders usually provokes abruptness of execution.

Brought about in this manner, the change of lead will most likely be bumpy, jerky, convulsive, or in the French manege expression "piqué" (staccato or choppy) which much diminishes its artistic value.

Finally, we may also wonder whether this lightning-localisation is essential, and even whether it is useful.

If it is, it only proves an alleged instantaneous obedience, which surely cannot be obtained from the start, and, after all, can only be confirmed by a progressive education.

As we cannot dispense with this progressive education, it seems preferable on the contrary to regulate it in order to obtain a "deferred" obedience, an "ultimate" one, giving the horse as much time as possible to change with both his pairs of legs without *jostling* him during the duration of the last stride of the original canter.

The second time of the canter is difficult enough to sense, and the interval of time between the second and the third is hardly perceptible; on the other hand, the first time is clearly sensed by the ear and the seat.

By making the beginning of his indication coincide with the beginning of the last stride, the rider will have "plenty of time" to give his orders without precipitation, with all the "softness" necessary, and the horse will have all his own (time) to change behind and in front with least abruptness.

The only possible disadvantage would be the risk of provoking a premature change in front, as both fore legs are in suspension up to the moment of the second time. This risk would indeed be considerable if the horse had already been trained to the change of lead by a "sudden attack", but we are not interested in this particular case.

The horse we have in mind is precisely the one which has to be "trained".

He does not know the order: "change the lead", and before he becomes familiar with its execution, he will only be able to obey by a series of attempts, at first over a period of several strides. This period will progressively become shorter, as the horse's ability improves with practice.

As soon as the horse's intelligence registers that the first regular stride on the new lead is always rewarded—rest, caresses—*his instinct* will be a much better guide than any of the rider's actions in getting him to execute it with a minimum of effort, and therefore a maximum of gracefulness.

Before schooling to the changes can start, certain conditions must be completely fulfilled.

—To start with, the strike off *from the walk* to the canter, and the transitions from the canter *to the walk* must be perfect, and perfectly symmetrical. The horse must strike off from the walk into the canter on either lead, in a perfectly straight position, at the same even rhythm, and with the same amplitude of movement.

From the canter on either lead, he must come back to a perfectly regular walk with the same promptness and the same ease.

The importance of flawlessness in the transition from canter to walk is, no less than in the transition from walk to canter, and it is almost always because the rider has neglected this that he faces serious difficulties in the education to the changes.

The transition to the canter *from the trot*, and especially from the canter *to the trot* must be absolutely avoided during the whole of the period of the education to the changes, and this applies to all horses but especially to those which have even a distant trotting ancestry. These have a marked disposition to insert a trotting stride in passing from one canter to the other. With them, it is not always easy to avoid this even if we insist firstly on perfect, direct transitions from the canter to the walk which is difficult enough in any case, but once the horse has been allowed to perform the change in this manner, the fault often becomes ineradicable; it robs the changes of all value and eventually makes the changes at every stride *impossible*.

To allow the horse to change behind first without difficulty, as he must always do, his quarters must be very free, and therefore considerably unloaded.[1] Consequently, in the first attempts at obtaining a change, the horse must be allowed to lower his forehand, his neck should not be shortened

---

1. It is for this reason that ticklish mares that buck in resistance to the rider's leg change the lead only too readily. It is also why the "change in the air"—which we practise frequently—was considered by the old masters to be a difficult movement. Their horses were considerably more "on their haunches" than ours, and the overloading of the hind-quarters made the leap of the hind legs, which permits the change, difficult. The old masters practised particularly a "two-time" change, also called "de ferme a ferme" (i.e. with a transition to and from the halt).

much, and the angle of the poll should be a little open rather than too closed. The rider should avoid loading the loins heavily by bringing his shoulders back.

The canter should be neither too slow, nor too collected. A longer and lengthier period of suspension greatly increases the ease with which the inversion of the limbs can be made. It follows that a rather extended and horizontal pace is especially favourable to the production of the first changes.

THE LESSON OF THE CHANGE

The horse must be perfectly relaxed and calm. In the preparatory work, the rider will only demand exercises and movements which the horse executes willingly, and will reward him with special generosity if they have been performed well.

The rider then, for example, will take the track to the right, at one end of the manege, where the large circle is circumscribed by three walls. After several circuits at a free walk, the rider obtains the Mise en Main without insisting on a Ramener, just in order to obtain a good, perfectly regular four time walk, a little short, but *active* even so.

He will then get the horse to strike off at the canter *on the right lead, always at the same* part of the circle. The choice of the right place is not unimportant. In view of further progress, it is advisable that it should be at that part of the circle which is circumscribed by the walls, in the centre of the narrow side of the school, for example, so that the horse can be kept on the circle without any interference from the rider.

Each strike off should be followed by only a few strides at the canter, with a return to the walk after approximately a half-circle. Every time the rider asks the horse to strike off, he uses the customary aids, and accompanies them by the indication of the voice, "mezzo voce", "canter up". This work is persevered with, until the horse strikes off almost automatically on the command of the voice, the other aids becoming almost unnecessary.

Once this first "convention" is well understood by rider and horse, the latter is again allowed to do one or two circles[1] of the manege at a relaxed walk, then is put on the bit again, and cantered *on the left lead* after he has gone *well past* the centre of the narrow side of the school. Still cantering on the left lead, when the rider reaches the centre of the short side, he *quietly* gives his indications for the canter right, accompanied by the aid of the voice, and waits while renewing his indications *without at any moment increasing their intensity*.

Usually the horse instantly manifests a quickening of his attention—and his perplexity—and *attempts* "something", but with some hesitation. He

1. Still on the right rein (Note of the 2nd Edition.)

attempts to change the gait and its regularity is lost; he may put in a number of false beats in front or behind, and after a certain time, maybe rather a long one, succeed in changing to the right lead. The rider should *immediately* and lengthily caress the horse, allow him to canter for a circuit or two, come back to the walk, and give a long period of rest.

If the horse does not react to the demand for the canter on the right lead —and this is seldom—or if he stops reacting before having achieved the change of lead—this is not so rare—the rider should quietly come back to the walk[1] and ask for a canter right by the means used previously, caress the horse, come back to the walk after a few strides and start again.

We should only resort to this procedure if the horse does not react to some extent or at all. For as long as he manifestly shows that he is trying to obey his rider's indications he must be allowed to go on attempting to do so. It is very seldom that his attempts do not succeed if all the conditions indicated above are fulfilled. In any case, it is only if the horse has not succeeded in changing to the right lead and, by the absence of any reaction, gives the impression that he thinks that he has obtained the result sought by the rider, that he should be brought back to the walk and be asked to strike off from the walk to the canter right.

To give his indications of a change, the rider should hold his seat towards the pommel, hold himself with suppleness in a vertical position, and support his weight rather more on the stirrups than on the saddle.

The right heel should be firmly closed on the girth, with a degree of firmness which must depend on the sensitivity of the horse and on the necessity of giving him a clear but completely painless indication.

Touches of the whip on the right hip produce rapid and reliable effects if the horse has been previously worked in hand and can also be used with other horses providing that they do not show excessive fear when this aid is used.

The reins should then be gathered in the passive left hand, very exactly placed between both shoulders, held low and ready to follow the movements of the neck, with the fingers rather more tightly closed on the right rein than on the left.

If the first change of lead has been obtained without too much difficulty, as is usually the case, and after continuing at the canter for rather less than a half circle, two or three consecutive demands can be made during this first lesson, each one separated from the other by a long period of rest, so that the horse can be confirmed in his understanding of the meaning of these demands,

1. To come back to the walk, the rider, although using both reins, should close the fingers more firmly on the right rein. It is on this rein that he will obtain yielding as soon as the walk is established and he should start cantering as soon as he has obtained yielding.

while no unfair advantage is taken of his co-operativeness; further lessons devoted to perfecting the exercise can be postponed.

If, on the contrary, this first change has presented prolonged difficulty, the rider should remain content with only one transition from canter to canter, then immediately dismount and send the horse back to the stable.

This rarely happens, and is nearly always due to insufficient preparation either of the transition to the canter or, and more often, of the transition *from* the canter to the walk, which will have to be practised again patiently and carefully before starting the work of the changes of lead all over again.

Once the changes from the outside to the inside lead can be executed neatly and easily on a circle, at a selected place, the rider should change this spot, until the horse changes equally well at any point of the circle.

He then leaves the circle and takes the track, asking for the first changes from the outside to the inside lead, and taking advantage at first of well rounded turns in the corners of the riding school.

Later on, and still on the track, the changes can be demanded from the inside to the outside lead, towards the middle of the long side of the school to start with, then anywhere along its length, but away from the corners.

In this part of the work, the rider's main concern will be the straightness of the horse's position, and preservation of this straightness during the change. The presence of the wall on the side of the new lead facilititates the rider's checking on this straightness, and also helps to prevent the haunches turning out to that side.

When the horse can execute both changes perfectly and easily, on both reins along the track, the same result must be sought on a straight line, away from the wall, further towards the centre of the manege.

Finally, the trainer will begin the work of changing from the inside lead to the outside one on curved lines at the start, on the largest possible arc of a circle which is progressively reduced to a circle of 8 to 10 metres diameter.

It is the degree of perfection of the change from the inside to the outside lead on a circle which gives most exactly the measure of the value of the results obtained in the single changes, this perfection being shown, furthermore, by the maintenance of the straightness of the horse, by his calmness, by the ease, the neatness and the amplitude of the inversion of his canter.

SUCCESSIVE CHANGES OF LEAD

To obtain successive changes without difficulty or disadvantages, the single changes must be equally easy on both leads, and on any lines of a figure. However, even more than their perfection, it is their symmetry that matters and the absolute evenness of their rhythm and length.

It is easy to measure the exact number of strides after which the change can be obtained *without turmoil*—it is the number after which the horse returns *to the walk* neatly, and resolutely, with immediate recovery of his balance and of the regularity of this gait.

On the one hand, therefore, the rider is very exactly informed about the interval he must allow between the alternate changes of lead. On the other hand, the progressive reduction obtained by practice of the number of cantering strides after which the horse returns to the walk provides the rider with the means of directly preparing the execution of repeated changes at close intervals.

Once the horse is perfectly trained to single changes, can come back to the *walk* imperturbably after *five* cantering strides for example, he is ready to change leads after every six strides.

If this first condition is not fulfilled, we may be able to "snatch" the changes at this rhythm, or even at closer intervals, but more often than not, past a certain stage, we subsequently come up against almost insurmountable difficulties.

The rider must, of course, confirm each stage of this work.

Having obtained and carefully confirmed the return to the walk after five cantering strides, he will ask for the first change on the sixth stride, on a circle, from the outside lead to the inside one, then on a straight line, then from the inside to the outside lead etc., with the same patience and calm perseverance as for the first single change demanded from the horse.

Before we proceed with a change on the fifth stride, the horse must first have learnt to come back perfectly to the walk on this stride, but it is equally necessary that the changes on the sixth stride should already have become flawless on circles and straight lines, on both reins.

In this way, we can usually come to the changes after every two strides without too much difficulty.

To proceed then to the change at every stride, "a tempo", it is helpful to break down the progression even more meticulously in the following manner.

Once the horse is perfectly able to execute from the walk *one cantering stride only* and to come back immediately to a regular walk, the rider asks for the canter, on the right lead for example. By reversing his indications at the rhythm of the canter, the rider asks for *two* successive changes. Therefore, the order of the last *three* strides will be: one; right; two: left; three: right. As soon as the horse succeeds in achieving these two reversals approximately correctly, the rider caresses him, returns to the walk, and gives a period of rest. He then repeats the same work but striking off on the other lead.

This exercise in two successive changes should be perfected at length on both leading legs, until complete symmetry is obtained between the strides to the right and to the left.

The rider can then proceed with three successive changes, the four last strides, from a strike off on the right lead, being thus:

One: right; two: left; three: right; four: left.

Once this result is obtained, the horse is virtually doing changes "a tempo". The fourth change of lead, so long as it is not demanded prematurely, is easily obtained, and so are the next ones providing the rider avoids increasing the number of changes before they have become perfectly symmetrical, can be executed with maximum ease and succeeded by returns to the *walk* of the utmost regularity.

Before we can teach the horse the changes "a tempo" on circles, we must wait until he can perform at least ten of them on straight lines with complete ease. We should still, of course, start with very slight curves, enclosed, as far as possible, by the walls, or by fences.

If the ease necessary for the performance of the change of lead prohibits any loading of the hind-quarters, a horizontal balance of the horse in changes at close intervals is even more imperiously required.

For some horses, which are heavy in the croup, it may even be necessary to put them on their shoulders to a slight extent once the changes become more closely repeated. It is convenient for this purpose to make use of a slightly uphill slope, so that the horse can assume of his own accord the instinctive corresponding attitude.

This very slight over-loading of the fore-hand, or at least absolute horizontality is almost always essential to the changes "a tempo". The amplitude and gracefulness which they can assume will much depend on this position, but even more on the freedom given to the neck, the smooth oscillations of which give a harmonious rhythm to this sort of "cantering amble", which constitutes the successions of alternative strides on each lead.

Performed with a fixed neck carriage, the changes "a tempo" are always jerky and lose much of their artistic quality.

TWO TRACK WORK AT THE CANTER
TEACHING THE HALF-PASS AT THE CANTER

Teaching the half-pass at the canter necessitates certain precautions, but these are not difficult to take if the pupil is a horse trained to strike off with the direct rein and leg aids, and particularly if he has already received the lesson of the change of lead.[1]

A horse cantering on the right lead that has been taught to change to the left canter by the aids of the left leg and left rein might possibly respond to a demand for a half-pass to the right by changing the lead. However, the action of the left leg to demand the half-pass is not the same as the one which indicates a change of lead. The point of application of the left heel is markedly different, but a "muddle-headed" horse could be confused, and this is a possible cause of confusion which should be and can easily be avoided, if the following procedure is adopted:

The horse, *walking* rather slowly and rhythmically, or if he is inclined to be heavy at the ordinary walk, walking a little collectedly, should be made to half-pass for some time at this pace, along the diagonal of the manege. Then, in the course of one of these half-passes at the walk, the rider asks for a transition to the canter, followed by a few strides of the half-pass at this gait, returns to the walk, and finishes the change of rein with a few strides of the half-pass at the walk.

Gradually, the number of cantering strides is increased, the transition to the canter being preceded by fewer and fewer strides at the walk on two tracks. Finally, the horse is taken at the canter, on the track, to the *same* place where the diagonal change of rein was executed before, and this change of rein is then executed entirely at the canter.

The same "roundabout" procedure, through the walk, should be used to make the horse execute the half-pass in all manege evolutions, particularly on curved lines, with the haunches in or out, up to the tight volte on the haunches,

1. There is some advantage in teaching the change of lead before the half-pass at the canter to horses which have an excessively mobile croup.

a work which is particularly beneficial to collection at the canter and the preparation of the pirouette.

Counter-changes on two tracks at the canter can be performed without difficulty once the horse is perfectly able to change the lead on straight lines. They are especially easy when the horse can change lead with the sole aid of the direct leg, and can do the half-pass with the sole aid of the indirect rein. However, it is essential that the number of two-track strides to either side be, at least, equal to the number of strides the horse has to make between changes of lead on straight lines.

PIROUETTES AT THE CANTER

The Pirouette at the canter can be directly obtained from the volte with the haunches in, by gradually reducing the radius of the volte.

But, as always, considerable difficulties are avoided if we start by working on certain preparatory movements which are easier to execute.

We must begin by gradually increasing the obliquity of the half-pass on straight lines. To this purpose, it is convenient to resort to the change of rein on the diagonal, at first leaving the track as usual immediately after the second corner of the short side and progressively further and further away (from the corner), on the long side. We should be careful to keep the horse exactly parallel to the long wall all the way and to pay great attention to the manner in which we leave the opposite track, always impeccably, always exactly at the same place, and always immediately with a return to the walk, and a rest. Gradually, we will manage to strike off closer and closer to the second corner of the long side, until we can half-pass, with the haunches in along the short side, so that the horse is parallel to the long side, i.e. half-passing at an angle of 90 degrees.

We will usually find out in this work that the lateral mobility of the shoulders is, and remains, greater than that of the haunches. We can remedy this by frequently executing the exercises of the *haunches out* on the circle, while still resorting to striking off to the canter from the walk.

Not all horses succeed in reaching an angle of 90 degrees in the half-pass, or at least in executing it with ease, and yet we can still get them to perform correct Pirouettes as long as they can very nearly achieve this inclination.

The Pirouette also should be started at the walk, and should be executed impeccably at this gait, as regards regularity, rhythm and particularly perfection of the Mise en Main. Once these are obtained, the rider asks for one or two cantering strides, comes back to the walk and continues the Pirouette, while re-establishing lightness and calm. The number of cantering strides is gradually increased, very progressively, never more than one or two extra ones in each lesson, until a complete Pirouette can be executed, always striking off from the walk. Finally, we can ask for a transition to the canter at the beginning of the Pirouette.

However, the execution of the Pirouette from the canter on straight lines also requires to be achieved in progressive stages, because the necessity of considerably reducing the pace at the moment of execution of the Pirouette risks disturbing the gait, and especially depriving it of its liveliness which should, on the contrary, remain particularly vibrant. In fact, the gait is frequently transformed into the "terre-a-terre".

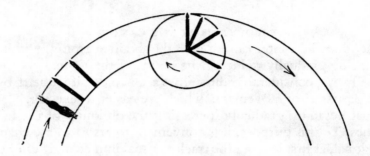

To reduce this difficulty, we must resort to the intermediary of the canter on two tracks, with a progressively increased degree of obliquity. The horse, proceeding with the haunches-in on a sufficiently wide circle to allow him to be constantly directed along a radius of this circle is asked to execute two or three strides of a Pirouette, to return to the walk while continuing the Pirouette, and once lightness is re-established at the end of the Pirouette, to half-pass on the circle once more with the haunches in. Gradually, the number of Pirouette strides is increased, until it can be executed entirely at the canter.

Finally, once this result is completely obtained on both reins, the following progression helps to avoid all disorder in achieving a Pirouette from the canter on straight lines.

In the example of a Pirouette to the right, the rider demands the execution of several Pirouettes from the walk in the first corner (A) of a short side (sketch p. 207)—always the same one.

He then drives the horse on, on the left rein and the right lead, turns as straight across the school as possible (at 1, towards the centre of the manege) and, as he gets to the wall puts the horse into a two-track canter to the right, head to the wall. As he reaches the corner, where the horse has just previously executed a few Pirouettes from the walk, he makes him execute two or three strides of the Pirouette, which he finishes at the walk. Gradually, the Pirouette

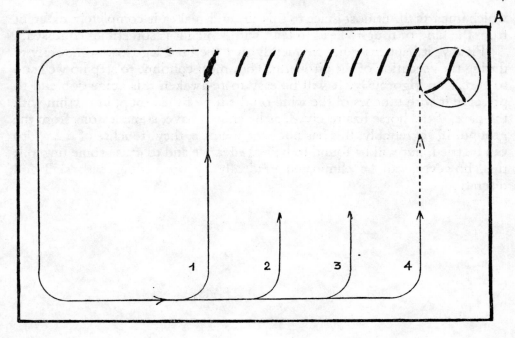

can be executed completely at the canter, and be followed with a period at the walk, a rest, and caresses.

The rider turns across the school closer and closer to the short side, at 2, 3, 4, thus reducing the length of the two track progression, head to the wall, which precedes the Pirouette. Finally, by turning across at six or seven meters (two lengths) from the short side, he arrives in the corner at exactly the right spot for the Pirouette, which the horse, placed in the corner, performs easily, without any previous strides head-to-the-wall.

A horse that has been trained from the beginning according to the progression outlined will always have a tendency, in the Pirouette, to advance too much. In order to curb this tendency to a suitable measure, it is necessary to come back to the walk frequently and to re-establish the Mise en Main as soon as the horse increases the tension on the reins; however, we must avoid destroying this tendency completely and making the horse dull, as he must remain vigorous and active in his Pirouette. At any moment, after a stride of the Pirouette, it should be possible to drive him forward and straight ahead in a lively manner, and to re-assume any extended gait quickly.

It is thus, by judiciously alternating transitions to the canter on straight lines and transitions to the walk while continuing the Pirouette, that the rider will be able to bring his horse to the state of moral and physical poise which imparts the utmost grace to this air, and makes it completely different from the kind of rough "head to tail" with which it is sometimes confused.

Finally, it happens quite frequently that the hind legs lose some activity during the execution of the pirouette. They must continue to step up well and to thrust up vigorously. It will be easy to re-awaken this animation and to preserve it with touches of the whip on the top of the croup, in rhythm with the pace, if the horse has received, as he should have, some lessons from the ground. If, regrettably, this has not been the case, they (touches of the whip) can be tried, but will be found to be less effective and to cause some turmoil; this, however, can be eliminated gradually by proceeding with skill and discretion.

Appendix[1]

UNMOUNTED
PREPARATION FOR
ACADEMIC DRESSAGE

Preparation of the horse from the ground is not an essential part of schooling. In some forms, it is even of very little use. Such, for example, is the work between the pillars, despite the fact that it was resorted to by most of the riding masters of the old school.

This is because the aims they pursued in the schooling of their horses were not quite the same as ours. They tried to obtain an attitude of their horses in which the haunches were constantly much more lowered than in the attitude which is suitable for modern international tests in which, on the contrary, the horse should be able to modify his balance, sometimes even to a horizontal position, as is required for example for the execution of closely repeated changes of lead at the canter.

There is little point, therefore, in detailing here the complete progression of work between pillars which is still used in France, in military schools, for the schooling of leapers. However, because of their persistent use, it might be of benefit to indicate how this can be modified if perfection of the piaffer is its only purpose. A few pages further on have been devoted to this work.

The same remarks apply to the work in long reins, which is however held in much esteem at the Vienna School. Its real utility for dressage work is small, and there would be little point in discussing it here, were it not that it provides an accessory and convenient way of overcoming certain difficulties

---

1. The General has dealt with this additional part of dressage with such precision and minutiae that it constitutes a handbook on its own. Although a few modern authors have described work on the lunge and in long reins (2), and in any case only very briefly and mainly with a view to training horses to jump, none of them since Faverot de Kerbrech and La Gueriniere has mentioned at sufficient length work in hand and work between the pillars (Note: 2nd Edition.)

encountered in the work between the pillars. It is solely for this reason that its use is detailed in this book.[1]

On the contrary, the work in hand with the long switch or with the lunging whip is so effective, and its drawbacks are so small compared with its benefits that we cannot recommend it too highly to all trainers. They will gain a twofold advantage from it: firstly, by educating their horses, and secondly, by developing their own feeling and their own skill. This work from the ground will provide them with points and means of observation for which no substitutes exist, even in a manege equipped with the best system of mirrors.

The principal object of this third part of the present work is therefore the preparation of the horse in hand. It can be practised immediately, without previous preparation by lunging, but if it is grafted on to the latter properly executed, it can be developed with greater facility.

For this reason, this particular manner of working on the lunge and utilising this work, forms the first chapter of these appendices.

[1]. An excellent booklet has been written in English by Mr. Schmit-Jensen, which was greatly esteemed by General Decarpentry: "Schooling of the horse in long reins". (Note: 2nd Edition.)

Appendix I · WORK ON THE LUNGE

Books of Reference:
EARL OF PEMBROKE MILITARY EQUITATION
GENERAL DESCOINS PROGRESSION DE DRESSAGE

In France, work on the lunge is hardly practised, except in the breaking in of the riding horse, and to exercise him when he cannot be ridden.[1]

The use of the lunge, as it is described hereafter, is a preparation for dressage proper as a sequence to breaking-in, and especially for dressage aimed at academic equitation.

The first purpose of this work is to drive the horse into his reins, up to his bit and to get him to maintain a general attitude which will promote the gymnastic development of the basic gait of dressage, which is the trot.

In the first stage it is intended to tension the horse rather than to supple him, to put him on the bit by means of fixed side reins and of an active, but uniform impulsion sustained by the whip.

In the second stage of this work, the tension must gradually be transformed into a Mise en Main (yielding of the mouth). The fixed side reins are replaced by the *hand* of the trainer, exerting a direct action on the mouth through the intermediary of the lunge, specially fitted for this particular purpose. *Uniformity* of impulsion is replaced by its progressive development to a speed regulated by the whip.

A judicious opposition of the hand to the impulsion demanded by the trainer brings the horse to the "Mise en Main", which is the first stage of "Rassembler" (collection).

When this is how it is conceived, work on the lunge prepares the horse not only for mounted work, but also for work "in hand" with the long switch or the lunging whip, which is of such great value in dressage for academic equitation.

---

1. Schooling for jumping, for which purpose lunging is so useful, is not considered here.

THE LUNGE

The lunge should be round, *slippery* (a very flexible cotton rope, softened by long rubbing with a piece of dry soap is most suitable), light, and of the thickness of one's little finger.[1]

Length: 6 to 7 meters at least.

One end should be finished with an eye to hold a strong snap-hook; the other, with a strap and buckle.

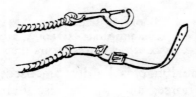

Couplings for lunging the horse from the snaffle rings

THE LUNGING WHIP

The lunging whip should be rather rigid from the butt end down to about the second third of its length, the third part becoming increasingly pliable towards its tip.

It should be light and slender, but the butt end should be *very heavy*, so that the whole of the whip, shaft and lash included, is perfectly balanced by the butt in the trainer's hand.

The lash should be thin, supple, light and finished with a string plait and a tassle.

The total length from butt to tassle should be about four and a half to five meters, so that it can "touch" easily on a circle of a radius of five to six meters.

(The circus whip is much longer, as the regulation diameter of the track is 13·50 meters: the optimum dimension for voltige.)

Ideally, the length of the lash should be about the same as that of the shank.

1. The cord can slip through the fingers and sear them. A convenient compromise is to make up the lunge of two equal lengths of 3·5 or 4 meters respectively: the first part, to which the snap hook is attached, being made of a round cord (nylon is perfectly suitable); the second part, finished with a loop, made of flat braiding, about 2 to 2·5 cm. wide. (Note: 2nd Edition.)

How to Drive the Horse up to the Bit

The basic principle in this stage of the work is to keep the horse constantly enframed between the whip at one end and the reins and the lunge at the other.

It follows that:

(1) The distance between the trainer and the horse should never be greater than one where the first can touch the second with the lash by just stretching out his arm.

(2) The lunge must be taut all the time, and give the trainer a light but steady contact with the horse's head.

(3) The horse's head position must be set by the side reins adjusted to the *limit* of freedom necessary for the head and neck but never enforcing by their tension an attitude other than the natural one which should be shown by a horse trotting calmly, energetically, and well up to his bit.

Preliminary Preparations

(1) Teaching the horse to turn away from his trainer.

(2) Adjusting the side-reins.

(*a*) Leading the horse in hand, from the near side, make him turn right by lifting the left hand towards the head, while we, ourselves, turn to the right.[1]

Repeat this work a great number of times, until the horse moves unhesitatingly to the right upon the slightest indication of the left hand. This work is then repeated, but with the horse turning left and the trainer leading from the off side.

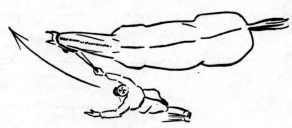

(*b*) Adjust the surcingle, making certain that it cannot move *at all*. The best way is to put it over the saddle, after having allowed the latter to settle as far forward as it would be if the horse were ridden, and having tightened the girth in that position.

Place the surcingle in the deepest part of the saddle and arrange the girth to fit behind and up against the saddle-girth. In this manner, the pommel of

1. As the groom must do when showing the horse in hand.

the saddle above, and its girth underneath, will prevent the surcingle from sliding forward.[1]

If the horse is frightened or violent, he must be accustomed to the surcingle by wearing it in the stable.

Work on the lunge with side-reins which are not completely fixed is always harmful. This is particularly so with side-reins provided with springs which yield when the horse goes into his bit and continue to pull after he himself has yielded.

Ensure that the side reins are of absolutely equal length.

Measure out a length of lunging rein corresponding to the length of the whip (shank, lash and trainer's arm).

Any kind of stable surcingle provided with rings can be used for this work on the lunge,[2] but the pattern illustrated below is convenient to use and prevents many of those small difficulties which we come up against in practice.

SURCINGLE FOR ATTACHMENT OF SIDE REINS

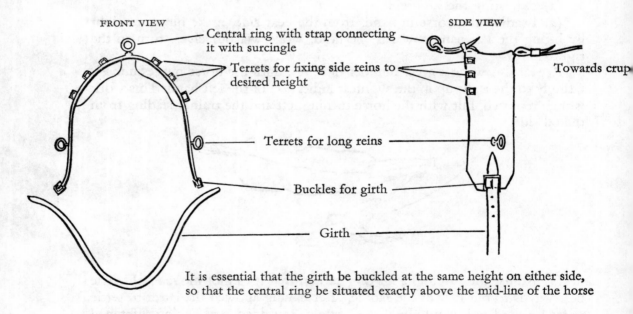

FRONT VIEW   SIDE VIEW

— Central ring with strap connecting it with surcingle

Terrets for fixing side reins to desired height

Towards crupper

Terrets for long reins —

Buckles for girth —

Girth

It is essential that the girth be buckled at the same height on either side, so that the central ring be situated exactly above the mid-line of the horse

1. In the rare cases when this arrangement is not sufficient (to prevent the surcingle from sliding forwards), a crupper would have to be used.
2. The saddle also, at least with horses which are not too excited. We can also buckle the side-reins to the rings of an ordinary hunting breast-plate; however, we then have no possibility of varying the height of the attachment. (Note 2nd Edition.)

PROGRESSION
WORK AT THE WALK ON THE MANEGE TRACK
USE OF THE SIDE REINS

At the ordinary walk, the neck should not be held in a set position; on the contrary, it should oscillate freely, and it is essential to use the walk for a few lessons to avoid the risks of disorderliness which the novelty of this work could cause at a livelier pace.

The side-reins therefore should be fitted at a sufficient length, for some time, to avoid hindering these oscillations of the neck, and they should merely impose upon the horse a very slight constraint, a sort of call to "Attention!".

As soon as the horse understands, at the walk, the meaning of his trainer's indications and starts being worked at the trot, which is the gait suited to the purpose of this work, the side-reins must be adjusted to correspond with the natural position of the horse at this gait, and the walk should be used as little as possible from now on.

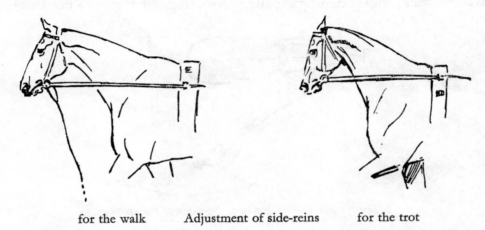

for the walk   Adjustment of side-reins   for the trot

The horse, on the left rein, is halted on the track of the riding school, the bridoon reins hanging loosely and their buckle-end attached to the centre strap at the top of the surcingle; the side-reins are adjusted in a manner that allows as much lengthening of the neck as is needed for an active, rhythmical walk, without slovenliness.

The trainer stands level with, and close to, the horse's left shoulder and fastens the divided end of the lunge to the rings of the bridoon,[1] and then holds the lunge in his right hand, at a distance of approximately 30 centimeters from the horse's mouth.

In the other hand, and with his arm hanging down vertically, the trainer

1. Or the extremity of the lunge to a coupling connecting the rings of the snaffle.

holds the loops of the lunge and also the whip, which is held parallel to the horse's body, its tip level with the hocks and the lash trailing the ground.

The trainer sends the horse on with a click of the tongue, and—only if necessary—a threat or a touch of the whip produced by a rotation of the left wrist. He moves forward with the horse and is careful to avoid any backward pull on the lunge, which the horse himself must stretch just sufficiently to ensure a contact with the mouth.

When, after a few circuits of the track, the horse walks out properly, does not hesitate or hold back, the trainer gradually moves away to the left, allowing his pupil to get ahead of him by letting the lunge, still drawn taut by the horse, slide through his left hand.

If the horse slows down when the trainer moves away, or shows signs of hesitating, the trainer, instead of continuing to move away, should walk in a parallel direction with the horse, at the same speed as the latter, and stimulate him with the voice and whip, though no more than necessary to re-establish an active walk, while carefully avoiding provoking disorderliness but keeping the lunge rein taut.

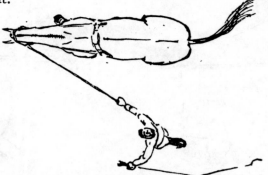

Making the horse walk along the sides of the manege
(preparation for lunging)

If the horse leaves the track and attempts to come towards the centre of the school, the trainer lifts up his left hand, stretching out his arm towards the horse's head.

To give greater authority to this gesture, he can allow the shaft of the whip to protrude obviously from his hand, but he must remain careful not to frighten the horse.[1]

1. If the horse displays an obstinate tendency to move towards the centre of the manege the trainer can shorten the right side rein appreciably, but this expedient should only be resorted to in case of unavoidable necessity and with extreme circumspection; it does not always produce the desired result and then a risk is run of teaching the horse to run out towards the left by refusing to obey the right direct rein. In any case, the reins must be adjusted again to an even length as soon as possible.

If the horse's capers are too lively to be easily contended with or threaten to turn into a resistance, the trainer, to impose greater restraint, can shorten the side-reins *temporarily* by a few holes, but he should lengthen them adequately again as soon as constraint is no longer necessary. Towards all manifestations of high spirits and liveliness occurring in a forward direction, the trainer must remain very tolerant, and he should calm the horse with his voice, and resist with his hand only to a necessary extent, always without brutality and with forbearance.

Finally, the horse must get into the habit of walking straight forward on the track, without showing any tendency to move towards the centre of the riding school, while the trainer walks on a level with his haunches, at a distance of two or three strides, and the lunge remains constantly and evenly stretched by *the horse*.

At the beginning, to halt the horse, the trainer must take advantage of a corner, so that he can move quietly towards the head and demand the halt, by a progressive resistance of the hand, and only when he is in a position from which he can prevent any attempt of the horse to turn off the track during the slowing down and the final halt.

The same work should be repeated in the opposite direction.

The horse should be confirmed methodically and patiently in this work on straight lines, which requires a lot of tact and *much time*.

PROGRESS TOWARDS WORK ON THE CIRCLE
(ON THE LEFT REIN)

It is only when the horse is accustomed to walking perfectly straight forward on the track that the trainer can start teaching him a change of direction towards the left.

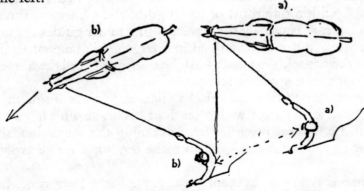

The trainer moves obliquely towards the left and the front from a) to b).
As the lunge comes to be perpendicular to the horse, the latter moves obliquely towards the left. To send the horse back to the track, the trainer lifts up his left hand.

The horse should execute this change of direction solely in response to an indication from his trainer, without relaxing the tension on the lunge, and should go back to the original straight line as soon as the indication ceases to be given.

The trainer's indication is given by a change in the direction of the lunge in relation to the horse, effected as the trainer himself advances towards the left. The more he advances towards the left, the more the lunge becomes perpendicular to the horse, and the sharper the resulting change of direction.

To start with, the trainer should demand no more than a slight oblique, and after a few strides should send the horse back to the straight line by lifting his left hand and slowing down to get back to his place, level with the haunches. The horse must then continue walking parallel with the wall.[1]

Once the horse understands, and performs this work calmly, the trainer alternates left obliques and straightforward walking along the wall, and even right obliques, controlling the direction by his own displacement and progressively limiting the role of his left hand until its movements become unnecessary.

The horse must be trained for some considerable time to execute these alternating changes of direction until he is able to guide himself unhesitatingly from the position of his trainer.

The latter then demands several consecutive left obliques, and shortens the distance on straight lines between them, while increasing the degree of obliquity in the changes of direction, so that finally the horse manages to turn across the school, from one track to the opposite one, in a series of consecutive left obliques.

This turning across the school must now be executed at one end of the riding school, within one third of its length if the manege is three times as long as it is wide, as is usually the case, and the trainer guides the horse along a roughly regular polygon, inscribed in a large circle tangent to the nearest short side of the school. This work must be continued until the horse gradually adjusts his track to the wide circle.

The trainer himself then describes a concentric circle inside the first one. He must remain all the time within reach of his horse with his whip, so that he can keep the lunge taut either by quickening the impulsion, should this diminish, or by using his left hand to make the horse move away from the centre.

The horse should not be kept on a circle for a long time, but should instead be straightened on the track of the long side, made to walk straight

1. If the horse displays a tendency to turn left too willingly the trainer must prolong his gesture with the left hand until the horse returns to the track by obliquing to the right.

Getting the horse to move on a circle is a series of oblique lines, at one
end of the manege. The circle, of irregular outline in the early stages, is
circumscribed on three sides[1]

forward again, be put on to a second circle which he should describe once or
twice, be straightened, and so on, in order to promote and to foster his
constant tendency to leave the circle at a tangent and, therefore, to stretch
the lunge all the time.

All these preceding lessons are given at the walk solely to ensure calmness
in the work at the trot.

The ordinary walk with its normal oscillations of the neck is not suitable
for this task of fixing the neck which is the purpose of work on the lunge in
side-reins.

It is only at a collected walk that the neck can be set in approximately the
position it has at the trot. To try to obtain collection directly at the walk
entails many serious drawbacks and usually leads to destroying the regularity
of this gait.

It is only when the horse is perfectly confirmed in a slow and shortened
trot that we can slow this down more to get the horse to execute a few strides
at the collected, or School, walk.

However, this is not the purpose of this work, but is in the nature of a
test to prove the results obtained at the trot.

WORK AT THE TROT

When the horse executes these changes of direction easily from curved lines
to straight ones, and from straight lines to curved ones, the trainer should
start working him at the trot.

This work is useful only if the side-reins are perfectly adjusted, i.e. if their
length corresponds exactly to the neck carriage fitting to a properly cadenced trot.

1. Work on the right rein. The acting part of the lunge must now be passed from the
trainer's *left* hand into his *right* hand, and the whip from the right hand to the left. Hence-
forth, this will be the normal way of holding these instruments. (Note: 2nd Edition.)

If the side-reins are too long, the jolting which they communicate to the bit and their flapping on the neck will provoke movements of the latter and also of the head.

If they are too short, they will cause the horse to seek some way of avoiding restraint. He will soon discover that because of the fixed fastening of the surcingle, his efforts to free himself from the pressure of the bit by pushing against it are useless, and he will employ one or several of the many ways suggested to him by his instinct to achieve his purpose.

If his tongue is too thick to allow him to flatten it at the bottom of its channel, thereby releasing it from the painful pressure of the bit, he will pass it over the latter; or he will try to separate the jaws, and he will then permanently "yawn". If the nose-band prevents him from doing this, he will fight it also and attempt to get rid of it by shaking his head. Then, again, he may seek relief by altering his neck carriage, either by caving it in, or over-bending it. The loin which has not yet been suppled, will not be able to endure the resulting constraint, which spreads through each vertebra from the neck down.

If the base of the neck collapses, the loin loses some of its upward and downward flexibility, and remains somewhat arched. If the horse over-bends his neck when the head is drawn back towards the body, the flexibility of the loin diminishes in the opposite direction, and it remains somewhat hollow. In both cases the hind-quarters will lose some of their suppleness.

The correct adjustment of the side-reins, therefore, necessitates careful and unremitting attention and can only be achieved by trial and error.

To start with, the trainer must have a picture in his eye of his pupil trotting at complete liberty, at a settled, calm, but animated pace, and on the basis of this preliminary observation he should make a first tentative adjustment. Thereafter, depending on the energy shown in the gait, and on the attitude of his pupil, and on the possible appearance of attempts to fight the restraint of the reins, he alters their adjustment until the horse "composes himself" without stiffness, and preserves willingly and without loss of impulsion, a position of the head and neck which ensures, through the tension of the reins, a light and constant contact between surcingle and mouth, with no backward pull of the one on the other.

Both reins must be equally taut, and a lateral bend should not be sought at this stage of the work, the purpose of which is not to flex the horse on the curved line of his circle, but rather to obtain straightness of his longitudinal axis, and symmetry of tension in his muscular system.

It follows that a horse moving on a circle and reined in equally on both sides can only turn by executing a succession of tangential lines, and this should not worry us.

This is, in fact, the procedure used by the horse at liberty in all turns of a wide radius and is therefore the one suited to the normal service expected of him.

The only requirements are that the circles imposed upon the horse by his trainer should not be too small (a radius of 4 to 5 metres approximately) and that the straight lines in between the circles should be of about the same length as the curved ones.

As soon as the horse settles nicely to the trot (on the left rein) the trainer changes his way of holding the lunge and the whip, and takes the first in his left hand and the second in his right hand, letting the butt end of the whip protrude behind his little finger. He should hold the tip of the whip very close to the ground, directed towards the horse's middle, and he should avoid touching the hind-quarters with it, to prevent any turning out of these towards the right. The whip should be used in an upward direction, in the direction of the girth or even of the *horse's shoulder* if the horse shows the slightest tendency to slacken the lunge.

The work aimed at driving up to the bit at the trot can be performed in a large riding school but can be practised with better results on a larger arena, as this helps to regulate the horse's course according to the necessities of schooling rather than to the proximity of the walls.

The course can then be varied, and the trainer can demand straight lines or circles depending upon necessity and opportuneness.

The walk should not be used in these lessons, except to slow down smoothly from the trot to the halt. Relaxation should therefore only be granted at the halt, and the side-reins must *be released immediately* the halt is achieved.

The work should only last for as long as the horse is able to preserve his attitude without showing signs of fatigue. As soon as he tries to alter the

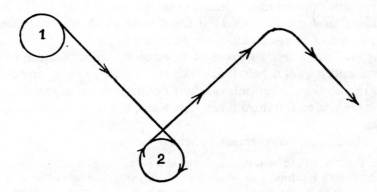

position of his neck, either by lowering it, or tossing it up and down, we should stop and grant a few minutes of rest. Gradually, these symptoms of fatigue will become fewer and farther between, and progressive training will secure a permanently correct position.

The horse, in the end, should easily be able to tolerate two or three periods of five minutes at least per lesson.

WORK WITH THE LUNGE ATTACHED TO THE BIT

When the horse goes into his bit, and can remain full of impulsion without losing the steadiness of his attitude at the trot for periods of from five to ten minutes it is time to substitute for the passive effect of reins attached to the surcingle, the active effect of the lunge enframing the neck and controllable at all times by the hand of the trainer.

Thus the work of the Mise en Main gradually continues the work of driving the horse to the bit.

It would have been possible to start this seeking of the "Mise en Main" from the beginning of work on the lunge, and to have dispensed with the work of getting the horse to stretch out to the bit by using the fixed side reins. However, in this case, some degree of overall muscular slackness would have been present instead of the essential "elasticity" required by a proper "Mise en Main", which demands the *firmness* which we tried to obtain in the first part of the work (on fixed side reins).

The duration of the first part of the work must therefore depend on the state of muscular tone of the horse. A colt should be exercised for some considerable period of time. For a made horse, properly confirmed by work out of doors, this first part can be shortened, but remains indispensable nevertheless as a verification of the horse's condition and a preparation for the second part.

To the resistance of the surcingle, which is fixed and unmoving, the trainer must not oppose more than a constantly equal degree of impulsion, corresponding to a certain speed. In the system of direct attachment of the lunge to the bit, a flexible resistance is possible, and the trainer is able to increase at will the horse's degree of impulsion, while, on the other hand, slowing the speed down below the degree corresponding, in the horse at liberty, to the amount of impulsion demanded. This arrangement, therefore, enables the trainer to obtain the Mise en Main, which is the starting point of the Rassembler.

Then again, certain dispositions of the lunge[1] also permit a slight inflexion

---

1. However, these signs can be due to laziness, and occur long before the true "cramp" of fatigue. The trainer's intuition must warn him of this, and a touch of the whip lash in the region of the girth or on the shoulder will then have to check these attempts.

of the neck, which in the *Mise en Main* and only in the Mise en Main causes the horse to incurve the whole of his spine, from one end to the other, and thus to conform to the curved line of his circle.

For the subsequent purposes of schooling, the lessons will have to be modified in this second part of the work on the lunge.

The horse being inflexed on the curve of his circle will become more and more supple, and the lateral elasticity of his loin will develop while its elasticity in a vertical direction from back to front improves as a result of the inflexion produced by the thrust of the hind-quarters.

Any attempt at obtaining this inflexion without obtaining first a Mise en Main entails the risk of provoking lateral resistance in the neck which spreads to all the other parts of the spine, causing the haunches to come off the circle, and thus teaching the horse to swing the hind-quarters out in all his turns.

The suppleness of the loin from front to back, in the vertical plane of the spine, is closely linked to its lateral suppleness, and conversely. Any progress made by the one immediately reacts on the other.

However, lateral suppleness is usually less than vertical suppleness, because the horse rarely makes use of it, and then only to execute infrequent movements, such as turning round in his stall—while on the other hand, in a vertical direction, his loin is active at all paces and especially at the walk and at the canter.

At the beginning of the work, it is to the development of lateral suppleness that we must devote special attention as it is this which will help us to improve the flexibility of the loin without difficulty.

It will be therefore by combining variations of the bends with variations in impulsion and in the opposition of the hand, that the trainer will be able to bring his horse on, little by little, towards a more elastic, more elevated, more collected form of the gait, which finally assumes the form of the "school trot".[1]

Finally, if we want to prepare the horse for work in hand, we must continue slowing down this permanently active trot to a pace which allows us to accompany the horse on a straight line whilst remaining ourselves at a good walk, without being obliged to run.

The lateral suppleness of the horse is never naturally equal on both sides, and we should consequently avoid exercising both sides equally. The inflexion of the naturally convex side should be pursued with tenacity, and the horse must be worked on the corresponding rein until equal suppleness of both sides is achieved as completely as possible. It follows that a horse

1. And even, in the case of horses with good aptitudes, the form of the "soft passage", as the old masters called it.

being worked on the rein corresponding to his convex side should not be directed as frequently onto a straight course, and not held to it for long, in order to avoid increasing his natural tendencies to a certain incurvation.

On the other hand, straightening him is especially useful on the rein corresponding to his concave side. Frequency and prolongation of straight lines are favourable to contending with this "congenital or acquired warping" of the horse, as long however as he does not escape incurvation towards his trainer's side by throwing out his haunches.

Therefore, the trainer, although he must watch the general attitude of his pupil, must be particularly vigilant as regards *the position of the haunches*.

As soon as the latter show the slightest tendency to turn out, the horse must be driven vigorously forward on a large circle by a touch of the whip just behind the shoulder and impulsion must be re-established and allowed to develop freely before the hand progressively opposes again.

Different dispositions of the lunge will allow the trainer to vary this work and to adapt it to the special kind of suppling exercise he wants to practice.

No. I arrangement, in which the opposition of the hand acts upon the horse mostly in a backward direction, with the least lateral effect, is suitable to direct pursuit of collection through the Mise en Main. In this manner of use, the horse can be driven onto the bit and made to bring his whole body towards it by the effect of the impulsion produced by his trainer, and his loin is thus rendered more supple from back to front in the Rassembler.

In No. II arrangement, there is greater lateral opposition of the trainer's hands. This is therefore better suited to produce and to increase the lateral inflexion and the lateral suppleness of the spine.

No. III arrangement becomes especially useful when the horse starts to bend easily on the circle, as it permits control of incurvation and opposes an excessive one. The lunge then acts principally as an indirect rein by pressing against the outside of the neck and thereby preventing the horse from throwing out his shoulders by exaggeratedly turning his head towards the centre.

In the case of many horses, arrangement No. III soon becomes the most useful one, and gives the best result (in any case on the rein corresponding to the horse's naturally concave bend).

However, we should also note the fact that on all straight lines tangential to the successive circles, the horse cannot be held straight when the rein is adjusted as in No. II. On all these straight lines, his attitude will be more or less pronouncedly that of the shoulder-in. Even with arrangements Nos. I and III, he cannot be made to go absolutely straight, although his bend will be less pronounced.

ARRANGEMENT OF THE LUNGE
Working on the left rein

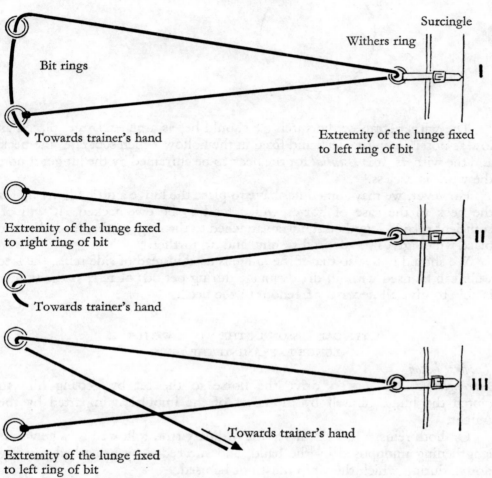

I. View from above of the arrangement of the lunge, horse circling anti-clockwise.—The lunge runs from the trainer's hand through the left bit ring, behind the chin groove and through the right bit ring; from there, along the right side of the neck, through the withers ring, along the left side of the neck to the left ring of the bit, to which it is buckled.

II. The lunge runs from the trainer's hand to the left bit ring, through this and along the left side of the neck; through the withers ring, along the right side of the neck to the bit ring, to which it is buckled.

The lunge runs behind the chin groove to the right bit ring, through this and along the right side of the neck; through the ring at the withers, then along the left side of the neck and is buckled to the left bit ring.

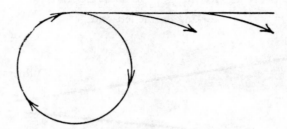

The wither strap of the surcingle should be, as a general rule, placed as low as possible on the neck and fixed in the hollow which separates the neck and the withers. It is *essential* for the neck to be enframed by the lunge; if not, the work is useless.[1]

However, we may sometimes have to place the lunge a little higher up on the neck in the case of horses which tend to be ewe-necked. It will be sufficient then to lengthen the strap attached to the ring, so that it reaches the place which gives the desired results, and no further.

We should note also that if the lunge is used instead of side reins, the free walk can be used without disadvantage during periods of rest, as the trainer is able to give all necessary freedom to the neck.

A TYPICAL LESSON IN THE WORK WITH THE
LUNGE ENFRAMING THE NECK

The first lesson

Arrangement No. I—To drive the horse to the bit by getting him to tauten the lunge himself by the effect of the impulsion imparted by the trainer.

On both reins, a few circuits at the ordinary trot, followed by a generous lengthening unopposed by the hand, and succeeded by a marked slowing down, during which the whip must not be used.

5 minutes on each rein . . . 10 minutes
A period of rest on a slack lunge rein.

The same work is repeated with a few slight oppositions of the hand when the pace is lengthened, and a final lengthening of the stride, with the horse on the bit, the hand allowing complete impulsion but not losing contact with the mouth.

2 to 3 minutes on each rein . . . 5 minutes.

Arrangement No. II—Shortening and increasing the radius of the circle, and

1. Which excludes the use of the cavesson. (Note of the 2nd Edition.)

interspersing straight lines. Spirals at a uniform rate of speed, with strict prevention of slowing down when the radius of the circle is shortened.

2 to 3 minutes on the concave side
7 to 8 minutes on the convex side . . . 10 minutes
Rest—Alter the arrangement of the lunge.

Arrangement No. III—Lengthening of the stride, with the horse on the bit, and a straightening of the course, $2\frac{1}{2}$ minutes on each rein: 5 minutes.

Approximate total: 30 minutes.

In subsequent lessons, changes of speed are combined with alterations of the size of the circle.

Little slowing down when the radius increases.

Watch the impulsion when the radius is decreased.

If the haunches show a tendency to turn out, immediately enlarge the circle and drive on actively.

Always start and finish the work with a few pronounced lengthenings of the stride, but always on a contact, and allowing the impulsion to develop to the greatest extent.

Appendix II · WORK IN HAND

The Italian Riding Masters of the Renaissance[1] have left written descriptions of the preparation and suppling of their horses by unmounted work with the lunge, the long-reins, the pillars, the whip and the long cane. It is very likely that these methods were not new at the time, and that these Riding Masters had been taught them by their own masters who were themselves heirs to a long tradition.[2]

Pupils of the Grisone, Pignatelli, Fiaschi, etc., who went to teach riding in all parts of Europe introduced the use of these methods which in the course of time were to be modified to suit the evolution of equestrian art and the resulting transformation of the type of saddle-horse bred to satisfy the different requirements of various times.

The lunge, with the whip, and with or without the cavesson is still in use almost everywhere. The German School usually lunges the horse in side-reins. In France, although side-reins[3] are described and advocated by Count d'Aure in his "Cours d'Equitation",[4] they have fallen from favour probably because in this country (in France) the lunge is used mostly to prepare the horse for jumping, where complete freedom of the neck is required.

The pillars, which are still used in Central Europe to cadence the horse, are almost unknown, in France, outside the military schools and even there their use is restricted almost solely to the schooling of the leapers (les "Sauteurs").

The long reins, very frequently used in Italy in the XVIIIth century,

1. And those of the end of the XVIIIth century, especially Mazzuchelli.
2. However, no trace of this can be found in the equestrian literature of the Arabs, who in all other branches of science and art have had considerable influence on the Italian Renaissance.
3. French riding masters of the XVIIth and XVIIIth centuries do not mention side reins, and Aubert, as well as Lancosme-Breves state that side reins were imported from Germany at the time of the Restoration by the Emigres. (Aubert, Traite d'Equitation, 1825).
4. Officially adopted by the Minister in 1853, and still prescribed, in the absence of any decision to the contrary.

prescribed in the British Army regulations until quite recently, much in favour at Saumur in 1925, and still in use at the School of Vienna, are nowadays less favoured although they are still utilised by some.

As for *work in hand* with the whip or the schooling cane, this is still used in riding schools on the other side of the Rhine and it is prescribed in the German Army. Apart from its use in the training of the leapers at liberty, it is not well known in France and its practice has more or less fallen in disuse.

Like their predecessors, the two innovators of the French School in the XIXth Century, Count d'Aure and Baucher, both resorted to work in hand.

D'Aure prescribes teaching the horse to range the haunches particularly with the assistance of the wall, the lunge, the schooling cane or the lunge whip.

Baucher, during the greater part of his life, only used work in hand to prepare his flexions of the mouth and the neck. It was only after the accident in which he broke both his legs that he extended this work from the ground, with the whip, to obtain Pirouettes and collection and even the Piaffer.

However, his pupils, and especially his more or less avowed dissidents had anticipated him.

Raabe first, then Gerhardt, developed work with the schooling cane and described it in their books.

Guerin, Montigny,[1] and nearer to us Captain J. B. Dumas attached great importance to work in hand in the progression of their dressage.

The work which we propose to describe here is limited to the obtaining of a cadenced collection progressing on to the Piaffer (without which the School leaps are no more than rather disorderly bounds, devoid of any artistic merit).

ADVANTAGES OF WORK IN HAND

Work in hand is no more indispensable to dressage than work on the lunge, but like the latter presents great advantages as against very few disadvantages.

When it is combined, as it should be, with work on the lunge, this work in hand allows us to bring the horse on to a very advanced stage of readiness for mounted work, as it avoids the effects of 'surprise" which are at the root of most resistances.

In fact, it ensures a continuous transition from primary education to dressage proper.

1. Before he was Riding Master at the School of Saumur, Count de Montigny had been a pupil, then a riding master at the Spanish School of Vienna, where work in hand was—and still is—much practised. Furthermore, subsequently, he attended Baucher's courses.

It is the very important education given by the groom[1] in the stable, and when strapping and walking the horse, which constitutes the foundations of work on the lunge and of work in hand and these two combined with mounted work can bring the horse on step by step to an understanding of the rider's aids, which he thus gains by degrees, as he proceeds all the time from "the known to the unknown".

Furthermore, after the period of breaking in, work in hand allows us to subject the horse to certain lessons which greatly increase in difficulty when he has to carry a rider, as the weight of the latter makes him contract in his back and overburdens his shoulders; work in hand allows him to preserve the free play of his natural movements.

From the point of view of the rider, this work in hand is equally useful. To the means of observation which he disposes of when he is mounted, he can associate his eyes, which otherwise can only be trained on one part of the forehand, and from an almost unchangeable observation point.

During work in hand, the trainer can see the whole of the horse, his attitudes, the disposition of his mass, and the movements of his limbs. After this, he will be able to develop his feel considerably by comparing the impressions of his eyes with those communicated to him by his seat. He learns better to recognise what is happening underneath him, better to judge his horse's action, and better therefore to regulate his own actions.

As against these important advantages of work in hand, the sole possible drawback is that the work is tiring, particularly if the horse is very big and the depth of sawdust in the riding school makes walking difficult.[2]

The work in hand detailed hereafter can be started directly without previous recourse to the work on the lunge described in the preceding

1. In the stable, any horse quickly learns to move sideways to allow his groom to bring him his oats, and to turn about in his stall to go to the drinking trough.

When he is being groomed, he learns to move the quarters around the shoulders when the order "Turn" is given, etc.

To obtain directly from the saddle these movements, essential to schooling, the indications available to the rider are too different from those used by the grooms to enable him to resort to these to help to make his own indications understandable. Work in hand is used as a link between the two.

Similarly, the first lessons in teaching the impulsive effect of the legs are not difficult in the course of work on the lunge once the horse moves forward unhesitatingly at a sign of the whip and a click of the tongue. The restraining action of the reins is taught in the same conditions, the whip and the lunge being used as the interpreters of the legs and the reins.

2. With a little practice, the initial awkwardness soon disappears. Obviously, if we can find rather firmer going, we must take advantage of it, at least for the first trotting lessons. The depth of the surface of military maneges is intended to soften the falls of the recruits, but is nearly always excessive for the freedom of movement of the horse, particularly when the sawdust is saturated by damp in winter.

chapter. This is really an unsatisfactory procedure but we thought that as it has sometimes to be resorted to it was necessary to consider it.

However, in order to avoid the repetitions which would have been needed if both manners of proceeding had been explained separately, the following chapter was written in the conditions set out here:

The *text* of the chapter explains work in hand when it is grafted on to the work on the lunge with all its advantages.

On the other hand, the plates which illustrate the text have been drawn bearing in mind the contingency of having to resort to work in hand directly, without previous recourse to work on the lunge.

The reader may find surprising the wealth and the minutiae of precautions prescribed hereafter in the description of work in hand. He will find them justified by the following considerations:

In the first place, this work in no way constitutes a distinct period of the academic education of the horse, but should, on the contrary, be pursued together with schooling from the saddle, although it probably is an advance on the latter as it prepares the new lessons during the period of time which directly precedes them. It lasts, therefore, as long as the whole course of dressage, and goes on for months if not years. The trainer has therefore at his disposal all the time he requires to confirm every step in the direction of progress. He would be very wrong if he did not take full advantage of this to attain perfection in minor details, as this eventually commands perfection of the final result in any kind of dressage.

Furthermore, experience proves that omission or neglect of these details leads inevitably to blind alleys from which we can extricate ourselves only by retreat and starting all over again from a point which we must first discover. Apart from the waste of time involved (a real one this time), we will have to bear with the necessity of rectifying, which is always more difficult than schooling, as results are always impaired to a certain extent by their corruption in the beginning.

With experience, and with increasing ability gained by sufficiently long practice, the aspiring riding master may be able, later on, to discover certain short cuts depending on the naturally favourable aptitudes of certain horses. However, until this obviously remote time happens, we cannot dissuade him sufficiently from trying them out before he has experimented for a long time with the methodically detailed progression set out here, and before he has been successful in the perfect schooling of several horses—a rare occurrence.

EXECUTION OF DRESSAGE "IN HAND"

Schooling in hand must be practised concurrently with other methods of education of the horse—the lunge and mounted work.

To start with, lessons in hand will be given towards the end of periods of work on the lunge, once the horse is relaxed, calmed and suppled up by the latter.[1]

Later on, this schooling in hand is combined with the education given from the saddle:

Before mounting the horse, which will have been relaxed previously by lunging or by being led in hand if necessary, the rider should spend a few minutes on the ground, rehearsing the exercises which will be the object of the mounted lesson and which have already been taught the horse by work in hand.

At the end of the lesson, when the rider dismounts, he should once again devote a few minutes to the advancement of the horse's schooling by continuing with teaching in hand.

The lessons in hand must always be short: a period of ten minutes following twenty minutes on the lunge; or five to ten minutes before the mounted lesson, or better still at the end of this are sufficient.

PROGRESSION OF WORK IN HAND

Work in hand, similarly to work from the saddle, should never be executed without first ensuring full impulsion.

It is this which constitutes the basis of all the lessons which we give the horse, and

The conquest of impulsion must be

—To start with: the sole preoccupation of the trainer.

—In the course of schooling: his continuous obsession.

The nature and the degree of difficulty of the lessons which can be given, and should be given, to the horse, will depend before anything else on the amount of impulsion that he has acquired.

No suppling or other kind of exercise should be practised before the horse is entirely confirmed in what we can term "elementary" impulsion.

Elementary impulsion can be deemed achieved when:

1. We must make a very clear distinction between the *work* the horse must be given, and the *lessons* which he must receive in view of his schooling.

In the course of *work*, the rider strives to develop the horse's strength by exercise, and limits his demands to the bare minimum necessary to ensure his mount's conservation and his own.

For his *lessons*, the horse already settled by his *work*, must be made attentive, and all causes of distraction and excitement must be avoided; the rider must strive to be *understood*, to obtain gradually and then to perfect obedience to his indications. The horse cannot be held to this constraint for too long. He becomes upset or bored, depending on his temperament. The intuition of the rider must inform him of the time limits within which the horse remains in a "receptive" condition.

(*a*) The horse, at *the halt*, never attempts either to step back, or to lean back ("acculement");[1] during forward movement, never tries to slow down or to stop.

(*b*) At the slightest *indication* of whip or cane or click of the tongue, he unhesitatingly moves forward into a walk—or better still into a trot—"valiantly pulling his cart", and without swerving from a straight course.

(*c*) He goes well up to the bit, and stretches both reins equally.

Once this result is obtained, we can:

(1) Leave the track, by straight lines or circular ones;

(2) Start asking for lateral displacement of haunches or shoulders;

(3) Request *a few* flexions to improve the contact with the bit.

Every one of these lessons begins and finishes with the development of impulsion. At the end of the lessons, our demands can be made more imperious, with the object of educating the horse to produce a more instantaneous and more energetic impulsion, which we can term secondary impulsion.

Secondary impulsion can be defined thus: upon a command from his rider, the horse, from the walk, immediately goes into a perfectly rhythmical trot, without attempting to snatch the reins, but, what is more important, *without losing the contact.*

Once this *secondary* impulsion is secured, and *not before*, we can:

(1) Improve on the practice of the Mise-en-Main by flexions at the walk or at the halt;

(2) Increase the mobility of the haunches and of the shoulders by practising Pirouettes;

(3) Cadence and collect the walk;

(4) Start the rein-back.

The end of each lesson is devoted:

To the execution of continuously smoother transitions to the trot from a walk in the Mise-en-Main; these are repeated until the horse remains in the Mise-en-Main at the trot. The Mise-en-Main at the trot is obtained by the slightest closing of the fingers on the reins, and the stride is gradually shortened by oppositions of the hands but the energy of the gait remains constant.

The transitions to the trot should then be made with a gradual decrease of the number of strides of *the walk* between the halt and *the trot*, until the horse moves straight off *from a standstill to a trot*.

---

1. "Acculement": the body moves backwards, while the limbs remain in the same place. (The translator cannot find an exact English equivalent for this word.)

Superior impulsion is characterised by this immediate transition from the halt to the trot.

The study of the Piaffer can then be started without detriment[1] after the Mise-en-Main at the halt has been developed to the stage of complete collection (Rassembler).

1. It is possible to obtain the Piaffer without following the progression which has just been detailed, and even by neglecting it completely. The quickest way of bringing the horse to the Piaffer, after a fashion, is to hold him in place with the hand, while attacking him with the cane on the top of the croup, or alternately on either hip, or even behind the fold of the buttocks. In a short time the horse will begin to hop with the hind legs, then in diagonal opposites, in a more or less regular manner.

However, even if allowing the horse to move forward a little, even holding his head up, the movements of the fore limbs remain restricted and will always lack elevation in the Piaffer obtained in this manner. The croup *remains high*, and the transition from the Piaffer to the Passage can never be good—if it is at all possible—because the disposition of the horse's body obliges him to affect it by "falling" forward, instead of "springing upward".

We can avoid to a certain extent this preponderance of the hindquarters and the consequently faulty balance by using the lunging whip instead of the switch, in order to animate the horse generally rather than his hindquarters only. However, with an unprepared horse the whip used to this purpose often provokes resistances which even when they are destroyed impart an air of ill humour to the horse. His tail and his ears will reveal it, despite his obedience. The horse does not enjoy his "air", ("Ne se plait pas dans son air," as the old masters used to say.)

Pillars, if used by a trainer thoroughly conversant with their proper use—in particular by one who knows how to adjust their length and the height of their attachment to the pillars, according to the size of the horse and the normal position of his neck—nearly always help to obtain a regular, if not brilliant Piaffer. They have the capital disadvantage of forming a permanent and unsurmountable obstacle to forward movement. The piaffer obtained between the pillars becomes an air outside, and separate from, the rest of dressage, difficult to link to it, especially for the smooth and easy transitions between the Passage and the Piaffer, and the Piaffer and the Passage.

Finally, it is quite possible to obtain the Piaffer directly from the saddle, if the rider is very able. To avoid setbacks, the best solution is to conduct mounted dressage and dressage in hand in parallel, and to profit when mounted from the results achieved with greater facility from work in hand, while following a similar progression in both these modes of dressage.

This is the manner which will offer the greater chances of obtaining a Piaffer which will, at least, be correct. And the *Piaffer*, together with the change at every stride at the canter, constitutes the Riding Master's Diploma (General L'Hotte).

ELEMENTARY IMPULSION
(The work in hand "grafted" on to the work on the lunge)

Preliminary conditions

The horse, previously accustomed to being lunged in side-reins with a light contact, from the halt should smoothly and obediently walk on, trot on, directly or through the walk, continue at an easy and regular trot on a circle of a diameter of 7 to 8 metres, slow down from the trot to the walk and to the halt, and stand calm and relaxed.

Preparation (left rein)

At the end of a good lesson on the lunge, the trainer hands the lunge and the whip over to an assistant (whose role is explained further on). He moves up to the horse's shoulder, and strokes the neck, the flank and the croup, first on the left side then on the right, by passing his right arm over the horse.

Upon a command from the trainer, the assistant gets the horse to walk on, while the trainer walks with the horse and continues stroking him in the same manner, while remaining close to the near shoulder. Then, when calm and confidence are established, the assistant halts the horse at the command of the trainer, who lightly leaning with the top of his body against the horse, places his right fore-arm on the saddle, the elbow pointing towards the centre of the latter, the right hand, fingernails turned up, held in the depression of the neck in front of the withers,[1] the bridoon reins crossed in his hand and sufficiently stretched to give a light contact with the horse's mouth.[2]

Transitions to the walk, walking on the circle, and halts are repeated and are effected solely on the *assistant's indications* given to the *command of the trainer*.

1. By trial and error, find out the place where the hand remains steady between the neck and the withers, so that the reins are equally stretched on both sides of the neck, and a little shorter than the side reins (which must be long).

An upward flexing of the wrist should permit a little increased tension of the reins, a flexing of the right wrist tensing the right rein by loosening the left one, and conversely. The right arm must remain propped on the saddle "from the shoulder", the elbow properly supported towards the centre of the seat, and the wrist must remain free to act.

We should not start to walk before we have practised for some length of time these various movements of the wrist with the horse at a standstill.

2. Instead of crossing the reins, we can knot them to the desired length, and hold the knot in the hand. This method imparts greater stability to the hand, but allows of less suppleness in the handling of the reins. It is suitable particularly for an impetuous horse, or for one who shows a tendency to take too strong a hold.

SECONDARY IMPULSION

This is characterised by the substitution of the trot for the previously employed walk and is obtained by the methods used to produce elementary impulsion by improving on the results achieved.[1]

Preliminary Conditions

In daily work on the lunge, the horse must first have been taught to move easily on a circle of a diameter progressively reduced to six metres approximately, at a steady and energetic trot, although a shorter one than previously.[2]

In this work at the trot, the trainer may walk backwards only when the horse is perfectly able to move off very calmly from a halt to such a slow trot that the trainer can accompany him without difficulty, to slow down to the walk and to the halt easily and sufficiently frequently to make it possible for the trainer to limit with ease the periods of trotting without jostling the horse. *Repetition of all the previously detailed exercises but without the lunge.*

Precautions

1.—During the first lessons without the lunge, the assistant should still follow the horse, at a distance of 5 to 6 metres, and be prepared to intervene with circumspection, firstly with a click of the tongue and, if necessary, with gestures and threats or flicks of the whip, to obtain or to confirm the forward movement demanded by the trainer.

2.—In the case of violent or nervous horses, or of horses which do not accept willingly the tension of the reins, the side-reins should be kept on for

1. We must again remind the reader that the *natural* position of the neck is not the same at the walk and at the trot. At this gait, the movements of the neck are considerably less— and even nonexistent—than at the walk. The neck becomes steadier and is held in a higher position than at the walk. Therefore the length of the side reins cannot be the same for both gaits. At the beginning of schooling on the lunge, the side reins are adjusted merely to set certain limits to the freedom of movement of the neck, thereby putting only such restraint on the horse as will prevent unruliness. If the reins are suitably adjusted for this period to allow the walk, they will be found to be too long for the trot.

Later on, if we want to *work* the horse effectively at the trot, with the view of "fixing" him between the reins, the side reins must be adjusted to correspond with the horse's attitude at the trot. The reins will then be too short for a free walk, which should be used as little as possible. If the trainer wishes to let the horse relax, either at the halt or at a free walk, he must release the side reins.

This adjustment of the side reins in any case incites the horse to go into a trot, because of the attitude which it enforces. The number of strides between the halt and the trot is reduced, and the horse learns gradually to move from the halt directly to the trot, which is one of the aims sought eventually in dressage when trying to obtain superior impulsion.

2. This result is easily obtained if the closing of the circle is done sufficiently progressively; otherwise, the haunches are turned out, and the trot loses its regularity and rhythm.

some time, but fitted rather more loosely than the bridoon reins held in the trainer's hand and tautened by a horse going confidently into his bit.

Progression

The progression should be the same as in work on the lunge and must be completed ultimately by exercises aimed at getting the horse to take a suitable contact with the hand and at enabling the trainer to guide him in all directions.

(1) *The trainer facing forward (fig. Ib and IIb) On the left rein:*

The horse standing on the track is made to move forward by the trainer as when he was on the lunge, by clicks of the tongue, by the whip or the schooling cane. Walk on, lengthen the walk, slow down, halt.

Some time must be devoted to keeping the horse absolutely straight[1] with a good thrusting, elastic contact with the hand. Occasionally, the trainer takes and yields by flexing the wrist upwards and downwards, slightly elevating his forearm while supporting the elbow firmly on the deepest part of the saddle.

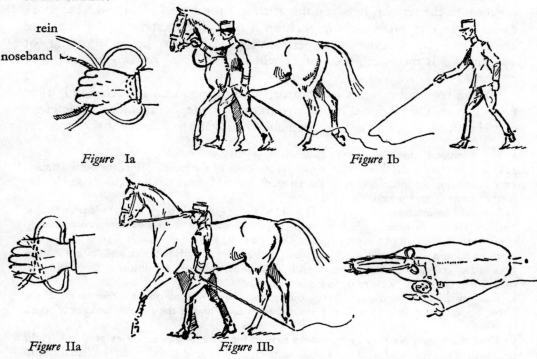

rein

noseband

Figure Ia   *Figure* Ib

Figure IIa   *Figure* IIb

1. At the beginning, it is often useful to have the right rein a little shorter (on the left hand) to prevent the horse from coming off the track and moving towards the centre of the school —as he almost always tries to do.

Good use must be made of the corners to develop the effect of the left rein, and to get the horse accustomed to turn on its indications.[1]

The same work is then repeated on the *right rein*, with the trainer *on the left side of the horse*, on the track, and as close to the wall as possible. The whip or the schooling cane in this instance should be used as little as possible[2] as the haunches must not deviate inwards. Particular attention must be given to *right* turns, effected with the *right* rein.

(2) *The trainer facing to the rear:* (Work on the left rein).

Once the horse's contact with the bit has become trusting and elastic, the trainer should face towards the rear,[3] and repeat all the previous exercises, in the same order.

At the beginning, it is level with the shoulders that he should be most of the time. However, he should get into the habit of being a little ahead of this position, even level with the mouth, so that he can use the cane on the breast, and practise flexions and collection, which is done more easily from this "advanced" position.[4]

For every kind of exercise—and for every different horse—a certain position of the trainer, between the girth and the mouth, will make the work easier and more precise. This position can be discovered only by trial and error, and by frequently experimenting. Whether he is standing or whether he is mounted, the trainer will find *that skill can only be acquired by practice.*[5]

When the trainer faces backwards, holding one rein in each hand, as in fig. VI, it should be noted that a turn to the outside, commanded by an effect of the rein on this side can be particularly difficult to achieve if the pressure

1. Very discreetly, for the reason explained in (1) above.
2. It is better to do this work by using solely the click of the tongue, the cane on the breast, or if necessary, the intervention of the assistant, placed behind the horse, but considerably further away from the wall than the horse.
3. Some riding masters start training in hand without going through the whole programme outlined above, or even neglect it completely. It is difficult for an experienced trainer to obtain satisfactory impulsion in these conditions. The trainer who is less familiar with work in hand must follow the procedure described above with patience and without omission of any stage, from beginning to end, if he wants to avoid an almost certain failure in subsequent dressage, because of *lack of impulsion.*
4. This position of the trainer, facing the horse, allows him to observe the whole of the horse when he stands level with the mouth, and this is one of the real advantages of work in hand.
5. When the trainer is closer to the mouth than to the girth he can easily let go of the right rein with the right hand, and hold both reins crossed behind the chin, in the left hand, in order to get an even tension on both reins. The horse must then be taught for some time to go well into the reins and to obey the indications of the hand, until he is completely accustomed to them.

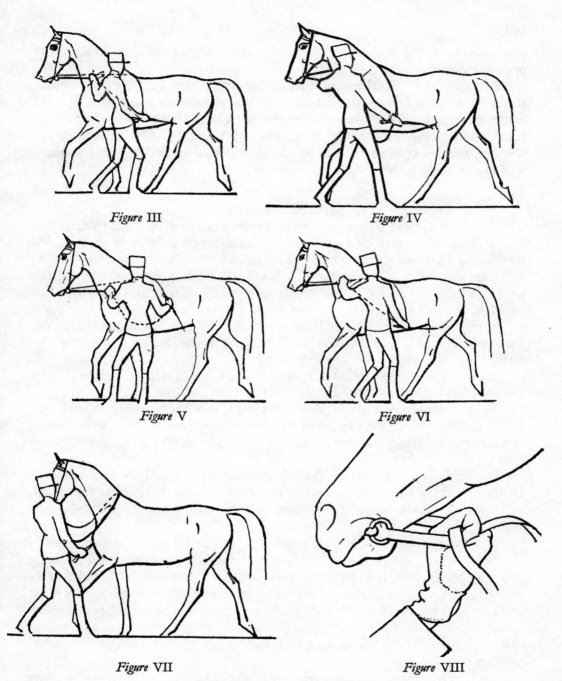

Figure III

Figure IV

Figure V

Figure VI

Figure VII

Figure VIII

Change from the position 'facing to the front',
to the position 'facing to the rear'.

PLATE I

on the neck of this rein, when it is firmly stretched, produces an effect in the opposite direction.

To counteract this effect, the trainer standing on the left side of the horse slides the left hand down the left rein as far as the mouth and with this hand firmly pushes the horse's head towards the right to determine a turn to the right. As the horse becomes better accustomed to being guided in hand in this manner, the intervention of the left hand will be required less and less and will finally cease to be necessary.[1]

SUPERIOR IMPULSION

This is characterised by an immediate transition from the halt to the trot, and is obtained by reducing gradually the number of walking strides needed by the horse at the beginning to move on from the halt to the trot. In practice, this can only be achieved after the horse has been suppled up by all the previous exercises performed with "secondary" impulsion, and once the Mise en Main can be obtained as easily at the trot as at the walk.

In this work the trainer will be working facing backwards most of the time, and should face to the front only when he demands a lengthening of the stride.

In work in hand as well as in mounted work, NOTHING useful can ever be obtained without IMPULSION.

As long as the horse, at a touch of the cane, is not irresistibly urged on by his *obsession* to move forward, and to overtake his trainer, the latter should not aim for anything else than instilling this fixed idea into the horse's mentality.

Until this stage is reached, no other lesson should be given to the horse in this work in hand. We could not devote too much time or too much attention to this fundamental lesson, which must produce the following results:

(1) The *essential*, the *foremost*, effect of a touch of the cane, on any part of the body, must be to make the horse move forward, straight ahead, frankly drawing on the reins held by the trainer. It is only after this result is definitely secured that various effects of the cane can be used, in combination with influences of the hand, to advance the horse's schooling by: changes of speed and of direction on one track (longitudinal mobility); work on two tracks (lateral mobility); the "Rassembler" (producing a special form of the output of impulsion).

(2) Even without any intervention of the cane, the horse should acquire

1. This difficulty is much reduced if the first turns are requested in the corners, as the latter oblige the horse to turn.

the irresistible habit of always trying to move ahead of his trainer, by at least the whole length of his neck. He should have learnt, and should never forget, that it is only when he is in this position, in relation to his trainer, that the impulsive action of the cane ceases to be felt and that he can expect some complete or relative peace.

The lesson of the impulsive effect of the cane must be given not only by touching with it all the parts of the horse's body where it will be applied in subsequent exercises, but also by using it from any kind of situation in relation to the horse, in which the trainer may have found himself during the performance of these exercises.

The trainer should never get someone else to hold the horse, either by the lunge or by the cavesson. This would be an unforgivable abdication.

On the other hand, it is often helpful, at the beginning of schooling, to support the impulsive effect of the trainer's whip or cane with a second whip used by an intelligent, prompt and obedient assistant, *behind* the horse.

Never, in any circumstances, should the horse be allowed to halt or relax in the position, in relation to his trainer, illustrated in fig. 1. Every time he does so—this is unavoidable at the beginning—he should be sharply punished by touches of the cane on the breast and driven forward until he is ahead of the trainer by at least the whole length of his neck.

The horse must automatically, without the intervention of his trainer, move of his own free will beyond the trainer, until the saddle is level with the latter, as in fig. 2.

Halt and rest

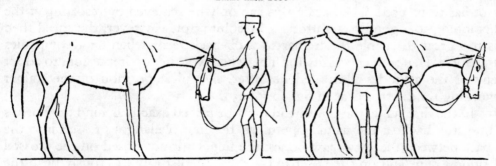

Figure 1. Never do this   *Figure* 2. Always do this

It is only when the horse has definitely acquired this habit that we can start flexions. Then the trainer, facing the horse, arranges the bit to suit the purpose of the flexion he has in mind, fixes his fingers on the reins which he has adjusted accordingly, and displaces his body backwards—(without displacing his hand)—until it is level with the horse's head. He then stops. The horse, by habit, will then try to overtake the trainer, thus going into his reins of his own will, and up to the bit which is fixed: he himself will produce the flexion, in forward movement. As soon as he feels the yielding of the mouth, the trainer opens his fingers, allows the horse to overtake him, and to rest when he has properly done so.

Any flexion produced by a *backward* traction of the reins, however slight, teaches the horse to *come behind the bit*.

The same habit assures continuous impulsion in all work on one track or two tracks, but it is especially in the Piaffer that its benefit can be felt. For as long as the horse is not ahead of his trainer, he should want to get back to his proper place and endeavour to do this spontaneously by advancing. The trainer, moving backwards inch by inch, keeps up the impulsion which must be permanent, automatic and as imperious as an obsession for the horse.

OBEDIENCE TO THE WHIP
(*The trainer faces forward*)

Preliminary observations

Work in hand can only achieve very restricted results when it is practiced at the walk. To obtain more substantial ones, a short, but energetic and cadenced trot has to be used. Then again this can only be achieved by resorting at the beginning to a good straightforward resolute trot. However, the speed then is too great to enable the trainer to walk backwards when he accompanies the horse. Hence the necessity for him, when working on impulsion, to adopt any of the attitudes illustrated hereafter. A typical position of the trainer working on the trot is as in fig. Ib, p. 237.

In the first stage, the right hand must be placed exactly behind the horse's head, the back of the hand uppermost, the first phalanges pressed into the space between the lower jaw bones, the fingers firmly closed on the crossed bridoon reins and on the noseband, so that the fist can vigorously push the head forward (fig. Ia, p. 237).

The trainer must use the whip without excessive gestures, only by turning his left wrist, and must try to find out where to touch the horse to provoke forward movement without tickling him (the best place is usually found between the buttock and the hock).

In the second stage, the right hand holding the reins crossed and adjusted must be firmly pressed in the depression between the wither and the neck, the back of the hand held uppermost, the elbow resting on the horse. (fig. IIb, p. 237).

Impulsion has already been confirmed by previous work (fig. Ia, p. 237), and the trainer now takes position b. The first work is done on the track to use the restraining effect of the wall; gradually the trainer can move away from it and lead the horse on straight lines off the track then on successive obliques to the right and to the left, on serpentines, circles and voltes to both hands. The same work is repeated, with the trainer on the offside.

Main purpose of this work: to get the horse to take a good contact (rather too much than too little). *Accessory purpose:* to teach obedience to the direct rein, acting by a lateral inflexion of the wrist.

At the beginning, the click of the tongue must be used simultaneously with a touch of the whip; at a further stage, the whip is used a fraction of a moment later, but only if the clicking was not sufficient to produce forward movement; finally, clicking of the tongue alone is used, although the whip is held in reserve.

LESSONS OF THE WHIP AND OF THE SWITCH
1st Lesson
THE WHIP

The Trainer faces forward
The trainer holds the whip in his left hand, as in fig. Ib and IIb, p. 237.[1]

At the same time as the assistant, upon the command of the trainer, sends the horse forward by the methods used in work on the lunge, the trainer clicks with his tongue and with his left arm outstretched and a turning out of his left thumb to the left, lightly touches the horse with the whip held parallel to the ground.

The moment forward movement is produced, the trainer moves on with the horse, keeping his hand firmly supported on the base of the neck to avoid involuntary actions of the reins on the mouth.[2]

1. Obviously, all precautions should be taken to avoid frightening the horse with this whip, which the trainer must hold behind his back, with the lash on the ground, as he approaches the horse.
2. If the horse *shoots* forward, do not prevent him from doing so, and attempt to go with him, while calming him with the voice, without increasing the tension on the reins. On the contrary, allow them to slide between the fingers, and firmly grasp the pommel and hang on to it to remain level with the shoulders and avoid being kicked.
   It is only if the unruliness turned into a resistance that the assistant, always and only upon the command of the trainer, would intervene with the lunge and the cavesson, and this only if all seems "lost". Impulsion is too precious a quality to risk destroying.

IInd Lesson
SUBSTITUTION OF THE CANE FOR THE WHIP
(The trainer facing forward)

The Cane Used on the Flanks

Figures IX, a, b, X, a, b. How to hold the cane, the trainer supporting the back of his hand against his back, below the waist, and flexions of his wrist producing various actions of the cane on the flank (touching, pressing, hitting or attacking).

Fig. IXc. The region of the flank where the cane must act (place of the leg); avoid touching further back, as this can provoke tickling.

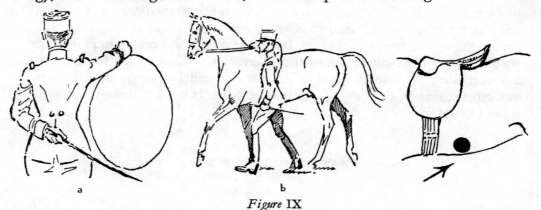

a   b

Figure IX

IIIrd Lesson

The Cane is Used on the Shoulder, then on the Breast

This is an especially important stage, as the aim is to substitute application of the cane to the breast for its application to the flanks. This method of touching on the breast is the only one which does not cause a lateral deviation of the horse from the line of his course away from the side on which the cane is used. It is the only way to increase equally the impulsion of both hind legs and to avoid a predominant activity of one of them. It is also the only way of developing the Piaffer at a later stage and of increasing the elevation of the forelegs in this air.

Baucher in the work in hand started using the cane *on the breast* from the very beginning; however, as we are not Baucher, we almost invariably obtain disappointing results if we try to proceed like him. The least of these would be this: it is relatively easy to induce the horse to move forward until he stands *level with the trainer,* but not any further and the horse makes no attempt to advance *beyond this,* which is essential. We can obtain thus only a small degree of impulsion, a diminished one and a narrowly limited one.

To obtain the halt, the trainer uses the usual command "Whoa", and

Figure Xa

Cane at the point of the shoulder,
right hand as in fig. 1b

Figure Xb

Cane on the shoulder as in fig. 1a

Figure Xc

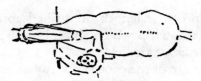

Cane at the chest

PLATE II

tightens his fingers on the reins without displacing the hand, while his assistant simultaneously gives the customary indications used in the work on the lunge.

In repetitions of this lesson, the trainer's commands gradually anticipate the indications of the assistant, and these continue to be given on the order of the trainer and only if necessary, to reinforce the first command.

Once the horse moves on without hesitation at the command of the trainer only—given at first by the combined use of the tongue and the whip, and later on by the one or the other alone—he is allowed to rest, is rewarded by caresses and is sent back to his stable; the lesson is repeated the next day until results are completely established.

The work is repeated with the trainer walking on the outside of the circle, on the off-side, with the left hand holding the reins above the wither.

The work is repeated again, but with the horse on the right rein, and the trainer walking on the offside, and then on the nearside.

N.B.—*The last two paragraphs apply only when the horse has been trained on the lunge before receiving the lessons in hand, and when the latter work has been grafted on to the first.*

Although this lesson, intended to teach the horse to obey the command of the cane applied to the breast, is the most important of all, the other lessons are nevertheless essential as they must teach the horse to develop his forward impulsion regardless of the subsequent particular effect of the cane, depending on the point of its application on various parts of the body.

The cane should never tickle, but should touch, either by being positively "pressed" against the horse, or by tapping more or less severely. The trainer should stand a little further back if he wants to touch the shoulder (near the point), or a little further forward if he wants to touch the breast, and he must hold the cane horizontally, and at a right angle to the horse's body.

Note: The cane should be 1 m 10 to 1 m 20 long, rather rigid, and slightly curved at its tip.

A fragment of a whip of the length prescribed above is quite adequate.

It is the blunt end of the whip which should be used to touch the horse, as the pointed end can prick or tickle.

If the continuous pressure of the cane is not sufficient to awaken a reaction —and this is rare—it should be used in rapid taps.

However, violent blows must be avoided, as the horse's sensitivity is quick to fade and can never be restored afterwards.

If the horse is unduly insensitive, the assistant must intervene with his whip.

IVth Lesson
The Cane used on the Shoulder or on the Flank

We illustrate hereafter the various attitudes and positions of the trainer which can be used to straighten or to maintain straightness in the case of horses which are inclined to avoid the impulsive action of the cane by turning their quarters away from the side where the cane is applied. Illustration p. 287.

Figure XIa   *Figure* XIb

(These positions are equally suitable, in furtherance of work in hand, to ensure a correct execution of the volte with the haunches in, and then of the pirouette on the haunches, which is the foundation of collection.)

Vth Lesson
The Cane used on the Flank, the Shoulder or Breast
The Trainer walks backwards, facing the tail (fig. VII, p. 239)

The trainer very gradually alters his position so that instead of facing forwards he finally walks facing the tail. Little by little he slides his left hand down the rein towards the bit until he can hold both reins close to the snaffle, and adjust them to a contact, just behind the horse's chin. (See fig. VI, p. 239). The right hand slides back on the right rein and maintains a contact on this until the left hand takes over on both reins. The right hand can then let go of the rein, so that it is free to use the cane wherever necessary.

THE PREVIOUS LESSONS ARE REPEATED WITH
THE TRAINER WALKING BACKWARDS

Finally, when all the preceding lessons have been inculcated upon the horse, the trainer repeats them one by one, but he now walks backwards, as shown in fig. IV, V, VI, VII, p. 239.

He holds the left rein in his left hand, the right rein which passes over the neck in his right hand, and adjusts them so that he can keep the neck perfectly straight, in a normal position, and maintain a permanent and light contact with the horse's mouth.

This backward facing position being indispensable for work on two tracks and for the pursuit of collection the trainer must get used to it by frequent practice, so that he can work the horse like this at the walk and at *the trot*.

THE ASSISTANT'S ROLE IN THE CONQUEST OF IMPULSION

At the beginning, *only* the assistant's indications conduct the horse, and they must conform strictly to the orders of the trainer.

As the horse becomes better used to the presence of the latter, more attentive to his indications which he learns to understand and to obey, the assistant's role becomes increasingly limited to only rare interventions, intended to confirm the trainer's indications if the horse were not sufficiently obedient. The assistant must now just hold himself *in reserve* at the disposal of the trainer. His role finishes as soon as the trainer has finally gained the horse's obedience.

SUPPLING EXERCISES EXECUTED WITH ELEMENTARY IMPULSION
At the Walk

1. *Changes of Direction*

The trainer is on the *nearside* of the horse, faces in a forward direction, and walks on the track, *in a clockwise direction*. He uses in succession all the means of obtaining impulsion employed before.

After the second corner of a short side, leave the track by a right oblique (flexion of the right wrist). Straighten the horse, come back to the track by a left oblique (left rein), thus getting the horse to trace a serpentine of shallow loops to start with, becoming progressively more pronounced.

Alternate between the walk on straight lines and on serpentines, until changes of direction can easily be obtained by a mere tightening of the fingers on the corresponding direct rein.

Sustain the impulsion attentively, using the whip or the cane on the breast. The cane should not be used on the flank.

When the horse is able to execute changes of direction easily and especially without loss of speed or of contact, he can be made to walk on a large circle, the trainer walking on the outside of the circle, and the diameter is gradually reduced to approximately 6 metres.

The execution of this work must be very painstaking because it is a preparation for "voltes with the haunches in", which induce a lowering of the haunches and collection.

Work on a circle, with the trainer between the horse and the centre of the circle should be practised also, but with great caution, because when the radius of the circle diminishes, the horse's natural tendency is to throw the haunches out; this puts him on his shoulders and enables him to disobey his trainer, who is not properly placed to overcome this turning out of the haunches which soon becomes a resistance against subsequent orders to the horse to collect himself.

The work is then repeated, with the trainer facing backwards.

Changes of speed

Lengthen the stride—. Slow down—. Halt—. Walk on.

Pay attention to: *resolute* forward transitions and lengthenings of the stride;

—*continuous tension of the reins* in downward transitions and halts;

—*immobility* at the halt with uninterrupted contact for a few moments, until the horse is allowed to rest on loose reins.

All these exercises should be repeated until their execution is flawless regardless of the means employed to produce impulsion and of the position of the trainer, on all courses, in all directions.

II.—*Mobilisation of the Haunches*

Preliminary observations

Mobilisation of the haunches leads on to work on two tracks which, when it is judiciously employed, helps to prepare collection.

However, if it is to be of any use in the preparation of collection, work on two tracks necessitates *activity* of the haunches in their *oblique position,* and the horse almost invariably attempts to avoid the discomfort of this attitude, either by altering the obliquity of his hind-quarters, or by diminishing the energy put out by his hind legs.

The trainer must insist therefore on:

(1) The croup remaining in exactly the position prescribed by the aids, without escaping it by a lack, or an excess of, obliquity;

(2) An undiminished activity of the hind-legs and of the length of their strides.

There is only one remedy for these resistances, be they employed separately or simultaneously, and this is: to drive the horse on, energetically, straight ahead, on a single track.

In practice, with most horses, *useful* two-track work demands *increased* impulsion, to an extent which must vary depending on the natural generosity of each individual.

It is the judicious opposition of the hand to the impulsive effect of the cane on the flank which must cause the haunches to deviate laterally.

When used alone, without an opposition from the hand, the cane must determine forward movement, regardless of where it is used: on the breast, on the shoulder or on the flank.

The purpose of the lessons up to this stage has been to reach this agreement with the horse. It must be enforced every time the horse shows the slightest tendency to disregard it.

Opposition of the shoulders to the haunches, which is effected by the hands, and causes the deviation of the haunches, can only be effective if the neck is sufficiently rigid; its lateral flexibility diminishes with its elevation. This is the reason why the opposition of the rein on the same side as the application of the cane, which produces a deviation of the haunches, must be exerted *upwards,* rather than from front to back, while the other rein, on its own side, limits the bending in the neck to the amount strictly necessary to allow the opposition of the shoulders to the haunches.

Opposition of the hand always has some restraining effect against impulsion. Therefore, it should be limited from the start, to the minimum necessary to produce the deviation of the haunches, and must gradually decrease as the horse becomes better able to step sideways upon a mere indication.

Execution (on the left rein)

The trainer, on the nearside, and facing backwards, by use of the cane on the flank, demands a succession of *energetic* forward transitions and *lengthenings* of the stride, on the track to start with, then within the manege, in all directions, on perfectly straight lines.

He then places the horse with the croup close to a short side of the school, and parallel to the long side, the horse facing towards the other short side, and approximately 4 to 5 metres from the track, and he drives him forward. Once forward movement is confirmed, without the necessity of constant interventions of the cane, the trainer makes an opposition of the left rein and uses the cane, so that the horse moves back to the track with a few sideways steps. Once the track is reached, the horse is allowed to relax, is rewarded by caresses and a rest.

When the horse has acquired the habit of moving forward resolutely the moment he is allowed to straighten himself out, the same work is repeated but from a point situated further down the long side of the school; *before* moving back to the track, he must be straightened and driven forward on a straight line.

Later on, two-track work and work on a single track must be practised alternately all around the riding school until the horse is definitely confirmed in his tendency to move again *as soon* as the opposition of the hand ceases to demand the deviation of the haunches.

In all this work, the obliqueness of the horse in relation to his initial direction should always be slight (25 to 30 degrees) because the *forward*

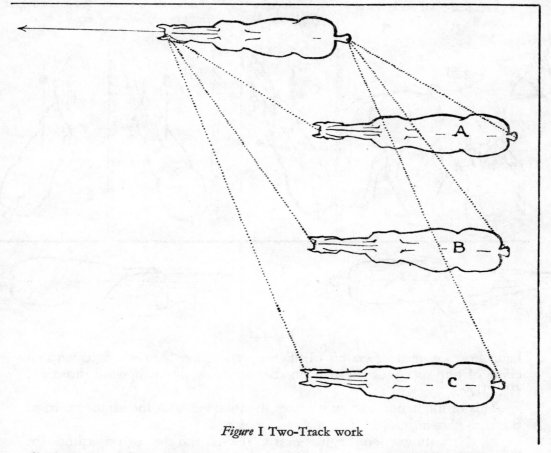

Figure I Two-Track work

displacement of the limbs must always be greater than the *lateral* displacement.

In any case, obliqueness must never exceed the amount ordered by the aids, and any exaggeration must be severely repressed by energetic forward driving.

Two-track work should not be developed more than this before secondary impulsion is completely assured. Once this secondary impulsion is confirmed, the horse can be worked at the shoulder-in and at the haunches-in and the haunches-out.

If the hind-quarters are unwieldy and the conformation of the horse makes it difficult for him to displace his haunches laterally, we must lighten the hind-quarters by allowing a lowering of the neck. (Pl. III, a, p. 253.)

Arrangement b, Pl. III, p. 253 facilitates this lowering.

However, if the horse *resists by fighting* our demand to displace his

Left half-pass, the trainer on the near side   Shoulder-in, (right hand)   Half-pass (Renvers position: right hand)   Half-pass (travers position): right hand

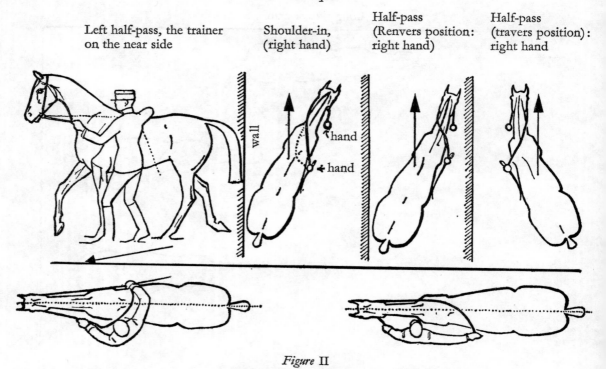

Figure II

haunches, we must *enforce* his obedience by keeping his neck rigid with an effect of opposition of the rein on the same side, in an upward direction. (Pl. III, c.)

This lifting action can be more easily obtained with the arrangement of the reins shown in d, Pl. III.

Pl. III, e, shows a correct half-pass to the left and the correct attitude for horse and trainer.

Two-track position facilitates transitions to the trot for horses who find some difficulties in executing them properly.

III.—*Flexions of the Jaw*
Preliminary observations
These first flexions are aimed solely at obtaining a mobilisation of the tongue without any alteration in the position of the head and neck.

The symptom of the horse's yielding to the flexion requested by the trainer is a movement of the tongue similar to the movement performed in the act of swallowing, which does not resemble the action noticed when the horse is chewing; the mouth must open only *just enough* to permit this movement.

At the very moment when the lips separate and the tongue starts to rise,

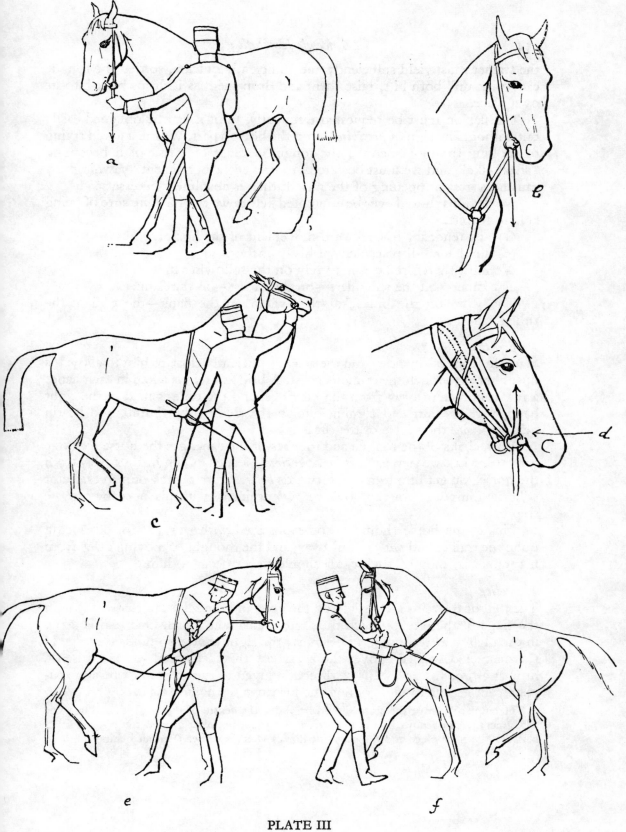

PLATE III

the trainer must yield sufficiently and sufficiently quickly, so that the tongue can "pick up" both bits, raise them and drop them as it drops back into its own place.

The flexion must be requested frequently, until it can be obtained easily but without any sign of *precipitation* on the horse's part. We must avoid trying to prolong the movement of the tongue because of a risk of it becoming "snake-like", and we must be careful to prevent a permanent "yawning" by causing a greater opening of the mouth than is absolutely necessary.

No flexions should ever be attempted before we can be quite sure of being able to forbid:

(1) any tendency to backward movement of the horse;

(2) any lateral displacement of his haunches.

We must therefore be able to rely on the following means:

The cane:—on the shoulders—on the breast—on the flank.

The whip on the buttocks—the switch on the flank—the wall of the riding school.

Preparation

Stand in front of the horse, on the track, sufficiently close to him to allow his nose almost to touch the trainer's chest. A bridoon rein is taken in each hand, a few centimeters away from the bit rings, and the cane is held in the right hand, with its butt end coming out on the side of the thumb, and its tip held opposite the centre of the breast.

With clicks of the tongue and touches of the cane, get the horse to move forward, while we step back *at the same time*. Next, standing further away from the horse, we get him to move forwards *before* we step back ourselves. Later still, we must wait for the horse to *push us* firmly with his nose before we step back.

Finally the horse should become obsessed with this idea of advancing upon the trainer and *pushing* him away, and the thought of moving away from his trainer by moving backwards should never occur to him.

Execution

The join of the reins at C is laid on the poll, and the reins are passed through the rings of the bit, to which they must remain attached. One rein is taken in each hand, at M, thumb uppermost; the right hand also holds the cane in the manner described above; the hands are then separated and are raised a little at a time towards M. The direction given to the reins must be approximately an imaginary line joining the bit rings to the horse's ears.[1]

1. The emplacement of the seam should be above the centre of the head piece, but some adjustment will be required for each horse, as one particular place gives better results, either between the head piece and the ears (for horses which overbend) either behind the head

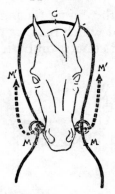

In this way a purely localised effect is produced on the corners of the lips, which rapidly induces an opening of the mouth and a raising of the tongue; the latter tends to be drawn back towards the larynx.

If the horse shows any tendency to move backwards, or even to lean back, the flexion must be stopped and he must be made to move forwards; the work starts again until the horse stands perfectly squarely at the halt.

Preparation of the Ramener

As soon as the horse has acquired a good, elastic contact with the bridoon at the trot, he should be put in a double bridle[1] with a loose, but not dangling curb chain.

piece, more or less low on the poll (for horses that go above the bit). The right place will therefore be discovered by trial and error.

The same applies to the direction given to the reins, which must never act upon *the body* through the neck, or modify the angle made by the head and the neck. The steady contact of the slightly taughtened reins in a suitable position is usually sufficient to induce mobilisation of the mouth, because of pressure of the bit on the corners of the lips. If this did not happen, a few vibrations on one rein or both reins would soon bring about the desired result.

1. If the horse is already accustomed to the double bridle there is no point in putting him back into a snaffle to proceed with dressage in hand; it will be sufficient to knot the curb reins to a length which will prevent the bit jolting in the horse's mouth, and to use only the bridoon reins. The best way of accustoming the horse to the double bridle is to let him wear, for a while every day in the stable, a bridle without reins with a bridoon and a curb bit with *very short cheeks*, and to let him have some oats and bran in the manger during that time. The attempts at chewing and swallowing which the horse will not fail to do are excellent "flexions", and the rapid success of these attempts give the mouth and the tongue the kind of mobility which is exactly the yielding that must be sought and achieved in the Mise en Main. The cheeks of the bit should be short enough so that they do not touch the bottom of the manger when the horse takes his oats.

At the beginning, the curb chain should not be worn. It can be put on later, but sufficiently loosely to avoid interfering with mastication of the food. Hay should not be given, as it forms plugs which are difficult to swallow.

In the course of the work, the trainer (facing forwards) takes all four reins, equally stretched, in one hand which he fixes on the withers, and the horse must in the end take as firm a contact on both bits as previously on the bridoon alone.[1]

Before attempting to obtain the Ramener, we must complete and regularise the elasticity of the contact on both bits by practising flexions of the jaw on the curb bit, until a mobilisation of the tongue equal to the one produced by the bridoon is obtained.

Direct flexions with the double bridoon on the curb bit

The easiest way to obtain flexion on the curb bit is to start from the flexion on the bridoon with which the horse is already familiar and gradually associate with it the flexion on the curb.

All precautions explained earlier concerning flexions on the bridoon must be taken at this stage, particularly against any tendency of the horse to move backwards or to lean backwards (acculement: see note 1, p. 233).

When the horse stands squarely at the halt, the bridoon reins are passed through the rings of this bit, and their joint is laid on top of the poll. The trainer stands level with the horse's ears and faces the left side of the head; he takes the ends of the reins which pass through the rings in his left hand, and holds them in *'front'* of the horse's forehead. He holds the curb reins in the right hand, fixed behind the horse's chin, and *without increasing* the contact, which remains *light*, he must be careful not to lose it.

The trainer then gradually lifts his left hand until he can feel a relaxation of the tongue, and yields immediately with this hand, but with the right hand, holding the curb reins, he yields a moment later.

Gradually, the movement of the tongue can be obtained by the tension of

---

1. Once this result is obtained, it is often helpful to take the curb off the hook on one side, and to pass it through the mouth, over the tongue and the bit, and hook it on to such a length that it rests partly on the tongue, a few millimeters below the curb bit, at its centre. (See sketch above). This arrangement induces salivation and prevents a "dead mouth", but we must beware also of provoking an excessive mobility of the tongue, and give up this method if the tongue showed signs of becoming "snaky".

the curb reins with less intervention of the bridoon reins, until the intervention of the latter becomes unnecessary.

The movement of elevation of the tongue produces a lifting of both bits, and when these are dropped when the tongue is lowered the typical clicking denoting complete relaxation of the mouth in a double bridle is produced.

At this moment, the right hand must yield immediately.

Lateral flexions of the poll

Very frequently, the poll lacks the necessary suppleness which permits a perfect Ramener and it can only be obtained then by practising localised suppling exercises called "lateral flexions".

The only horses which will not require these exercises are those which have perfectly set on heads, for which the following conditions must exist:

—sufficiently long and elastically coupled Atlas and Axis vertebrae;

—the lateral processes of these vertebrae must not extend too far forwards;

—the cheeks must be sufficiently cut away at their posterior edge;

—the maxillary must not be excessively developed in length or in height;

—the parotid glands must not be too large and must move freely in their groove.

Many horses, and especially Anglo-Arabs and Norman horses, have a faulty set of the head, and this sometimes makes the kind of Ramener demanded in the High School quite impossible for them.

Lateral flexion is developed from direct flexion, which has already been obtained in the manner described above.

When the horse yields upon an equal tension of both curb reins, the trainer, instead of relaxing the tension simultaneously on both reins, opens his fingers on one rein and, with a lateral flexion of his wrist tightens his fingers on the other rein. The horse prolongs his yielding for a short while, and slightly turns his head to the side on which the contact is maintained.

At the beginning, a very slight flexion is all that is required, but it is essential that the poll should flex without any twisting of the head, i.e. the poll should not incline in an opposite direction to the nose.

If the flexion is correct, the ears remain at exactly the same level. In the opposite case, the outside ear is lowered and the inside ear (in relation to the flexion) is raised. The trainer thus possesses a convenient way of checking on the correctness of the flexion.

To correct any tendency to crookedness of the poll, or better still to prevent it, the trainer, while using the curb rein on one side to obtain a flexion, resorts to the bridoon rein on the opposite side, with an upward action, creating an effect of direct opposition to the lowering of the head and to the outward inclination of the top of the head produced by the twisting of the poll.

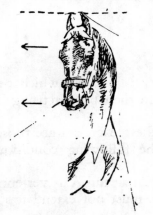

Correct lateral flexion
of the head

Faulty lateral flexion
with tilted poll

Lateral flexions are very slow to produce their effect. They must be practised frequently, for only a few moments at a time, and we should remain content, for a long period of time, with progress reduced to a few millimetres. Any attempt at enforcing the flexion would cause the horse to contract his jaws and to twist the poll. However, in the end we should be able to get the horse to look frankly to the right or to the left of his body, while maintaining suppleness of the mouth and mobility of the tongue.[1]

1. At the beginning, an assistant standing on the side towards which we wish the horse to turn his head draws the horse's attention by rattling some oats in a scoop.

The door of the manege also has a powerful attraction on the horse's eye. There is no reason why we should not take advantage of this.

Elevation of the neck

The Ramener should always be obtained with an elevation of the neck as high as can be produced without causing the horse to move backwards or to lean backwards.

Therefore, to start with, we must teach the horse to stand squarely with his neck held as high as his conformation permits. At the slightest sign of a backward movement of the limbs, or of the body in relation to the limbs, we quietly touch the horse on the breast with the cane and make him move a few steps forward; then we halt him and start all over again. If the loin is excessively hollow, we *gently touch it* with the tip of the cane.

The horse should not only assume this elevated attitude of the neck, but he should also retain it without supporting himself on the reins until the trainer lowers his hand; the hand continues to act as explained above regarding flexion on the bridoon.

Practice of the Ramener

Once this result is obtained, then we hold the curb reins crossed in the left hand, close to the bit, with the finger nails facing the underside of the horse's neck, and the back of the hand facing the space between the jaws, and take a contact with the mouth. (The trainer facing the head).

(1) Quietly make the horse move forward by touching him on the breast with the cane and yield only just enough to allow the forward movement. Halt after a few steps by increasing the opposition of the hand. Repeat a number of times, until the horse moves frankly forward "by advancing over the hand", i.e. by advancing the top of his head more than the lower part, so that the forehead approaches a vertical line passing through the end of the nose, the advancing of the latter being slowed down and limited by the opposition of the hand.

(2) At the beginning we should be satisfied with the smallest sign of the forehead advancing in relation to the nose, and we must endeavour to reduce the number of forward steps each time, until the horse takes a bold step forward with one leg only, the other one remaining stationary.

See that each foreleg executes this movement with equal facility. The leg which steps forward with more difficulty or which takes a shorter step must be exercised more frequently, until the length of both steps is the same.

(3) Gradually reduce the length of each of these steps from the very beginning of the forward movement. Then alternate long and short steps, regulating the length with the action of the hand; this, subsequently, in the study of the Piaffer will enable us to keep the horse perfectly straight and square by making him, if necessary, advance, in line with its neighbour, the foot which has a tendency to be left behind.

A.E.—18

(4) When, upon an indication of the cane, and against the opposition of an increasingly fixed hand, the horse can advance each foreleg boldly but only by a few centimetres, the trainer should gradually ask for a more considerable advance of the trunk towards the head until the line forehead-nose is perpendicular, *while the forelegs remain perfectly vertical.*[1]

Ramener at the halt

The hand must remain absolutely still. It is the horse that must *advance* his whole body to bring it closer to his chin

If the progression set out here has been followed without any omission, the hind legs will usually move forward of their own accord to a vertical position.

If, on the other hand, the hind legs have a tendency to move further forward than this, because of insufficient elevation of the neck and insufficient flexion of the loin, the cane must be used on the breast to make the horse move forward, and the hand is slightly raised to fix the hind legs.

Preparation of the Ramener is a long and exacting task which requires patience and great attention to detail, and continues until an absolutely correct vertical position of the head, and more important still, of all four legs is obtained. The trainer must remain particularly vigilant to prevent a position in which the horse is *under himself* in front, or behind, or with all four legs, a position frequently and very wrongly mistaken for collection.

At the beginning, the last minutes of each daily lesson should be devoted to the study of lateral flexions and of the Ramener; the first sign of obedience must be rewarded in the manner to which the horse is most sensitive, i.e. by immediately leading him back to his stable. Later on, the teaching of the Ramener should precede and follow all the exercises practised in each training session.

1. This vertical position of the forelegs in the Ramener, and later on in the Rassembler is of the greatest importance. It is upon this that the perpendicularity of the canons of the forelegs depends when they are in suspension in the Piaffer, just as the horizontality of the fore-arms depends on the vertical position of the head in the Ramener.

Once the Ramener is easily obtained at the halt, and when the horse can hold this position without attempting to elude it or to shift his limbs away from the vertical, the trainer can make him move on while trying to keep him in the Ramener; he halts whenever the horse's body fails to move at the same time as the head and the poll falls behind the vertical of the nose. He then re-establishes the Ramener and the perpendicularity of the legs at the halt, makes the horse move forward again, and so on.

The pace must be very slow at the beginning, one slow step after another. Impulsion is then gradually increased until an active and perfectly regular four-time walk is obtained.

All the work on one or on two tracks at the walk must be repeated now in the position of the Ramener, and the activity of the pace must be watched; however, "jogging" which is due to the hind legs taking short and hurried steps must be most carefully avoided.

Once the work is performed perfectly at the walk, the transition from the walk to the trot is demanded by touches of the cane on the breast. This transition must be executed most carefully. We should not tolerate an elevation of the hind legs greater than of the forelegs and we must prevent this by elevating the neck to the required extent without losing the Ramener of the head.

All the work on two-tracks must be repeated at a good cadenced trot, with well marked moments of suspension.

Gradually prepare the transitions from the halt to the trot by reducing the number of intermediate strides at the walk. In the same manner prepare the halt from the trot.

While working on the Ramener with the horse in movement, grant frequent periods of rest; as soon as the halt and the Mise en Main are obtained, yield completely and allow the horse to lower his neck and head. After the period of rest, and before moving forward again, re-establish the position of the head and of the limbs.

The Rein-Back

With the horse standing perfectly squarely and "Ramene", ask for *one* backward step by an action of the hand alone, immediately followed by several forward strides commanded by the action of the cane on the breast. Halt and re-establish the position. Repeat until the Ramener remains perfect in the rein-back as well as in forward movement and until both legs of each diagonal step back perfectly simultaneously.

Both diagonals must be exercised in turn.

—Ask for two backward steps, with resumption of forward movement immediately after the second one.

—See that the rein-back is executed *slowly*.

No more than four backward steps should be asked for, and they should start sometimes with one diagonal and sometimes with the other.

Never halt at the end of the rein-back. On the contrary, inculcate upon the horse the idea that the rein-back is invariably succeeded by forward movement.

From the rein-back move forward into the trot, as often as possible by using the cane on the breast; however, it may be necessary at the beginning to use it by touching the top of the croup, as the hind legs may require disengaging. The use of the cane on the breast must be returned to as soon as possible, to prevent an excess of elevation of the hind legs in the trot.

As a general rule, horses find it easier to move into the trot from the rein-back than from the halt. Both transitions must be practised alternately and the study of the Piaffer should begin only when the transition to the trot from the halt can be obtained with the greatest facility starting with one diagonal or with the other.

To start with the *right* diagonal, move the hand very slightly towards the left (the horse's left), in order to overload a little the shoulder on this side, and act with the cane on the point of the right shoulder. (In the beginning, on the point of the left hip, or on the left hind leg.)

PASSAGE AND PIAFFER

When all the preceding exercises, without any exception, can be executed easily, and when the transition to the trot from a stand-still is easily obtained at a touch of the cane on the breast, in an unaltered Mise en Main, we can without detriment start on the study of the Piaffer.

—We must start at both ends, i.e. work alternately on a slowing down of the trot on the one hand, and on transitions from the halt to the trot on the other hand.

In both exercises, we must particularly watch the overall position: elevation of the neck, Ramener, and perpendicularity of the limbs. We must prevent an elevation of the hind limbs superior to the elevation of the forelimbs, either by lifting the neck to produce a lowering of the action of the hind limbs, or by using taps of the cane on the breast to activate the action of the forelegs.

However, we should avoid continuously tapping with the cane, as the horse must be allowed frequently to find his balance on his own, and if the activity of the gait diminishes we should just use a clicking of the tongue.

—Both exercises must then be connected: transitions from the halt to the trot, a slowing down of the trot, halting as soon as the trot subsides, immediately moving forward again, and so on.

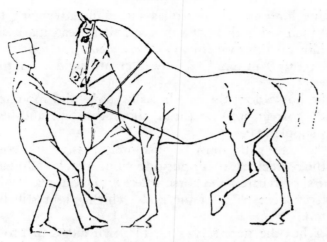

Moving directly from halt to trot

At the outset, forward progression must be limited more and more, but for a long time *we must avoid* obliging the horse to remain exactly on one spot. On the contrary, we must insist upon his maintaining his constant tendency to advance, which must be restrained only by a lighter and lighter opposition of the hand.

ALWAYS END THE LESSON WITH A RESOLUTE FORWARD START AND A PERIOD OF ACTIVE TROTTING.

—Once the horse has found his balance, (see illustration above) once he can maintain his balance and the unimpaired regularity of his whole attitude

As soon as the horse has discovered the balance, give him as much freedom as possible

when alternating long and short strides and while advancing by only a few centimetres at each stride then, at times, our hand can mark an opposition which holds him on the spot for *two strides*. Then for four strides, and so on. Never for more than ten. Carefully alternate strides on the spot with forward strides.

—When the horse does this work easily, have him mounted by a rider with a perfectly correct position (head, shoulders, hips and heels vertically aligned) and a supple seat.

The rider, to start with, must be absolutely passive and concerned only with keeping the correctness of his position while merely following the movement. Next, he should caress the horse wherever he can reach with his hands, and especially on those parts of the body which might still be contracted (poll, loins, etc.).

If the rider has the necessary skill, his own aids can progressively be substituted for the indications of the trainer, but the trainer continues to be in sole and absolute command.

As usual, we must proceed by advancing from the known to the unknown. At the outset, the rider's actions should coincide with those of the trainer, and the latter progressively diminish while the first remain the same and finally become the only determining ones.

This substitution requires an agreement between trainer and rider which is difficult to accomplish.

DEVELOPMENT OF THE PIAFFER

To obtain the Piaffer, we must prolong the suspension of each diagonal, extend the period between the strides, and expand the gesture of the forelegs.

It is the action of the hand that enables us to achieve this result, and the trainer is more likely to succeed if he mounts the horse, as the necessary rein effects cannot be produced as well from the ground.[1]

Books of Reference:
GENERAL FAVEROT DE KERBRECH
RAABE
GERHARDT
WACHTER
J.-B. DUMAS

1. It is possible, however, to obtain these results by work in hand, but great skill and much time are required, and no great advantage is derived in the dressage as a whole.

Appendix III · LONG REINING

Long-Reining when practised by an experienced and skilled horseman is a useful method of quick breaking in.

However, it can also be used in dressage, in adjunction to lunging, to prepare the horse for work in hand, especially between the pillars.

It is in relation to its complementary role as a preparation for dressage that it is discussed in this section.

ADVANTAGES AND DISADVANTAGES

The main advantage of long reining compared to lunging is that it gives the trainer the faculty of leaving the circle to drive the horse straight ahead, which is particularly helpful when the horse attempts to move closer to the centre in order to come behind the bit; this is the most common, and the worst, form of evasion of the horse, when he is worked on a circle, be he mounted or worked in hand.

However, this only becomes a real advantage when the work is executed on a space big enough to allow a sufficiently extended straight course, so that the trainer is not obliged to allow his horse to turn, when, from the point of view of dressage, he should be keeping him straight.

The manege therefore is not, at least at the outset, a suitable place in which to practice long-reining.

With this method, and especially on straight courses, the presence of the whip behind the horse induces him to move resolutely up to his bit, to "go into his reins", and this it achieves better than any other method. It is therefore a very practical manner of obtaining collection. It is for the same reason that driving a horse in harness, providing it is done intelligently, of course, and by the trainer himself, is an excellent exercise for saddle horses (effort of traction).

On circles, the outside rein enveloping the quarters and pressing on them is also favourable to collection, but to a lesser degree, as the whip in this position cannot act from back to front quite as positively.

On the other hand, the weight of the reins, their friction on the rings and on the horse's body considerably impairs the right degree of communication between the horse's mouth and the trainer's hand. The compliance or the resistance in the mouth cannot be felt clearly by the hand, and is usually felt too late for the hand to resist or to yield opportunely and in the right measure, and consequently the trainer often yields too late, and sometimes at the wrong moment.

In theory, the advantage of long reins on the lunge is to replace the fixed side-reins by the trainer's hand with its ability to yield or to resist. Therefore, long reins ought to permit not only the "*mise sur la main*" (driving the horse up to the bit), but also the *Mise en Main*. In practice, this is only true to a limited extent because the frictions mentioned make the actions of the hand too confused.

This is why long reins, despite their undeniable advantages, should only be used with caution *in dressage*. Their employment requires a great deal of tactility on the trainer's part, and in the absence of this they involve a great risk of making not just a *hard* mouth, but also a completely spoilt one.

EQUIPMENT FOR LONG REINING

Spanish Riding School, Vienna

At the Spanish Riding School of Vienna, the riding masters attach the long reins directly to the bit without passing them through any intermediate terrets on the surcingle or the collar.

They work solely on straight courses, with the trainer immediately behind the horse, or very slightly to one side when working along a wall. The horses of this School are so gentle, so well schooled and so well handled that the trainer can often walk right up to the horse's hocks, sufficiently close to be able to stroke the croup continuously in the course of the exercise.

This method could not be applied without some drawbacks to the kind of horse which we have to use. Furthermore, it does not assure sufficiently an enveloping of the hind quarters, and is difficult to apply to the work on a circle.

Neapolitan School

The Neapolitan School, in the XVIIIth century, made considerable use of long reins, and passed them through the terrets of a collar similar to the one used nowadays in harness work, before buckling them to the rings of the bit.[1] This school does not appear to have enveloped the quarters with the long

1. This method is still utilized by Mr. Schmit-Jensen, who achieves remarkable results from it.

reins, as is the modern practice, but used the reins to perfect work between pillars, or rather between low parallel walls which were substituted for pillars in the furtherance of dressage, in order to avoid maintaining the horse on one spot. (Mazzuchelli.)

England

The British, who make considerable use of long reins, practise especially the work on a circle, with the outside rein enveloping the quarters. They pass the reins through the stirrups, and adjust them so that they act rather behind the latter, approximately level with the stifle. (See Cavalry Regulations: Capt. M. H. Hayes, The Book of the Horse.)

This method is fraught with many dangers. Unless the stirrups are kept steady by a strap joining them under the belly, they shake continuously and they constantly jolt on the reins. On the other hand, when the stirrups are firmly fixed by this strap, the reins run through them, and the actions of the hands become harsh and uncertain. The principal disadvantage, however, lies in the direction of the reins from the bit to the stirrups, which is much too low and rapidly causes an overlowering of the neck and over-bending.

France (see De Mauleon, Donatien Levesque)

The most practical arrangement and the most elaborate one consists in a collar and surcingle provided with lateral terrets, or a driving pad equipped in the same fashion. The terrets of the collar should be high enough to ensure a direction of the reins similar to the one existing when the rider holds the reins when he is in the saddle.

The terrets of the surcingle must be situated at about 40 centimetres from the centre of the latter, so that when the reins are stretched their position behind the terrets of the surcingle is approximately level with the stifle.

The surcingle previously used in lunging is very suitable for long reining.

In the absence of a collar, we can pass the reins directly from the terrets of the surcingle to the rings of the bit, but in this case, the terrets are better situated a little higher than previously, and the lifting effect of the reins can be enhanced to a certain extent by passing them through the rings of the bit so that their extremities are joined to a ring placed in the centre and behind the head piece of the bridle.

Whenever possible, it is preferable to use a collar in order to prevent any lowering of the neck.

A.E.—19

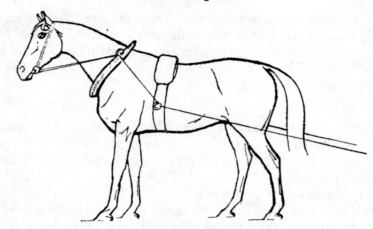

Ideal equipment. The harness collar could be replaced by an ordinary
hunting breast plate, providing that the reins are sufficiently thin to slide
freely through the rings

THE WORK IN LONG REINS

The special purpose of the work considered here is to increase the activity
of the hind-quarters at a certain speed, which the trainer is able to regulate
and to maintain constant.

Long reining on a circle, although it is not absolutely useless from this
point of view, can only produce limited results. Work on the lunge, when
conducted in the manner described earlier, should already have procured the
utmost benefits to be expected from unmounted work.[1]

In any case, work on a circle in long reins usually presents no difficulties[2]
when the horse has been trained on the lunge, as explained previously.

For the special purpose indicated above, long reining must be executed
along straight lines if it is to be of any use.

---

1. These long reins, however, may be useful in the case of horses who tend to carry their
haunches *outward* on a circle. The opposition of the outward rein enables us to hold the
hind legs on the same track as the forelegs. Quite frequently, however, the horse then falls
into the opposite, and no less serious fault of assuming a position in which the haunches
are turned in towards the centre of the circle, "the haunches-in", and in this case the long
reins are ineffective in straightening him; the whip and the opposition of the inside rein are
not always helpful.

In reality, the lateral inflexion of the horse on the circle, which is the foundation of the
"shoulder-in" can only be obtained, practically and effectively, from the saddle, because it
requires the intervention of both of the rider's legs.

2. The sole occasional one results from kicks provoked by the irritation of the side reins
on the fold of the buttocks. This is never long-lasting, but it is advisable to avoid it by
attaching to the stable rug, for some time, a rather loose fillet string.

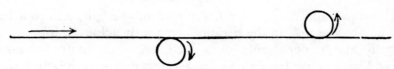

This can be achieved only by an intelligently graduated progression, in which straight lines are linked to curved ones, and the serpentine is transformed into a series of broken lines by a flattening of its loops and a widening of the angles formed by the broken lines, until it changes into a long, continuous straight line.

Progression

When the horse in long reins is kept on straight lines, his most usual form of resistance is to attempt to force the hand by rushing forward.[1]

Whenever the horse starts pulling, the trainer immediately engages him onto a circle, upon which he maintains him until calm is sufficiently restored to permit a return, by a tangent, to the original direction (diagram above). The course, therefore, will be roughly the one illustrated above, the length of the straight lines increasing in the same measure as calm is restored.

Subsequently, as the horse's attempts to run away become less violent, they can be contended with, without putting him on to a complete circle. A fraction of a circle will be sufficient to produce a result, and the horse's course can take the shape of a serpentine, of gradually flattened loops, and the changes of direction become less pronounced all the time.

Finally, the horse moves freely forward in the direction indicated by the trainer, who can then drive him on long stretches of straight lines, broken only occasionally, if the contact becomes too strong, by slight obliques, alternated to maintain the general primitive direction of the course.

The gait to achieve is a trot sufficiently slow to enable the trainer to follow at the maximum speed of a walk, without having to run. This trot must be energetic and well cadenced: it is precisely the kind of action which should have been obtained in previous work on the lunge, preparatory to work in hand, by a gradual shortening of the ordinary trot.

Once this result is obtained, the horse must be made to practise changes of speed, within a measure which still enables the trainer to follow him easily.

1. As these are the most felicitous resistances the horse puts up in the course of dressage, we must be content to avoid them in the least measure necessary without trying to destroy them altogether by severe punishment. The most favourable direction for work on straight lines is the one leading to the stable or to the gate of our practise ground, because this ensures natural impulsion.

These changes of speed must gradually lead to the halt, and to a transition from the halt to the trot, in the manner previously achieved in work in hand. Occasionally, the trainer should allow the horse to move unconstrainedly on a circle, and to develop the trot to the greatest extent compatible with regularity of the gait.[1]

TWO TRACK WORK

Once the horse trots boldly forward on a straight line, he must be accustomed to move away from it on two tracks. This exercise is not difficult in long reins if two-track work has previously been executed and perfected in hand —and no advantage will be gained from trying to perform it before then in long reins.

To achieve a half-pass to the left, with the horse walking straight ahead, the trainer moves to the left and forward, and tightens his fingers on the left rein, while relaxing them on the right rein. When the horse displaces his forehand towards the left, the trainer closes the fingers of the right hand, and

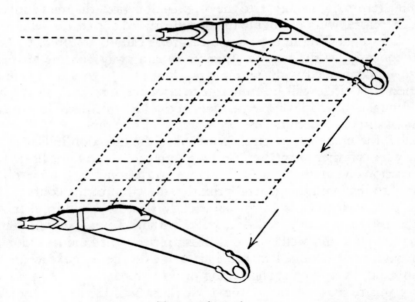

Two-track work

1. As regards a full halt and complete immobility, the trainer should be exacting only at the end of the lesson, for the last halt, after which the groom, having patted the horse generously, should detach the reins and take the horse back to the stable. On the contrary, resolute forward movement must be demanded after every halt, and some tolerance should even be shown towards a certain "turmoil" at the beginning.

presses the rein against the horse's buttocks. The horse then displaces his quarters towards the left, and the trainer yields as soon as the hind legs are behind the forelegs in the original direction.

In this manner, the horse will have executed a more or less correct half-pass for one stride towards the left.

We should remain satisfied with one stride in each direction until this is executed boldly and correctly without any loss of impulsion, and the horse moves forward and quite straight immediately afterwards. We can then demand two consecutive steps of half-pass, then three, but there is little advantage in prolonging movement on two-tracks in this manner.

On the other hand, it is essential and very profitable to alternate half-passing to the right and half-passing to the left, and to teach the horse to change rapidly and easily from one movement to the other.

The resulting little counter-changes have a remarkable effect of regularising and cadencing the gait, which becomes sometimes a little hurried and distorted when the horse is excited; this effect is particularly noticeable when we can reduce the half-pass to one stride in each direction, by opposing the rhythm of the forelegs with each rein alternately.

If the horse has been taught the Passage by mounted schooling or schooling in hand, and when he has acquired sufficient practise in alternating counter-changes in long reins, then by alternating the half-halts on one rein and on the other, and combining this with an increase of impulsion (use the clicking of the tongue, or the whip), we will be able to get him to execute the Passage in long reins.

However, this work is of no real advantage unless we want to make use of the pillars to perfect the Piaffer, which must have been obtained previously by schooling in hand or from the saddle.

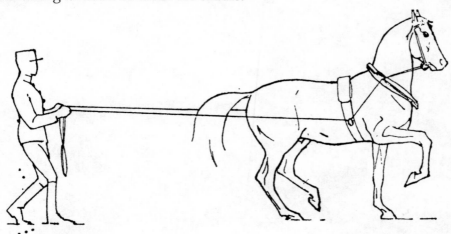

PREPARATION FOR WORK BETWEEN PILLARS

When the work described above is properly confirmed, the trainer starts preparing the work between the pillars by driving the horse, held quite straight in the long reins, through the centre of the pillars, and getting him to move through them, very frequently and always perfectly straight, in the direction of the entrance to the manege or the outdoor arena.

At the outset, the gait should be resolute and uniform, before entering the pillars, between the pillars, and afterwards.

Then the trainer slows the horse down *before* reaching the pillars, and allows him to lengthen resolutely as he goes through them and away.

Finally, after obtaining by degrees more pronounced slowing down before the pillars, the trainer gets the horse to halt frankly between them, and to trot on energetically immediately afterwards.

It is the last stage which imparts value to this work, because it gradually associates in the horse's understanding the pause between the pillars with the forward start, and unless this idea becomes an obsession, work between the pillars can have a detrimental effect on impulsion.

This lesson must be repeated at length before real work between the pillars can be started. During the pause, absolute immobility must not be demanded; on the contrary, were it to occur, the horse would have to be driven forward immediately and energetically.

Most horses go quite quickly into a relatively correct Piaffer when they are held between the pillars in long rein, and they do not attempt to turn the haunches out, as they necessarily must do if we start to obtain the Piaffer by "swinging" the quarters. In any event, if two-track work in long reins has been properly confirmed, the long reins enable us to straighten the horse quite easily.

Appendix IV · THE PILLARS

The utility of the pillars for dressage as a whole is very limited.

In the pursuit of collection, they achieve relatively rapid results, but at the detriment nearly always of impulsion, which is often destroyed by their use

To a certain extent, they facilitate the preparation for the "School Leaps", although the latter can be obtained just as well by work in hand outside the pillars.

The only real advantage of the pillars compared to work in hand is that they leave the hand free, which controls the horse's mouth in work in hand. However, this loss of control is not without some disadvantage, as the tactility of the trainer is replaced by the fixity of the pillars.

We may nevertheless have to resort to them when other means fail us, or to train the "Sauteurs aux piliers" (horses trained to perform leaps between pillars), traditionally used in military schools to strengthen the seat of the young riders.

PLACING THE HORSE BETWEEN THE PILLARS

Work between the pillars can only be utilised to the extent to which the horse acquires, maintains, and manifests an unfailing desire to pass through the line joining the pillars and to move out of the gap, in a forward direction, in a perfectly straight position, without deviating from a straight track.

When this desire and its manifestation decline, the horse starts "holding back". Work between the pillars ceases then to be useful, and because of the lack of impulsion, it rapidly becomes injurious.

The desire to pass out of the pillars is always instinctive with the horse[1] but he manifests it unwaveringly and in an exclusively forward direction only after the first half of his body has moved past the pillars.

During the time that the major part of the horse's body is still behind the

---

1. And we must very carefully avoid diminishing this by holding the horse within the pillars when he is not being worked.

pillars, the horse, despite the whip, remains undecided about the direction in which to satisfy his desire to get out.

His impulsion, whether natural or inspired by the trainer, remains hesitant as to the direction it should take, forwards or backwards. He is "behind his reins".

For all horses, the pillars are just a kind of door, and any rather narrow door inspires some anxiety in the horse who must go through it, probably because of a fear of hitting himself on it. When the horse is held between the pillars, he imagines himself "trapped in a doorway", and his apprehension manifests itself in the agitation of his movements, which become all the more jerky and restricted the closer he finds himself to the pillars. Depending on which pair is nearer to the pillars, either his forelegs or his hind legs will become more restricted in their action.

The activity of all four limbs will only be uniform when the pillars are at an equal distance from the forelegs and from the hind legs.

If one were sufficiently misguided to place between the pillars a half-trained horse, the least detrimental way of putting him in motion without causing excessive disorderliness would be to displace his hind-quarters alternately to the right and to the left, to "swing the haunches".

In this case, the hind-quarters would have to be moved further away from the pillars, by shortening the pillar reins, to make more room for the lateral displacement of the hind legs.

However, when the time comes to transform the "swinging" of the quarters into "forward engagement", the horse must be advanced between the pillars in a manner which enables us to establish absolutely and definitively a straight and forward action.

As the length of the pillar reins are the means of determining the position of the horse in relation to the pillars, it will have to be adjusted frequently and carefully.

When the pillar reins are short, and the horse has not penetrated between the pillars with the front half of his body, the Piaffer remains a "stamping" in front and more or less of a "hopping" behind. The impulsion remains feeble.

When the length of the reins brings the middle of the body level with the pillars, the activity of the forelegs and the activity of the hind legs are fairly uniform.

Finally, if the trainer subsequently wishes to develop the gestures of the forelegs, he gets the horse to advance further and lengthens the reins to make the horse penetrate between the pillars almost as far as his hips (Montfaucon de Rogles). The freedom of the forelegs and the lightness of the forehand increase in measure with their distance ahead of the pillars.

The height of the point of attachment of the reins needs adjusting as carefully as the length of the reins, as it effects the position of the neck, which influences the balance of the horse and his general attitudes.

In the case of a horse with good conformation and a naturally correct position, the points of attachment can be situated in such a way that the pressure put by the horse on the cavesson or on the bit is applied horizontally, and that they cause neither a lifting nor a lowering of the neck.

In the case of a horse that holds the croup rather high or arches his back, the reins must be fixed higher up, to provoke a lifting of the neck, and on the other hand, they must be fixed lower down with horses that hollow their loin and tend to stargaze, or with horses that are heavy in the hindquarters.

In each case, the arrangement must be modified depending on the resistances of the moment[1] and the results achieved.

WORK BETWEEN THE PILLARS

When the training in hand and in long reins has been conducted as explained earlier, no difficulties should be experienced in working the horse between pillars.

The horse will already have learnt in the course of being worked in hand to shorten his strides to a few centimetres, and to start frankly from the halt into a shortened trot. Long-reining will have made him familiar with the pillars and will have confirmed him in transitions from a halt to the same shortened and cadenced trot.

Before placing the horse between the pillars, the trainer must get the horse to repeat in hand a few transitions to the trot on the track, then he leads him between the pillars, without tying him to them. Standing alternately on the right side and on the left side of the horse, to the outside of the corresponding pillar, and against it, he repeatedly induces the horse, with the cane applied to the breast, to come out of the pillars, and he accompanies him afterwards, while generously rewarding him with caresses. Finally, having adjusted the pillar reins so that the horse's forehand moves well past them, the trainer gets an assistant to tie the horse to the reins, and stands level with the pillars, on the right or on the left side of his pupil, and facing the side of the horse. The hand which is closest to the horse's shoulders holds the cane, so that it can reach the forehand; the other hand holds the whip so that it can

1. On their inward aspect, the pillars must be grooved down their length, with a sort of ladder, the rungs spaced at approximately 2 or 3 centimeters, so that the hooks for the attachment of the pillar reins can be rapidly adjusted or released. The pillar reins are attached at one end to the pillar, and at the other, to the snaffle. The cavesson, and heavy reins can be utilised to train "leapers". They are not suitable for dressage to the Piaffer.

reach the hind-quarters. The assistant stands on the other side of the horse, but only intervenes when ordered to do so by the trainer.

With a clicking of his tongue, the trainer gets the horse to move forward as he previously did in hand and in long reins, and so seek a contact with the cavesson or with the bit.

As the horse has acquired the habit of Ramener and Rassembler in mounted work as well as in work in hand whenever he came against the resistance of the hand to his impulsion, he reacts in the same manner when he meets the resistance of the pillar reins, and executes a few strides on the spot; whereupon he is immediately rewarded with caresses from the trainer and his assistant.

The exercise is repeated a few times, and then the trainer and his assistant release the horse quickly and at the same time by detaching the reins, and allow the horse to move out of the pillars, and the trainer quietly takes the reins and accompanies the horse, while generously caressing him.

This lesson should last no longer than a few minutes, and by its repetition the horse is rapidly induced to regularise his action.

The trainer can then start to intervene, if necessary, to modify the form of the action. His intervention can assume the form of localised actions on the limbs or on the entire body of the horse, with the aim of getting him to move "forward" and "straight" in case he were not doing so sufficiently well.

For we should never lose sight of the fact that a faulty movement of the limbs[1] is always an effect, the cause of which invariably lies in a deficient impulsion or position.

If the superior articulations of the hind-quarters fail to flex sufficiently, the whip must be applied behind the hocks, at their lower part, or behind the fetlocks.

If the horse holds his forelegs underneath and grounds them behind the vertical, the *cane* can be used on either of them, just before they alight, behind the fore-arm, just under the girth groove.

If the feet fail to "spring" with sufficient activity, a touch of the *whip* in front of the hind cannons, or *of the cane* above the knees will increase their elevation.

However, the localised improvement obtained in each case is often accompanied by an aggravation of a more serious fault than the one which we have attempted to correct. For example, an excessive or impetuous activity of the limbs, although it may increase their elevation, also diminishes the power of the upward thrust, and of the resulting degree of "suspension of the body". Each diagonal, despite its elevation, touches the ground before the lifting of

1. Except obviously in the case of pain due to unsoundness.

the other diagonal. The horse is then executing a diagonal *walk* on the spot, which is not a Piaffer, because the Piaffer must be a trot, and can no longer be so when the moment of suspension of the mass between the two strides which is characteristic of this gait disappears.

If the impulsion shows signs of declining, the trainer can use the whip or the cane to animate it.[1]

The disadvantage of the lunge whip is that it provokes a turning out of the haunches away from the side where it is applied. The trainer is therefore obliged to stand behind the horse, so that the lash can act in a forward direction, without a predominant effect towards one side or the other. Besides the fact that the exactness of this touch is difficult and tricky to accomplish, this position has the additional disadvantage of depriving the trainer of the benefit of his position to one side of the horse, which enables him to observe the general attitude of the latter. Furthermore, the action of the whip on the hind-quarters also risks provoking an excessive engagement of the hind legs, which is no less detrimental than a lack of engagement.

The use of the cane on the breast, to awaken impulsion, presents many other advantages compared to the use of the whip.

It does not provoke the horse's tendency to turn his haunches out, or to excessively engage his hind legs, and it enables the trainer to retain the advantage of his lateral point of observation on the whole attitude of the horse.

Furthermore, the trainer can, by varying the points of application of the cane to the horse's breast, produce other effects besides impulsion. Towards the centre of the breast, the cane produces practically no other effect than impulsion, but used higher up, approximately where the underpart of the neck grows out of the trunk, it causes an elevation of the neck, and an advancing of the neck towards the head, or Ramener. Used lower down, towards the upper extremity of the fore-arms, the cane produces a lifting of the latter, develops "knee action" ("donner des genoux" was the expression used by the old masters), and forward extension of the cannons, which in a perfect Piaffer must be vertical.

The trainer uses the pillar reins to modify the general attitude of the horse, as has been explained earlier. However, the pillar reins can only modify the elevation of the neck, and are useless to straighten the crooked horse or the bent one.

---

1. Between the pillars, to an even greater extent than in work in hand, the utmost discretion is obligatory in the use of the aids. The most sensitive horse rapidly becomes "blasé" to the touches of the cane or of the whip. We should, therefore, whenever possible, be content to make a gesture rather than to effect a touch and resort to a touch only, in the case of the gesture being disregarded.

In the case of the crooked horse[1] the whip or the cane can straighten him temporarily, but they have to be resorted to repeatedly and they do not permit utilising the effectiveness of the opposition of the forehand to the hind-quarters. Shortening the pillar rein on the side towards which the horse traverses should in theory produce this effect of opposition, but this is not what actually happens; the horse flexes his neck towards the side of the shortened pillar rein, and escapes with his shoulders towards the other side.

To straighten the crooked horse, the long reins give quicker results and also more permanent ones, for when the horse has been trained to half-pass in long reins, they make it possible to act at the same time on the fore-hand, through the mouth, and on the hind-quarters by a pressure of the reins on the croup.

Placing himself behind the horse, and exactly opposite the centre of the pillars, the trainer firmly fixes the rein on the side of the traversing. Instead of acting intermittently, as he must perforce when using the whip or the cane, he resists and sets up an opposition to both extremities of the horse at the same time. The other side rein, used in the same manner, allows us to limit the horse's reaction, and finally to keep him straight. Furthermore, this fixed opposition requires little skill. It can be effected by the assistant, and the trainer can then return to his place in order, not only to observe, but also to intervene if necessary with one hand or with the other.

However, one rarely comes across a crooked horse that is merely crooked. He will nearly always be bent to some extent in the same direction. A horse placed centrally between the pillars may give the appearance of being straight, but careful observation will frequently reveal that one lateral pair of legs is more extended than the other. For example, the right fore will be slightly behind the left fore, and the right hind will be slightly in front of the left hind.[2] The horse is then more or less bent, concave on the right side, and convex on the left. His right legs carry more weight than his left, and the movements of his limbs are necessarily affected.

To correct this serious fault, the trainer can stand on the concave side of the horse, pass the rein from the other side over the neck, and hold it taut against the base of the neck, in front of the withers. In this manner he provokes a lateral bend of the neck opposed to the faulty incurvation. As it is

1. The same result can be obtained by the trainer, if he holds, instead of the whip, a lunging rein attached to the outside pillar and passing around the fold of the buttocks. This procedure has the advantage of avoiding an outward turning of the haunches towards the side which is away from the whip.

2. At the halt, the horse at liberty assumes this attitude to a greater or lesser degree. Similarly to man, the horse is never completely symmetrical and therefore never completely straight.

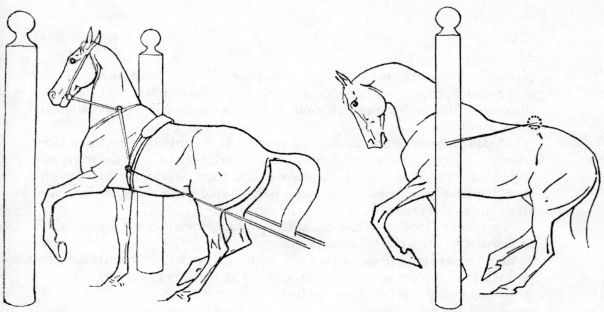

Manner of using the long reins to keep the horse straight, or to straighten him again, between the pillars. (The horse in this illustration is engaging the hind limbs excessively)

This horse is excessively engaging the hind limbs and is overbent. Give some well *spaced* but rather vigorous taps of the whip to get him to *buck* and attach the pillar reins higher

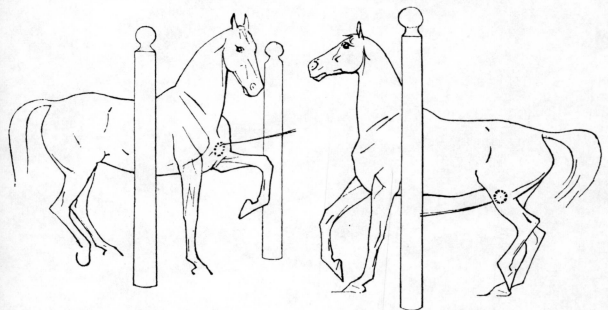

To obtain greater elevation of the forehand, give little taps at O, in rhythm with the diagonals, and just before their elevation

A horse that is not engaging behind, is hollowing his back, bracing against the forelegs and fighting the restraint of the pillar reins. Tap at O, at the fold of the buttocks, but *principally* attach the pillar reins lower down

physically impossible for the horse to dispose his spine horizontally in the shape of an S, the flexion of the neck inevitably produces a flexion in the same direction of the entire spinal column, and the horse is obliged to straighten himself out.[1]

Once the horse understands and complies, it is convenient to make him wear a training surcingle with terrets and to attach both reins to the terret on the concave side; the rein on the convex side must be adjusted to a length such that its diagonal bending action is only exerted when the horse loses his straightness and assumes a wrong bend again.

To sum up, long reins and the special surcingle with terrets are valuable accessories in the work between the pillars.

In order to preserve the horse's full impulsion, we will frequently have to go back to practising the exit from the pillars as much in long reins with the whip, as in hand with the cane applied to the breast.

1. It is obviously not sufficient to place the horse in a *straight* position to obtain permanent straightness. If we want to give a riding stick a permanent bend opposed to its natural one, we must hold it that way for some time. The same applies to the horse.

BIBLIOGRAPHY

F. BAUCHER: *Œuvres complètes* (13ᵉ et 14ᵉ éditions).

H. BAUCHER (son fils): *Aperçus équestres.*

Capitaine BEUDANT: *Dressage du cheval de selle.*

Capitaine J.-B. DUMAS: *Equitation diagonale dans le mouvement en avant.*

Général FAVEROT DE KERBRECH: *Dressage méthodique du cheval de selle d'après les derniers enseignements de F. Baucher.*

James FILLIS: *Principes de dressage et d'équitation.*

Lieutenant-colonel GERHARDT: *Traité des résistances du cheval.*

DE GASTÉ: *Le modèle et less allures.*

Lieutenat-colonel GOSSART: *Les allures du cheval.*

DE LA GUÉRINIÈRE: *Ecole de cavalerie.*

Général L'HOTTE: *Un officier de cavalerie. Questions équestres.*

Comte de MONTIGNY: *Manuel des piqueurs, cochers, etc . . .*

MONTFAUCON DE ROGLES: *Traité d'équitation.*

LE NOBLE DU TEIL: *Cours théorique d'équitation, de dressage et d'attelage.*

DU PATY DE CLAM: *La science et l'art de l'équitation.*

Lord PEMBROKE: *Military Equitation.*

Capitaine RAABE: *Examen du Cours d'équitation de M. d'Aure. Méthode de haute école d'équitation* (1863).

Dr RAU: *Aptitudes du cheval d'après sa conformation* (in German).

L. RUL: *Le bauchérisme réduit à sa plus simple expression.*

Gustav STEINBRECHT: *Le gymnase du cheval* (translated from the German by Commandant Dupont).

Lieutenant WACHTER : *Aperçus équestres.*